Everything Is the Way

Everything Is the Way

ORDINARY MIND ZEN

Elihu Genmyo Smith

SHAMBHALA
Boston & London
2012

Shambhala Publications, Inc.
Horticultural Hall
300 Massachusetts Avenue
Boston, Massachusetts 02115
www.shambhala.com

The chapter on Mu appeared first in a slightly different form in *The Book of Mu*, edited
by James Ishmael Ford and Melissa Myozen Blacker (Somerville, Mass.: Wisdom
Publications).

9 8 7 6 5 4 3 2 1

First Edition
Printed in the United States of America

⊗ This edition is printed on acid-free paper that meets the
American National Standards Institute Z39.48 Standard.
♻ This book is printed on 30% postconsumer recycled paper.
For more information please visit www.shambhala.com.

Distributed in the United States by Random House, Inc.,
and in Canada by Random House of Canada Ltd

Designed by James D. Skatges

Library of Congress Cataloging-in-Publication Data

Smith, Elihu Genmyo.
Everything is the way: ordinary mind Zen / Elihu Genmyo Smith.
p. cm.
ISBN 978-1-59030-972-8 (pbk.)
1. Zen Buddhism—Doctrines. 2. Buddhist philosophy. I. Title.
BQ9268.6.S64 2012
294.3'420427—dc23
2011038599

This work is dedicated to my Dharma Teacher,
Charlotte Jōko Beck
(March 27, 1917–June 15, 2011),
and to my wife,
Karen Cho-on Etheridge

Contents

Contents

Acknowledgments

This book is the result of many beings. My life and practice would not be possible without my late parents, Reuben and Bella Smith, to whom I owe a boundless debt. Many teachers to whom I owe unrepayable debts supported and nurtured me, most important among them, in chronological order of my practice life, Soen Nakagawa, Eido Shimano, Taizan Maezumi, and Joko Beck. I have also practiced with many people, including "my students," and learned and benefited immeasurably from them.

I have had the able editorial assistance of Ed Mushin Russell and Steve McCabe, who provided many useful suggestions about turning this material into book form. Without their help, this book would not exist. Some of this book was originally audio material that was transcribed by many people, including Faye Lesht, Cindy Seishin Cucia, and Nick Lee. However, there are many more unnamed transcribers, all of whom made this book possible through their efforts and to whom I express thanks and appreciation for their work. The love and support of my wife, Karen Cho-on Etheridge, and my children, Sara Ashley Smith and Gabriel Reuben Smith, sustained my ongoing practice and ability to produce this work. At Shambhala, David O'Neal's efforts insured the translation from text to book.

Introduction

Everyone is living the Way. This is so whether we know it or not, whether we want to or not, whether we are making efforts to do this or not, and whether we are skillful or not. Nevertheless, we often find that we are not at ease and not awake, despite being this universal life. Because we are not being at ease in the midst of our life and not being awake, we do all sorts of things that create difficulties and stress for our self and for others.

For many of us, encountering Dharma and the practice of Zen enables us to clarify and live more intimately and effectively this life that we are, this life of the Way. Practice enables, encourages, and supports us to be awake. We can see what we do, we can see what blinds us, and we can see what keeps us from this life and from being at ease. This ease is a natural manifestation of who we are. Functioning naturally, we manifest compassion, which is the empathy of responding to beings and conditions out of the wisdom of life.

I learned how to sit in late 1970 and began to sit regularly at that time. However, I had neither practice companions nor a group with whom to practice. My first ongoing teachers were books: *Zen Mind, Beginner's Mind* by Shunryu Suzuki, *Talks with*

Sri Ramana Maharshi, and a boxed collection of materials that later became *Be Here Now* by Ram Dass.[1] At that time, 1971 in Brooklyn, New York, I did not know of any group sitting regularly, any people who practiced, nor of any Zen teachers in the area, though there were some in Manhattan. Given who I was at the time, I probably would not have been willing to practice regularly with a group or teacher. I did begin attending public talks by various teachers such as Chögyam Trungpa and Swami Satchidananda. Though I found much of value in these public lectures and workshops, I was not drawn to further investigate organized practice.

Nevertheless, I needed help and support for my sitting and practice. So my Dharma books became my practice community, my Sangha. After sitting in the evening, I would read a paragraph or page of the Maharshi, Suzuki Roshi, or Ram Dass. At times I could not understand what I read. Despite my desire to understand these readings, to figure them out and add to my conceptual understanding and knowledge, not quite getting them was OK. I found that the readings touched me and clarified something even when I could not articulate what that was. Soon I found other Dharma books that resonated deeply with me, that encouraged, supported, and clarified my practice and life. I came to trust this resonance as a support for practice.

Even after I began to practice with a teacher, and even after I had practice companions, Dharma friends, and was part of a Sangha, I found that various Dharma books served my practice in vital ways. By sharing the words of Ancestors and teachers and resonating with their expressions, I was entering the Dharma realm they spoke from and wrote out of. This was and continues to be very valuable.

Practice is not a matter of learning new ideas and concepts from others but finding what resonates in this moment and clarifies this life. It is never a matter of getting something from someone else or somewhere else. And it is not self-centeredness, and it is not further aggrandizing habits of attachment. Practice is living this intimacy that we are. It is our own treasure that we realize; it is our own life that we encounter throughout the day, throughout the universe.

In this time of Zen centers and Dharma centers spread all over the globe, as well as the availability of lots of material on the Internet, what is actually helpful for our life and for our practice depends on countless causes and conditions. In fact, our whole life is the coming together of causes and conditions right now. In this world of interdependence, in this interbeing that is our functioning right now, there are many facets in this jewel of our life that enable us to manifest our light.

In this spirit, I hope this book can serve and support those who read it—to find in it something that they resonate with, to see what supports and clarifies this life-practice that we all are, and to make good use of that in living the Way. There are boundless life supports and boundless Dharma supports, but it is up to us to make good use of them, and to clarify what is so. By seeing what is so, we can make good use of what is so, and thereby live our intention and efforts to manifest this Boundless Way.

Elihu Genmyo Smith
Champaign, Illinois

PART ONE

Practice

1

Be Still

Sitting is a natural slowing down of this rushing, self-centered, mind-body chattering that we often live. This is the practice of realization, which is what we are, and this practice allows us to be who we are. As we practice, we discover who and what we are. This is the process of sitting, whether for one period or for many years.

My Dharma teacher, Charlotte Joko Beck, often quoted an expression from the Hebrew Bible: "Be still, know I am."[1] In a way, this expression clarifies and reflects realization practice; this being still is our practice, our *zazen* practice, our life practice. The truth of our life is that we are still, that we "know I am." Being still is not a means to an end; it is not that we should be still and then create something else or change. Being still is being who we are.

This might seem like a means-end process to us because we tend to see and understand our life in terms of a dualistic perspective; we tend to understand our life as self and not self, as before and after, as made of specific conditions. From that perspective and perception, we misconstrue who and what we are, and therefore rush around in all sorts of self-centered ways to deal with our fear in the midst of this impermanence, in the midst of this ongoing change that is being still, that is this unborn, that is this undying.

We try to do something to avoid the pain that we think is here, which is caused by our belief that we are dualistic, that we are self and not-self. So be still, be the stillness that you are; see that this is the practice. Suzuki Roshi used to say, "You are perfect as you are, and you can use some improvement." Improvement is your practice-effort in the midst of the perfection that we are. Perfection perfecting perfection.

Many teachers have their own expressions. Maezumi Roshi used to say, "Appreciate your life." Not change your life, not make your life more like it should be, but appreciate your life; appreciate this opportunity in the midst of the perfection that you are. Appreciation is your practice. In the midst of the stillness that you are, practice manifests as this life.

This is what we are doing. We get to notice this, maybe just a little bit, as we settle into zazen and into this moment. In a way, the forms and schedule of practice force us to settle, despite our wanting to rush around inside and outside; it forces us because we are this body-mind moment. Sitting still, settling our self into this moment, settling our self onto our self, settling "into" this that we are—that is what zazen is. We have the choice to settle where we are or to refuse to be where we are. Of course, we don't go anywhere else, but if we refuse to be where we are, we miss this life that we are. Instead, we can settle in the midst of ongoing change.

We are change itself. We often think of our life in terms of things changing: we like some changes and we don't like others; we want things to change in some ways and not in other ways. And of course, this moment of ongoing change is our opportunity for skillful, appropriate responses to the circumstances that reveal themselves, the conditions that reveal themselves as this moment. And yet, we are change itself. The Sixth Ancestor said, "Ongoing change is Buddha-nature." We are Buddha-nature itself, if I can say this in such a way. And Buddha-nature itself is the opportunity to be still, to be this that we are, to know this that we are. Stillness is ongoing change; they are not two different things.

"Be still, know I am" is not talking about knowing conceptually. This knowing is a knowing of not-knowing; this knowing is the deep *prajna paramita* of the *Heart Sutra,* which says, "Avalokiteshvara Bodhisattva doing / being deep prajna paramita." You all know very well that Avalokiteshvara isn't someone else. Being this wisdom that you are, you can see the emptiness of all the five conditions, you can see the boundlessness of the ongoing change that you are, and thus you can relieve suffering and pain. What suffering and pain? The suffering and pain that come from misperceiving, misunderstanding, and mistaking our self to be a duality of self and not-self.

As we live this practice life, we have little glimmers of this truth that we are. We have glimmers not because things change but because all of a sudden we see right where we are. We see being just this moment, and we see that we can manifest this compassion that we are—this compassion naturally comes forth in being just this moment.

To say it differently, being still is being this life as it is right now, which reveals this not-two. Of course, if we are just saying "not-two" or "nondual," these are just more words. We could say what is so; we could reveal what is so. Even that is just candy; it is just encouragement for us "to do," because by doing, we see and we are. We have to do our part, despite the fact that we are perfect as we are; we have to do our part, despite the fact that from the beginning we are this realized life. Yet because we are such, we can be such. Or to add the imperative: "Because you are such, hurry up and be such a person."

Because you are stillness, be stillness. This is really what we are doing here: you are allowing yourself to be who and what you are as this moment. We are being seamless; we are living a seamless life, a shadowless life.

Now remember, I write these words not because you have to agree or figure them out but rather to encourage us to do what we each can do as our own life. Because we each have this capacity to be seamless; we each have this capacity because this is who we are. We have this capacity in this breath, in this body-mind moment. So we don't have to add anything extra; we can simply allow ourselves to be right where we are.

2

The Four Practice Principles

Caught in the self-centered dream, only suffering.
Holding to self-centered thoughts, exactly the dream.
Each moment, life as it is, the only teacher.
Being just this moment, compassion's way.

These Four Practice Principles were formulated by my teacher Charlotte Joko Beck and written by her student Alan Kaprow. They are a restatement of the Four Noble Truths, which is a basic teaching of Shakyamuni Buddha. The Four Noble Truths are the suffering of existence, the cause of suffering, an end to suffering, and a way to the end of suffering.

The Four Practice Principles are a way of reminding ourselves of what brings us to practice, and how to make our practice efforts. It is valuable not merely to recite the Four Practice Principles but to allow them to be present and resonate in us.

Caught in the self-centered dream, only suffering.
Holding to self-centered thoughts, exactly the dream.

Zen is being intimate, being who we are. Holding to beliefs, expectations, and requirements are the barriers that keep us from being who we are. How can we not be who we are? And yet, we are able to cut off from our life!

This is the realm of practice. It is our delusion and attachment that maintain suffering in life. They separate us; actually, we separate our self from natural functioning Unborn Buddha-Mind. We separate our self from the Attained Way of "I and all beings of the great earth."[2]

By being attached to the self-centered dream that we mistake for life, we assure that we will suffer. Not seeing the dream for what it is, we blame circumstances for suffering. Self-centered thoughts—anger, greed, and all the variations of emotion-thought—are the bricks that continually build and maintain the dream. In order to avoid suffering, we attack life and try to change it to fit our thoughts. Or we try to change particular thoughts and feelings to avoid suffering. Sadly, the dream itself is suffering! But we "hang on for dear life" to the dream, in order to fight the suffering that we think comes from outside—and we don't know that it is the very hanging on to the dream that causes suffering. As we practice, we come to discover for our self what the dream is, and what life is.

Each moment, life as it is, the only teacher.

A teacher is not someone teaching us something. Rather, a teacher is someone who or something which creates opportunities for us to discover and clarify the dream for our self. Zen is not accepting a new set of beliefs as a substitute for those we have. We explore and clarify the beliefs we have and the consequences of these beliefs in our life, because holding on to beliefs is the basis of the dream and the suffering. The more we notice emotion-thoughts and the more we are the experience of bodily awareness, the more we allow the self-centered dream to be transparent, which is what it truly is.

"Life as it is" does not mean that "I don't need to practice; I'll just go on with my life and learn what is needed." That would be like saying, "Having food in the fridge is enough; I don't have to prepare it and put it in my mouth." The ludicrousness of this is obvious; yet often in our life we do not see the need to make an effort to practice.

To make effort is to take the responsibility for making life circumstances our teacher, as well as our practice venue and opportunity. Walking into a public bathroom with used paper towels all over the floor, do we just use the bathroom and think, "That's the janitor's job. I don't like to touch that sort of thing"? Right there, those beliefs are the barrier. One alternative may be to bend down and clean up the towels. Practicing means noticing our requirements of life, experiencing the emotion-thought, and being the bodily experiencing moment, and then responding right here.

What to do varies for each of us, moment by moment. What is important is the intention to practice. Taking responsibility means being the timekeeper in the *zendo* (practice hall). We do this even though we don't want to be there early to open the zendo, even though we are afraid people will judge the way the bells sound, and even though we don't want to "disturb" our sitting by keeping track of the length of the sitting period. Practicing is noticing requirements and emotion-thoughts, and nevertheless responding to the moment.

Making the effort to practice, we come to appreciate life's circumstances. Life, including emotion-thought reactions, is the practice-support that offers the opportunity of:

Being just this moment, compassion's way.

As beginners, we approach Zen practice in terms of what we can get for our self. We are in the midst of the self-centered dream;

practice is another attempt to make the dream work. By noticing thoughts and being bodily experiencing, the self-centered dream reveals itself as transparent, and it drops away of itself. Being natural functioning, and being unhindered by attachment to the self-centered dream, is experiencing the present moment and responding directly. Responding without being hindered by "self and other," we see what is needed, and we act accordingly. Not doing anything special, our life is revealed as the compassionate activity that it truly is. In this compassionate life, suffering has been resolved.

3

Embodying Life

A cool wind, bright green spring leaves blowing, a cloudless sky. Seeing this, feeling this, I am all of it. This alive world is joy! But if someone says, "You are a stupid and selfish idiot!" what then? When I am cursed, it is not easy to accept this intimacy of life, much less embody it. I may cringe and withdraw, or I may strike out. Life does not feel joyful; it feels like suffering and pain: "I do not want this, no way." This is difficult to even touch, much less to rest as and rest in. Embracing gain is fine; but when we are losing, we say, "No, not this!"

Can I face losses? Will I feel loss? Resistance to loss seems natural: "Yes, I should avoid this." Nevertheless, I am everything I encounter, you are everything you encounter. There's no need to agree, figure out, or believe this. To the extent that you can, embody this life as you are. When we are being this ongoing practice, life reveals life.

Sitting and being present, we may see and sense this interconnected life that we are. Yes, this aliveness is wonderful. Nevertheless, even when we see this interconnected life, this is hard to embrace. At times we are sure that what we encounter is not us! "I do not want this, not this experience, no way!" This life-moment is hard to embody and actualize. Uncomfortable or painful feelings arise: "This hurts, this is not me." Bodily pains and illness arise: "This is unacceptable, intolerable." Memories of past "mistakes" or "misdeeds" are not welcome.

What am I to do when this moment feels so bad? Naturally I want to avoid suffering. When suffering occurs, I think I should change something, the circumstance or the cause; I think I should try to fix things, or get away from the suffering. Paradoxically, truly "avoiding" suffering consists of being suffering when suffering arises. Yes—completely entering this moment of suffering, completely opening this suffering. Then we discover that joy is not elsewhere; joy and equanimity are not some thing that is opposed to suffering. Joy and equanimity are in the very midst of the seeming suffering, and that suffering is in the very midst of joy and equanimity. Can you rest as this moment, even as this moment of pushing away, this moment of "No, not this"? Waking up aching, can you be this?

Naturally, we like feeling good. It is great to feel that way. But since we often connect "feeling good" to particular conditions and circumstances, either external or internal, inevitably there are times when we do not feel good. When this is "not good," or feeling good does not arise, then what? When something is lacking, then what? We try to do something to change the feelings. We try to distance our self from what we don't like; we do all sorts of things to get away. One strategy we use to change our feelings is behaviors like drinking, partying, and so forth. Unfortunately, out of this very ordinary attempt to feel good, or to avoid feeling bad, some strategies just result in more difficulties.

There are people with whom you do not want to be, and there are people whom you can't bear to remember; thinking about them cascades you into hurt, anger, and frustration. There are people with whom you want to be but who cannot or do not want to be with you. All of us "lose" someone. We may blame this on others, our self, forces of nature, or the unknown. When "loss" occurs, you want to do something, or you feel helpless, even hopeless. So, what to do?

The Hebrew Bible states, "Love your neighbor as your self."[4] Something similar is stated in many traditions. This statement is often taken prescriptively, as meaning that you should imagine your neighbor is like your self, and therefore you should love him and treat him the way you would treat your self. Actually, the point is more basic and direct: your neighbor *is* your self! If you see this clearly, naturally you function as the love that is life; you function this way toward your neighbor and toward everything you encounter, which is your self.

Unfortunately, at times we even find it difficult to love our "self," namely the thoughts, emotions, feeling, and states of being that we judge, criticize, and want to reject. So, we have suffering. Fortunately, right here is the opportunity of opening, including loving our suffering. There is no need to try to change, add, or get rid of anything. Loving is simple and straightforward; it is just embodying this, being exactly as this moment is, being this body-mind-world, responding as this body-mind-world. Of itself, life is naturally revealed and naturally seen.

In fact, right now, body-mind-world are not separate; they are certainly not three things. Our encounter is always right now. Considerations of so-called past or future can turn this encounter into something else, and then we miss this, this which is nothing but our self. Past and future, as well as present, are right now. So by noticing that you are holding emotion-thought, you embody and function as this actualized life moment that you are right now. This is our practice opportunity; nothing lacking, nothing extra. Zazen is a way to do this. Zazen is being what is and inhabiting this moment of life.

Everything we encounter is exactly our self. Our life is serving everything we encounter, and our life is being served by everything we encounter. Serving and being served are positions we embody according to circumstances—exactly this life-death. If we limit serving and limit our self to what "I like" or what "I dislike," then there are difficulties. Ongoing practice is inhabiting this moment. Serving is inhabiting this moment, serving what appears, giving self away to self. Serving—whether I want to or not, whether it suits me or not.

But serving what does not feel good, serving what feels uncomfortable and even painful, requires our practice commitment, because our natural habit is to avoid discomfort. The opportunity of being this holding moment is right here in our clinging and sticking to positions and beliefs. Our practice-effort in seeing this holding allows us to inhabit this moment.

Seeing holding is likewise the practice effort if we are holding to a fixed position of "being kind" or "being compassionate." Unseen and uninhabited attachment to "kindness" and "compassion" can hinder responding appropriately to what is needed. Needed by what? By life—not as an extra or special effort but as exactly what is required by the whole of this moment, by this universe that is exactly our life. This is compassion; this is kindness. This life as is is exactly this wonderful opportunity.

There's no need for an idealized style. If we make mistakes, the practice is to do what is required next. We serve mistakes, serve selfish actions, serve foolishness and its consequences, and we even serve the reactive anger and more that might result. Responding to what is required allows what is needed to arise. Bowing to the mistake, we then clean up. It is human functioning, knowledge, and wisdom that enable us to see, act, and respond. Even knowledge and wisdom may get in the way, especially if they are unseen. If knowledge and wisdom do get in the way, no problem; the mistakes are our right-here opportunity. Mistake after mistake is the perfect way.

Honey and nectar are wonderful, but only a bee lives on these things; you cannot live on only honey and nectar. Yes, enjoy honey. However, attempting to stick to a life of honey will keep us from the life we are. A life limited to only the comfortable and the luxurious does not sustain. A practice that is too comfortable, a "country club Zen" that cushions us from circumstances and avoids fear, does not nurture life.

Practice is not a means to be safe and comfortable. A good practice is sustained in the midst of life, including life's inevitable discomforts and disappointments. Life as it is offers these discomforts; these are also supported and created by practice communities, sitting schedules, and *sesshin*. Ongoing practice makes good use of these things. We do not require only what is likable; we do not require only a diet of honey. The varied diet of arising circumstances, which are our life, is the nurturing of the joy we are.

"The Buddha turns the Dharma wheel and so reality is shown in all its many forms / He liberates all suffering beings and brings them to great joy." This is a Zen dedication after sutra chanting in a formal service. The varied tastes and flavors—sweet, sour, bitter, and pungent—all the arising circumstances are the present-moment diet that sustains us and sustains this great joy. Inhabiting this moment is being sustained. The many forms are the reality of our life; this great joy is seeing and being who we are. This great joy is our life as it is right now. So, being this joyful life, enjoy.

4

Zen Is Easy, Zen Is Difficult

Dogen Zenji writes in his *Shobogenzo* fascicle "Genjokoan" ("Everyday Life Way"): "When a fish swims in the ocean, there is no limit to the water no matter how far it swims; when a bird flies in the sky there is no limit to the air no matter how far it flies." Is this our life, a boundless life that supports and sustains us? What do you believe?

Unfortunately, we often fail to appreciate this life because we want our life to be other than what we think it is. Our life is this wonderful functioning, whether we call it Buddha-nature, emptiness, or whatever. We are in the midst of this, but because we do not know it, we search for air and for water as if there was something else somewhere else. Do we need to know what it is in order to appreciate our life? Truly, we have no need to "know it"; we are this, whether we know it or not. Functioning as our life, as the fish in water or the bird flying in the sky, the joy of life is always right here. How wonderful! Sadly, living out of self-centered attachment is suffering; thus we fail to see and appreciate what our life truly is.

Zen practice is not at all difficult. It is allowing the awareness that we truly are. I use the word "allowing" to emphasize that practice need not require tension and stress. Yet because we are caught up in habits of being that seem so natural and solid to us due to our self-centeredness, there is great effort in practice. The effort is in not-doing; the effort is in noticing and working with what is so habitual that it is like a deep groove in being, a groove that we easily slip into and that limits our life.

When we begin sitting, it may be difficult to remain still and to be present as the bodily sensations arise and pass. It may be even more difficult to notice and face being caught up in emotion-thought and to open to awareness, especially because noticing is not about analyzing or thinking. The ability and willingness to tolerate this may determine if we continue in Zen practice. As we continue, we develop the muscle of practice, the ability and strength to tolerate what seems outside this habitual pattern we call our self, and the ability to be present as the life that we usually run from.

How does suffering occur? We evaluate and measure others and our self by many expectations, with all of us inevitably falling short. Is this so for you? Because we break life up into "our" life and what we do not accept as our life, we believe that the circumstances and the other beings in our life create and sustain our dissatisfaction, stress, and suffering. Because we misapprehend the source of the suffering, we want to change or reject those circumstances and beings, and we react to them with fear or anger. Our actions often lead to more suffering. How sad! The work of practice is noticing, over and over, the specific thought, emotion, belief, or feeling that we are caught up in. These things have been the basis of our reactions because we assume they are an accurate expression of life and objective reality.

True sitting is allowing awareness throughout life. True sitting is being present as all the circumstances arise, including so-called internal and external circumstances, including others and ourselves. What do we not allow? What do we not accept? From the beginning, there is nothing excluded, nothing we can exclude. Even saying "allowing awareness" is extra. Being this life that we are requires no effort.

Is this so for us? Rarely. How come? Since we believe the self-centeredness and the habitual grooves, these things are so for us. That is where the work of practice is; it is in noticing and clarifying our specific dreams and our habitual grooves. And that is what we resist. The ongoing work is to embrace aspects of our life that we have been unable to be with, accept, and include. We face this in formal sitting and throughout our everyday life. This work requires effort because we are caught up in the dream and fiction of who we think we are, and what we think our life is. Noticing and being present is the resolving and dissolving of our problems and suffering.

The fish is swimming in the water, with nothing lacking and no limits. The water is the life of the fish. If we are caught up in our self-centered perspective, in our views of the water, then the water limits us. We may even try to use practice to stay in the grooves of our habits. This is why ongoing practice is repeatedly noticing and being present—during zazen, in our everyday life, and especially when we are reacting, which is evident if we are angry, sad, or depressed.

Sometimes we speak of practice with habitual patterns as "going against our system." Believing this expression is fooling our self; it is our system going against our system. Practice is fooling our self until we see that from the start, we have been fooling our self by believing that we are our system, and that we are our emotion-thought habit. To fool our self as the self-centered dream is the human condition. And practice is to trust our self.

What is "trust"? Trust is sitting; trust is allowing our self to be our self; trust is allowing awareness that is life. By clarifying and being present, we allow this wonderful functioning to manifest.

Swimming in the water of our life, there is no limit; we go freely, and we are not hindered by circumstances. Going against circumstances or flowing with them, we are supported and strengthened in the currents of our life. This is our life!

5

Mu: Mysterious and Subtle, Simple and Straightforward

Zazen is Mu. Even to say that is extra. Nevertheless, we need to say more in order to see that saying this is extra.

In the exploration of Mu that follows, the guidance of my teachers, my own teaching, and my ongoing practice are all intertwined. I will speak at times as a student, at times as a teacher, and always as an ongoing practitioner of Buddha-dharma.

I am grateful and fortunate to have practiced at various times with my teachers Soen Nakagawa, Eido Shimano, Taizan Maezumi, Bernie Glassman, and Joko Beck. Working with a teacher is vital in Mu practice, and yet Mu practice must be our own. Nevertheless, unless a teacher is consulted, it is easy to go astray or quit due to frustration. Even if we "accomplish something" in Mu practice, without guidance from a teacher it is possible to be satisfied with a little bit, with a shallow opening or understanding. The goal is not "passing" Mu, because Mu is a lifetime practice; it is not just a means to get somewhere or something. Over and over we clarify, realize, and actualize this life of Buddha-dharma, this ongoing practice of everyday activity.

When I began Mu practice, I was told, "Do Mu." After initial attempts, I asked for more instruction, and my teacher suggested that I look at "Joshu's Dog," the first case in *The Gateless Gate*.

> A monk asked Joshu: "Has a dog Buddha-nature or not?"
> Joshu answered: "Mu."

Reading the case and commentary, I thought that I knew what to do. Hearing *teisho* on Mu also seemed to point my practice in certain directions. (Teisho is a nondualistic presentation by a Zen master on a Zen case or text.) But very quickly, what I knew and my interpretations seemed to be of little value. Presenting Mu to my teachers, little by little I was disabused of the various notions and strategies I had adopted in trying to do Mu.

Mu practice was a natural deepening of my practice and my desire to grasp the Buddha's teaching, to see and be this joyful life, and to take care of my suffering. At the same time, in the back of my mind I had a notion that this koan would get me somewhere; it would allow me to enter a mysterious world that I thought was expressed in the various koans that I heard and read about but could make little sense of.

Being told to "Do Mu," I assumed that there was something to do. So I tried to figure out what to do. Because my zazen had initially been breathing practice (counting inhalations and exhalations, and later simply concentrating on inhalations and exhalations), breathing Mu seemed sensible. I combined Mu and breathing, so the out-breath was Mu, the in-breath was Mu. My teachers did not discourage Mu-ing breath. And in fact this is a good way to proceed; not just Mu breath but Mu whole-body breathing.

Doing and being seemed different to me, yet I was urged to be Mu. I was told, "Throw your self into Mu." At this point, practice was my self going forth and practicing Mu. I was doing Mu and being urged to be Mu; this was especially frustrating when my "trying to get somewhere" seemed to get me nothing except blows from my teacher. I assumed that blows from my teacher were a criticism, a negative evaluation of my presentation. What are blows? Are blows Mu? Blows are easy to misunderstand, especially if we are looking for Mu as "some thing."

In trying to figure it out, I kept coming back to the question: Is "being" different than "doing"? I had a sense of other practitioners forcefully Mu-ing, whether in the *dokusan* room or at other times. And in fact in teisho, we often heard just that: "Work on Mu in your lower abdomen" and "Become Mu yourself from morning to night." We were assured that by maintaining such a state, we would totally become such a state. This effort and concentration seemed to be what was called for, but it seemed to get me "nowhere," at least nowhere that I thought I was supposed to get to. What is Mu? What is being Mu?

The commentary by Mumon states: "Concentrate your whole self, with its 360 bones and joints and 84,000 pores, into Mu." Misunderstanding these and other "instructions" of Mu practice might lead one to think that a forced concentration effort is valuable. Unfortunately, practice that is primarily this concentration may create a sense of power and accomplishment, as well as a tension and subtle self-sense that actually perpetuate self-centeredness.

As Mu practice continues and various byways and dead ends of the "effort to accomplish" are abandoned and fall away, body-mind is more and more Mu. Concentration can lead one to attempt to push everything else away in an effort to just hold on to Mu, just Mu-ing. Although at times this may be necessary and useful, if pushing away is always the practice style, then a dualism is perpetuated, a dualism of Mu and not Mu. It's more useful to open Mu to include whatever physical and mental states arise. Everything is thrown into Mu: Mu swallows up our whole life,

Mu lives our life. Therefore, Mu is being body-mind present this moment as is, each moment as is. Not body versus mind but this emotion-thought body state, this being Mu. What is this?

What reactions, what emotional states, do we get caught up in? If there is gain, is gain experienced? Is gain Mu? If there is loss, is loss experienced? Is loss Mu? By seeing what beliefs we hold to as true and real, we see how we exclude Mu. Right here is the opportunity of bodily experiencing; right here is the opportunity of being Mu.

In deepening Mu practice, Mu pervades the whole of being; the whole of being is Mu. Zazen is Mu, daily activity is Mu. Mu washes up, Mu lies down. Mu breathes in, Mu breathes out. A state of clarity and presence may eventually develop. Yet this state is just that: a particular state. It may be important as an indicator of the quieting of body-mind, but it is just a "way station" of Mu. Though the state of body-mind is good, if we attach to it and think, "I have to keep this" or "That will interfere with this state," we are blinded by delusion. There is still some hindrance. We may remain stuck in this clarity and stillness until our teacher and our circumstances push us and expose this attachment.

Sometimes Mu practice includes a subtle hope and a search for an "experience" of a certain type. Hearing words like "opening," "enlightenment," "satori," or *kensho* (literally, "seeing into one's nature"), it is easy to expect there will be some "experience" or state of being that will come when working on Mu and when accomplishing Mu. We might even turn having this experience into the aim of our Mu practice. Unfortunately, this desire and hope is another sidetrack that detours practice, and may actually create attachment and delusion that further perpetuate self-centeredness.

It is also important to differentiate an experience, particularly body-mind states such as one-pointed concentration or deep stillness, from the often-heard notion of "experiencing for one's self."

The phrase "experiencing for one's self" is used to differentiate from ideas, notions, or beliefs received from others, whether through readings, talks, or intellectual analysis.

In Mu practice and in all our practice, the self-centered way of understanding world and mind (and the resulting functioning) is the problem. Unfortunately, these habits of body-mind seem natural and seem like the whole truth. They are not! If we see the "delusional" habits of body-mind for what they are, they are not a hindrance in the functioning of body-mind-world. Then, from morning to night, this life is only the functioning of Mu. Mu is thus walking the path that is not other than right here.

Mu is not an experience, but seeing. Seeing is not something created by us, by "my action." Though we may use the word "insight," seeing is not conceptual or intellectual. And seeing is not insight as opposed to presence or awareness. Seeing is experiential insight. Seeing is not something extra. Seeing is natural functioning of being, yet this natural functioning may seem unusual and special because in so much of our life, we are blinded by the lens of self-centeredness through which we see. Because our habitual seeing is through the lens of self-centeredness, in "Genjokoan" Dogen Zenji encourages us to forget the self; forgetting the self, we are awakened by the dharmas of life, to "see" and be our life functioning. Dropping away body-mind, Mu reveals our life, Mu is our life. This enlightening, this seeing, is experiential insight into the nature of our life and the life of the universe, which is not-two.

Again, seeing is certainly not some intellectual or conceptual matter, and seeing is not some extra "thing." Being Mu, Mu is seen; the functioning of great joy is encountering our original face. We encounter our face from morning to night. To pass the barrier of no-barrier is to pass through the self-centered dream that we maintain. Though Mumon says this barrier is set up by the Zen ancestors, there is no barrier except that we are unable to forget the self. We create the barrier—and because we create and maintain the barrier, we must pass this barrier of our ancestors. Only in forgetting the self, as Mumon says, "You will know it yourself and for yourself."

For the practice of Mu, explanations are of no use. Discussions of emptiness and Dharmakaya have no place in Mu. Explaining Mu is more than worthless. One might even believe the explanation to be some truth, which further entangles life in the self-centered dream, even if it is a new "enlightened" dream.

Seeing is our life as is; seeing is being thus. Therefore, the practice of Mu, the seeing of Mu, is whole body-mind; it is dropped away body-mind. A teacher can detect when a practitioner has "seen" Mu by the way they are, the way they walk into the room, and so forth. Seeing naturally manifests being; being naturally manifests seeing; there is not something extra.

Seeing Mu, being Mu, varies with each person and with each circumstance. It is so even if it is shallow, even if it is just for an instance. Depth and breadth vary. Yes, attachment and delusion may arise, habits of body-mind may arise. After an initial or early opening, or even after later practice, many ancestors went through periods where attachments and habits of body-mind arose. Hakuin Zenji's Mu enlightenment led him to believe that "In the past two or three hundred years, no one could have accomplished such a marvelous breakthrough as this." Nevertheless, by Hakuin's own account, after this statement his pride and arrogance earned him the pounding of his "delusions and fancies" by Master Shoju.

Even after resolving this matter further under Master Shoju, Hakuin was encouraged not to be satisfied, to instead devote efforts to "after-satori" practice. Hakuin Zenji would face body-mind habits arising over and over. More than ten years after his initial opening and after many more openings, Hakuin could say that "the understanding I had obtained up to then was greatly in error."

Ongoing practice is certainly life practice. In fact, after-satori practice is ongoing practice of original nature. From the beginning, our life is this original nature; therefore from the beginning, our practice is after-satori practice. Practice is in realization, as Dogen Zenji states. Nevertheless, awakening, seeing this for our self, is valuable.

And this ongoing practice continues. As Dogen Zenji states in "Genjokoan": "To be enlightened by the myriad dharmas is to cast off one's own body and mind, and the body and mind of others as well. All traces of enlightenment disappear, and this traceless enlightenment is continued on and on endlessly."

Ongoing practice deepens and actualizes insight. Habits of body-mind are opportunities of ongoing practice. Insight feeds and supports ongoing practice. Being Mu naturally manifests seeing Mu. At appropriate circumstances, being Mu manifests as seeing, as serving, as receiving, as our daily life. Step-by-step, ongoing practice is straightforward and ordinary.

6

A Single Hair Pierces Many Holes

Just this: a simple expression of our life, of Zen practice. Sitting, just sitting, "body-mind dropped away." Of course, thinking, "Does just this exclude that?" "Do I have to do something special?" or "How do I know if it is just this?" creates difficulties. Even saying "just this" is extra; saying "just this" is not just this.

Just do your best. This is the whole of practice, the whole of our life. All sorts of chatter comes up in the midst of the circumstances of our life. Something breaks, we clean it up or fix it up. Or we can start chattering about, "Why does this happen to me? Oh, I always do this. What am I going to do? What does this mean?" We all know the consequences of that. After speaking with someone, do we continue holding on to the discussion with "internal" chatter like, "Why did they say that to me? It's not fair that they say it to me." If that chatter—habits of reactions, habits of thoughts and emotions—arises, then right there in the noticed chatter is our practice. Just be chatter in the midst of doing, and allow chatter to pass. Bodily experience this. Or you can turn and look: Who chatters? Or you can cut it off, open it up, be just where you are, or various other practices.

What to do grows from and depends on our life practice, our capacity and capability. In the midst of daily functioning and activities, we often react, wanting particular reasons for doing something. This limits us. Until we can see that this is occuring, we have troubles and difficulties. Not because there is anything missing but because we hinder functioning and hinder our life. We do this, not someone else. Sitting is simple. It really is. Yet being so simple, it can be so difficult.

The last case of the *Transmission of Light* by Keizan Jokin Zenji, "The Fifty Second Ancestor, the Priest Ejo of Eihei," is the case of Koun Ejo Zenji, who was Dogen Zenji's successor.

Koun Ejo had practiced with Dogen for many years. At one point, Dogen brought up the expression, "A single hair pierces many holes." Hearing this, Ejo was awakened. That evening he made bows to Dogen and asked: "Irrespective of the single hair, what are the many holes?"

Dogen smiled, saying, "Completely pierced."

How do you see this case?

This moment, this intimacy. This is just sitting, this is just doing; this is being completely pierced. Nowhere are there any holes. But when we believe and react out of our story about something lacking or something missing—"I don't know enough to do my best, I need to do this before I can do my best"—then these are ways that we refuse to be this life. We believe there are many holes. Though we cannot miss this life, we miss this life, miss this single hair piercing. We miss this even though we have only this moment life, and even though we have only this moment doing. Because we believe "many holes," Dogen says, "a single hair pierces many holes." Do you see? This piercing is true no matter what the conditions, whether they are so-called inside conditions or so-called outside conditions. And those so-calleds are "nowhere are there any holes." Then, this is completely pierced. That is, unless we believe our stories.

This life is not a matter of figuring this life out. As Keizan says, "Do not be fond of much learning or become occupied with extensive studying. Even for a short time, for a fraction of a second, arouse a determination in which not a speck of dust can survive." Don't get some idea about this. This is doing, this is sitting. There is nowhere for a speck of dust to land, much less myriad holes. The words are to remind, encourage, and support us to be who and what we truly are; to remind us to see and be awake, if I can use such words. Do not allow the words to hinder; instead allow them to help us.

Practice is just, just, just: sitting, walking, eating, resting. If you are resting, rest. If working, work. Practice does not require a special state. There is nothing to attain, nothing to attach to. Practice simply doing what you are doing, and not doubting. Or if you are doubting, make doubting your practice; be doubting.

Keizan says further, "While not beyond conception, that which you will realize is certainly beyond the reach of thought." That's an interesting way of putting it. Another translation: "You will surely reach a place that thought does not reach. Even if it is inconceivable, you will reach a place that cannot be emptied." We often want to limit our self to what we can conceive, to what we can figure out. And if we limit our self that way, then indeed we seem to be limited in that way. We even do that with sitting: we want to turn sitting into how we imagine it, into what we conceive it is going to be. That itself limits us.

Don't believe your concepts of your limits. Don't believe your ideas of what sitting is, what walking is, what breathing is, what hearing is, what seeing is. Otherwise, if we believe stories about holes we can enter and holes we can't enter, stories about what states are or what states aren't, we miss this single hair piercing myriad holes. And not only that, but we do not see the point of the question, "irrespective of the single hair, what are many holes?"

Of course, saying this is extra. Extra in the sense that this is what is so, this is who you are. What need is there to say the obvious? Nevertheless we need to say this; still, this is extra. You depend on you to enter your life. So I say, just: just sitting and doing your best.

Some people respond, "Well, is my best good enough? I'm not sure if I'm doing my best. Am I just doing it?" These are just considerations. If those doubts come up, fine. Don't deny that they are there. Throw those into your practice. Let that be the fuel to nourish doing. Just doing, including the thoughts. Just doing, so that thoughts don't keep you up in your head, stuck in judgments about, fears about, chatter about. Realize and taste this.

You have to do this life practice because only you can do it. No one else can do this for you. Someone said to me, "You do it for me." No one can do it for you. You can have all sorts of supports, encouragement, even prodding and poking, but still this practice effort is yours to do.

I like this tea here. I am the only one who can drink this tea. I can't drink this tea for you, no matter how much I drink. You don't taste it. I can tell you about it, and if I am a poet, a musician, or an artist, I can do something with this experience of drinking tea and maybe offer you a resonance. I will do that. But you have to taste the tea of your life. And we discover that we share a life-tea. That is why teachers and ancestors can encourage and share with us. That is why they—and we—can transmit. You have heard the expressions "Transmitting the untransmittable" or "Mind-to-mind transmission." In fact, this is where the title *Transmission of Light* comes from. With mind, transmit mind. Then we can see ways to express this.

So Keizan says, "Even though myriad things are extinguished, there remains something that is not extinguished. Even though everything is gone, there is something that is not exhausted. It turns out to be as expected: utterly empty, marvelously bright by nature. Not a hair of doubt, not a whisper of false thought. It is like waking from a dream. Simply vivid alertness, so we call it vivid alertness." Vivid alertness is yourself, so we call it vivid alertness. "Calling it alertness means that you are very awake. Calling it bright is just that it is very bright." These words are pointers. Don't go looking for anything special.

"Space from the beginning has not admitted even a needle. Vast, nonreliant, it is beyond all discussion. Do not say that a hair passes through many holes. Empty and spotless, it is unmarked by any scars." Another translation: "It is naked and without blemish, beyond any trace of anything." Don't get trapped by words. This is just your life, just encouraging you in your practice. What is it? The determination to do what you are doing. Just be what you are.

Dogen and others encourage us: "When a person is seeking the Way, it should be like an ordinary person trying to meet a great beauty, or overcome a powerful adversary." In other words, determination: wanting and attending, determined to do something. "When determination is deep and strong, then even a thousand, even ten thousand people will acquire the way. Once you raise up a strong determination, you will have a deep experience of this."

What is this? This is just your life. So you do your part, and the rest is clear. It is clear because there has never been anything lacking, despite any beliefs you might have, despite any ideas you might have. There has never been anything lacking.

7

Intimacy and Commitment

Practice is intimacy, intimacy as the whole universe, intimacy as our life, as this moment. Because it is so simple and straightforward, for just this reason we find all sorts of ways to avoid our life, our practice, and our zazen. How does this occur?

In ordinary language and in ordinary life, we use the word "intimacy" and think we know what it means. We use "intimacy" in terms of specific relationships, specific activities, or we say that we feel intimate at specific times in activities such as music, arts, and sports. We identify intimacy as certain experiences. In fact, the enjoyable, nurturing, and enlivening aspects of various activities are related to being intimate. Nevertheless, understanding intimacy only in this so-called ordinary way, especially in terms of the pleasurable and almost seductive quality, the experience of intimacy we associate with only certain activities, especially some such as the sensuality of sex, may lead us to miss the most basic and underlying aspect of intimacy.

Zazen is intimacy. This is not an intimacy between you and others, between you and the universe. Zazen is intimacy; zazen is our life that is the universe. Not seeing this clearly is a problem that stems from the ordinary understanding of intimacy, whereby intimacy becomes another aspect of dualistic self-centeredness. We feel intimate with another in a relationship as long as they fit our expectations, as long as the experience is what I want. What is expected, what is included or excluded? I am intimate with my parents except when they are critical of me, demanding, boring, or needy. I am intimate with my partner except when they are troublesome, not enjoyable to be around, not the way I want, or when our relationship does not feel intimate.

Have these thoughts and feelings arisen for you? They have for most of us. Do you notice these thoughts? Do you believe these thoughts? Do you hold to these beliefs? Based on these beliefs, do you act as if you cannot be intimate with the person or the circumstance? This is a practice opportunity. Do you cut off this moment? Do you cut off your life? This "cut off" maintains self-centered suffering.

How is it when a person manifests habits that I don't like? How is it when someone is not doing what I want? What if they have terrible taste in clothes, music, and so on, or if they want to do something that is just stupid—or at least, something that I am sure is stupid? "My kids are just so silly, stubborn, foolish." Am I intimate when they act that way?

If my reaction is anger, right here is the opportunity to notice held emotion-thought, right here is the opportunity to bodily experience this. Intimacy is resting on the icy couch of this moment. Often I would rather run from this moment by reacting with anger, believing the expectations, or avoiding what seems to be too painful to experience. Notice that this self-dream is what interferes with intimacy. Holding to emotion-thoughts and reacting from them cut off the intimacy of life.

We often associate intimacy with certain pleasurable feelings of closeness in relationships, especially sexual relationships. Clarifying intimacy is tied to clarifying commitment. Do you say, "I like the intimacy of our relationship, but don't ask me for a commitment?" Do you want the relationship and intimacy when it feels good but not when it does not feel good or comfortable? Commitment is not dependent upon circumstances, and commitment comes from beyond self-centeredness. Whether it is commitment to practice or to a relationship, true commitment grows out of who we truly are, and true commitment manifests who we are.

On the surface, commitment may look ordinary, sometimes almost contractual. And yet commitment is vital to practice, as it is to all sorts of activities. All of us know this: if you want to learn to play a musical instrument, if you want to learn an art, a skill, a craft, a language, you must make a commitment. We make a commitment despite the fact that it gets hard, boring, dull, or unappetizing. Or I should say, some of us make a commitment. Some people do not commit; some people are not willing to experience what is hard, boring, or dull.

Commitment grows from what might be said to be "deeper than small self," even though at the start commitment makes sense and is rational. However, if we stay only on the rational level of commitment, then when commitment gets "too hard," we leave it. Contractual commitment is not adequate for a true relationship. What are we committing to in a relationship? Look closely. What is commitment when it does not go the way we like?

An aspect of relationship and commitment is evident with elderly parents. Some of you know this from caregiving for your parents; even when taking care of them is smelly, dirty, hard, or tiring, you are still committed to doing what needs to be done, despite anger, upset, or frustration. At times commitment related to an infant seems easier than commitment on the other end of life; it seems easier to change diapers, get barfed on, or respond to smelly, dirty needs in the middle of night. Many of us manifest this commitment to caregiving in our life. And yet if we are caught up in self-centeredness, we fail to see clearly because we are holding on to reactions of like and dislike.

At times we believe intimacy is unpleasant and something to avoid, since it doesn't feed the rational side of us that says, "I want, I like, I enjoy" or "It is not exciting enough, deep enough, does not produce the results I want; it is uncomfortable, and it does not go anywhere." We have all sorts of reasons to avoid intimacy. Sitting is being just this "does not suit me." Sometimes we talk about intimacy; we say all sorts of things and know all sorts of things about intimacy, but we refuse to be intimate. We may talk about practice endlessly, and yet talk does not reach. Avoiding is refusing this intimacy that is life; avoiding is refusing this bodily moment.

True commitment is vow. It is making a vow, not necessarily for others, though at times that is appropriate, too. In "Gakudo Yojin-shu" ("Things to Look Out for in Your Buddhist Training"), Dogen Zenji states: "Parents experience physical and mental hardships, and yet they persevere. After their young have grown up, fathers and mothers receive no reward. And yet, they have compassion toward their young. Even small creatures have this attitude. This is very similar to the Buddha's compassion toward all living beings."

Joko once said (I'll paraphrase): "When you know you can count on someone no matter what, then you know this is a relationship for you." See, intimacy is not dependent upon meeting some conditioned circumstance. Can you depend on yourself to be intimate?

Committing to practice, committing to who we truly are, does not mean that things are not hard at times, or that we never feel like running away. Yet we still commit: we make a vow of what we are, we make a vow of our life. See, intimacy is our life; it is not something added on, it is not something special we have to do. This is "raising the Bodhi mind."

Buddha is who you are: it is only the clinging to attachments, self-habits, self-discomfort, and self-thinking that confuses us and cuts us off and blinds us. All of you have discovered how easy it is to believe the stream of emotion-thought: "This doesn't feel comfortable (enough), this is too difficult," or too boring, or too dull. This avoidance seems natural, and therefore it may be hard to simply be present. We have all sorts of ways to avoid this intimacy that is who we are. Nevertheless, "Practice is from the beginning in realization." Being intimate is our life. There is nothing but intimacy.

Yet, the habits of attachment and beliefs seem to be who we are. At times life may seem hard, uncomfortable, unnatural, extra, even a strain, which we think "should not" be part of intimacy. Sometimes we try to "create intimacy" in the way "we want it," which is just more of this self-centered dream, this habit of attachment "doing itself," which is not at all intimacy. If we can be this bodily moment as is and forget self, then life functioning manifests naturally, and intimacy blooms.

Everyday functioning, morning to night, are the opportunities of intimacy. The whole of our practice is nothing but intimacy; the whole of our life is nothing but intimacy. So we can say, "When I, a student of the Way, look at the real form of the universe, all is this!" All is just this intimacy, just this opportunity, just this functioning of this life. The intimate universe, the turning of the Dharma wheel, is who you are. So please be intimate; please be the intimate life you are. Enjoy.

8

Enlightenment Practice, Everyday Practice

The Buddha Way is the Way of enlightenment. This is because from the beginning, practice is in realization. It is the manifested Way, the awakened life that we all are. Being so, we are able to realize. Realizing, clarifying, and actualizing: this is ongoing practice.

"Wonderful! Wonderful! All beings are the wisdom and the perfection of the Tathagata! But because of delusion and attachment they do not realize this." These are Shakyamuni Buddha's words upon enlightenment. They are the basis of practice.

Hakuin Zenji stresses, "All beings are primarily Buddhas!" Dogen Zenji states, "You should also know that basically we lack nothing of highest enlightenment. Though we are endowed with it, since we are unable to be in complete accord with it, we have a way of giving rise to random intellections, and by chasing them as if they were real, we stumble vainly on the Great Way." The realm of practice is self-centered thinking; this self-centered dream by which we are misled is always the barrier to the functioning of the realized life. Self-centered thought arises as the three poisons of greed, anger, and ignorance.

Unborn Buddha Mind is our natural state, which is manifested as experiencing. This natural functioning is covered over, cut off, and abandoned when we believe self-centered emotion-thought, and when we act based upon these emotion-thoughts. Everyday Zen is not a rigid concentration, nor a "neurotic mindfulness," to use Soen Roshi's words. Practice is not an effort to create or force a state. Buddha-nature pervades the whole universe, revealing right-here-now. Everyday practice is this moment, working with the self-centered thoughts that cut off this moment and prevent us from opening to this moment.

Experiencing the present moment always starts with the six senses, with the physical reality of our body-mind and our perceptions. However, even a thought such as, "I am experiencing such and such"—in other words, an awareness of the experiencing—may be self-centered emotion-thought. Our dualistic language-thought does not accurately express this direct experiencing. The striking of a bell, the sound it emits, and the process of hearing are thus separated by our self-centered beliefs. The sounds of the stream, the mountains, the office building, the traffic—all this is our very body, the body of the Buddha.

Thinking is a natural function of mind. It's not a hindrance, as long as we are not attached to and deluded by self-centered thoughts. Unfortunately, we are picking and choosing; we are believing self-centered thoughts to be an accurate description of life and a sound basis of activity. Having become habituated to living in and believing emotion-thought as life, it may require ongoing and at times enormous effort to not filter experience through emotion-thought but be this moment experiencing, which includes arising emotion-thought but is not limited by and to it. In practice, we extend and deepen our sensitivity to and awareness of emotion-thought, clarifying the ways that we cut ourselves off from natural functioning. This is where working with a guide or teacher is most valuable. Practice is not analyzing or explaining emotion-thought, but rather it is clarifying—becoming clear about—the subtle processes and patterns of our emotion-thought. Clarifying robs emotion-thought of its power to mislead: the more the seeming solidity and exclusivity of emotion-thought "melts," the more the natural awareness and joy of life blossoms. Enlightenment manifests of itself, like a flower blooming, like ripe fruit falling from the tree.

The effort in practice is always in terms of the self-centered barriers, and our tolerance and willingness to be the physical experience of the suffering and sorrows of the present moment when that arises. Mind and body are not-two. Allowing awareness of this moment, feeling this bodily moment, may be very "painful" and may require great effort and perseverance. The effort is in not being distracted or cut off from this moment, and thereby being the bodily-sensory functioning of life.

The inability and unwillingness to experience dissatisfaction and suffering are the barrier. Herein lies the virtue and importance of patience *paramita* (perfection). It is as if we had a "muscle of patience," which practice both requires and develops. In practice, the three poisons are transformed and revealed as the Three Treasures of Buddha, Dharma, and Sangha. Beginningless greed, anger, and ignorance born of our body, mouth, and thought are just this, just endless dimension universal life Buddha.

"You are putting a head on top of the one you already have," warned Linji. From old, practitioners have been disabused of the idea that the purpose of practice (or zazen) is to become a Buddha. An example is "Daitsu Chisho," case 9 of *The Gateless Gate*, where Daitsu Chisho Buddha sits zazen for ten *kalpas* and does not "attain Buddhahood."

Another case from classic Ch'an history (Jingde chuandeng lu, *Transmission of Lamp*) concerns Mazu.

Mazu sat zazen day and night, explaining, "I am trying to become a Buddha."

Hearing this, his teacher, Nanyue, began polishing a brick to make a mirror.

Mazu asked, "Can a brick become a mirror by polishing?"

Nanyue responded, "Can one become a Buddha by doing zazen?"

Because there is no need to do zazen, we must do it! This zazen is not a meditation practice of a sect of Buddhism; it is the very expression of Buddha's enlightenment. "Doing yourself, by yourself, with yourself," in Kodo Sawaki Roshi's words. This is our life, the life of the universe. It is our privilege to see and actualize this life as our ongoing practice.

9

Everything Is the Way

Our life is completely realized as it is. Always. Complete realization is not dependent upon doing and creating. Nevertheless, if in the midst of experiencing we hold to beliefs, likes, and dislikes, if we grasp and reject, then all sorts of reactions arise. As a result, the simple and straightforward truth of our life seems distant.

Being this moment is who we are. In being the awakened life we are, our practice effort is noticing what blinds us. These blinders are self-centered emotion-thoughts interwoven in forms, conceptions, and sensations. Practice effort may be defined as labeling thoughts and being bodily present, as noticing strategies and experiencing, as koan practice, as breathing, or just sitting.

If we are unclear, we may think practice is about making things better, about changing and improving. Though improvements may occur, they are not the aim of practice. Even in the midst of practice effort, we sometimes fail to see that practice is exactly experiencing, practice is exactly emptiness. Practice is experiencing. As the *Heart Sutra* states, form is nothing but emptiness. But even "emptiness" is another fancy word that we need to throw out. Emptiness is exactly form; form is exactly form. Dogen Zenji uses the phrase, "Practice realization."

PRACTICE

There are many different ways to practice with our self-centered habits of mind and functioning, and there are many different ways to clarify this matter—and this is because there are many ways of muddying up life. Practice is seeing the picking up, the holding, and the rejecting. In believing and holding to emotion-thoughts, even emotion-thoughts about muddying up, we miss our life in the midst of mud; we miss being this very muddy life. Our life is this practice opportunity. If we are not clear about what we are doing, we go off.

As a reminder and practice support, let us look at the opening sentences of the introduction to case 16 in the *Blue Cliff Record*, "Man in the Weeds." The *Blue Cliff Record* is a Chinese collection of a hundred cases compiled in the eleventh century, mostly concerning events that occurred in China from the seventh through tenth century. It was compiled by Xuedou with comments and verses, and later Yuanwu added introductions, capping phrases, and commentary. These cases have been collected in the *Blue Cliff Record* because of their value for our practice-life. It is valuable for us to clarify what is said, how it is expressed and handled.

Blue Cliff Record, CASE 16, "THE MAN IN THE WEEDS"

INTRODUCTION

The Way has no byroads; one who stands on it is alone and inaccessible. The Truth is not seeing or hearing; words and thoughts are far from it. If you can pass through the forest of thorns, untie the bonds of Buddhas and Zen Masters, and attain the realm of inner peace, then the gods will have no way to offer flowers and outsiders will find no opening through which to spy; you work all day without ever working, talk all day without ever talking. Then you can freely and independently exercise devices to break in and break out, using the sword that kills and gives life. But even if you can manage this, you still should realize that in the context of provisional expedients there is such a thing as uplifting with one hand while suppressing with the other. Yet that only amounts to a little bit—the fundamental matter is still out of range. What is the fundamental matter?

The introduction to the case begins: "The Way has no byroads." Life is clarified. The Way, our life, our practice, has no byroads.

"Nothing is not the Way; everything is exactly the Way." We are always right on the Great Way, always just this. Straightforward and simple, our practice and teachers are right here. Nothing more is needed; nothing is lacking.

As stated in the *Sandokai* (*Identity of Relative and Absolute*), "When you walk the Way, it is not near, it is not far." The Way is not elsewhere; our life isn't anything but the Way. Even saying this is extra. Nevertheless, we become caught up in and believe the story of our self-centered dream, we believe our strategies and reactions. Then, as the *Sandokai* says, "If you do not see the Way, you do not see it even as you walk on it."

The introduction to case 16 continues: "Not only that, but one who stands on it is alone and inaccessible." Not "alone" in the sense of "lonely." We must walk the Way and we must practice for our self. In fact, we are walking it!

A distorted belief that we are alone can be the great fear that we are running from. And we run by means of our various life strategies and habits. As a young child, I felt terribly alone and helpless after my father's death, and the terror of abandonment seemed the truth of life. All sorts of difficulties arose from my believing this and from my reacting to life based on this under-lying fear. Only by turning from such a core belief each time it arises, only by noticing and bodily inhabiting this moment, can we be the life that we are. We need to bodily inhabit this fear, this most painful moment.

Recently I met a number of elderly people for whom being alone and abandoned is the underlying theme that they believe pervades their whole life. This belief makes it difficult for them to function, because they react to circumstances based on this core belief, and this causes all sorts of suffering. They are truly cut off from their life. Working with the specific circumstances and needs of each person, the clarification of beliefs and fears occurs as we practice. Inhabiting this body-mind-world allows life to shine forth.

Some of you have heard the gloss that the word "alone" is really "all one." Several weeks ago we celebrated Buddha's birthday. The image of the baby Buddha has one hand pointing up and one down. The phrase attached to this image is: "Above the heavens, below the earth, I alone am the World-Honored One." This is "one who stands on it is alone."

Sometimes this phrase is distorted to mean that practice is for me, as opposed to beings for others. Such an attitude misses the interconnectedness of life, the fundamental serving of a Bodhisattva's practice. The vow to liberate numberless beings is a life koan of all who practice the Way. This is the practice of being present. A life koan such as the Bodhisattva's vow is not about conceptually or intellectually figuring out what to do but rather embodying the vow as our practice effort and intention. This does not mean that we need to memorize or even agree with these words. As I have said, what is important is how a reading or talk resonates and clarifies practice. Memorized words do not take care of this matter.

As the introduction to the case continues, "The truth is not seeing or hearing. Words and thoughts are far from it." Words may be useful, but they are not it. As you know very well, you can sit and tell yourself all sorts of words, but that is not sitting and that is not practice. Sitting is being this; sitting is experiencing. Even saying that is extra. Yet one word that resonates can clarify our life; a one-word koan can open up this matter. That is the point of Dharma talks and readings. Once this matter is clarified, awakened life is clearly revealed.

"If you can pass through the forest of thorns, untie the bonds of Buddha and Zen teachers, and attain the realm of inner peace, then the gods will have no way to offer flowers, and outsiders will find no openings through which to spy." Put simply, this is working with the strategies and the ways we are caught up in self-centered beliefs, "this forest of thorns." What are the bonds of Buddha and teachers? Do they tie or do we tie? How do we untie what is never tied?

In the *Heart Sutra,* we translate *shunyata* as "emptiness." Exploring "emptiness" is our ongoing task. Some recently proposed translating *shunyata* as "boundlessness." "Boundlessness" or "emptiness"—both are fine. They both point to the boundaries that we put on forms, sensations, and conceptions, the boundaries that we then believe are solid. These boundaries are then maintained by our self-centered strategies.

As we practice throughout our life, and particularly in sitting, we discover and clarify how holding to self-centered thoughts makes seemingly solid boundaries of this boundless emptiness. We discover this not by thinking but in our body-mind functioning, in our specific and appropriate efforts to work with our clouds. Practice, which means working with whatever clouds this unexcelled jewel, reveals the Way that we always are and reveals this boundless joy. As the introduction to case 16 continues: "If one is clear with this, then you work all day without ever working, talk all day without ever talking." This Bodhisattva functioning is our life. Who works? What work? Is something added?

Practicing together in sesshin is the experiencing that we always are. In the midst of complete realization, we practice; in noticing self-centered holding, we practice. Being present is the opportunity to be "clear with this." Yes, practice is working with ignorance-based reactions of fear, greed, and anger. Nevertheless, we are clarifying in the midst of clarity. Always our effort is exactly this Bodhisattva functioning that is our life, that is being just this.

Please enjoy this life.

10

One Bright Pearl

Master Hsuansha said, "The whole universe is one bright pearl."
He is not talking about some universe out there but this universe
that is our life. It is not a matter of inside or outside, it is not a
matter of big or small.

I was looking at Master Hongzhi Zhengjue's words regarding
"one bright pearl" and I came across something. In a previous talk,
I said, "The thing that erodes self-centeredness, the mischief in
our life, is the open experiencing of our life at this moment." Now
listen to what Hongzhi said in eleventh-century China: "You must
completely withdraw from the invisible pounding and weaving of
your ingrained ideas; if you want to be free of this invisible turmoil, you must sit through it." He goes on, "Attain fulfillment and
illuminate thoroughly, light and shadow all together forgotten."

Note the similarity in terms of the invisible pounding of
ingrained ideas and the self-centered mischief of our life, which
only erodes in the open experience, in the sitting through it, in
the experiencing of it. Always the same point, whether in the
eleventh century or in the twenty-first century. Life is in the
midst of this invisible pounding of self-centeredness, and yet it is
this one bright pearl.

Hongzhi says, "In a bowl the bright pearl rolls on its own without prodding. Yet, for a luminous jewel without flaw, if you carve a pattern its virtue is lost." Some take "carve a pattern" to mean that if we try to add something to who we are, if we see our practice as adding something, then we just take away from this bright pearl that is our life. How do you see this?

Master Dogen's commentary is: "For a luminous jewel without flaw if polished its glow increases." See, sitting is this experiencing; sitting is being who we are. Yet we may discover this tendency in our self to turn sitting into adding self-centeredness, even though sitting is intended to free us of self-centeredness. Nevertheless, this practice effort of zazen is an effort we must make; it is a polishing that increases the glow.

In a way, this is a subtle point; in a way, it is not so subtle. It is important to be clear on what it is we are doing and with what attitude we are practicing. Indeed, how do we see the mischief, the difficulties, and the suffering in life?

Dogen Zenji picks up this phrase in his *Shobogenzo* fascicle "Ikka Myoju," or "One Bright Pearl." Here Dogen expresses it a little differently from "For a luminous jewel without flaw if polished its glow increases." In *Shobogenzo* he says, "Though on the surface there may seem to be change or no change, enlightenment or no enlightenment, it is the one bright pearl. Realizing it is so is itself the one bright pearl. Confusions and doubts, affirmations and negations, these are nothing but the ephemeral, small responses of ordinary [folks]. However, still they are the one bright pearl, appearing as small, ephemeral responses."

This one bright pearl is always the life we are right this moment; right this moment, our difficulties and confusion are just this one bright pearl. Nevertheless, unaware of what the bright pearl is, Dogen says, "What it is and what it is not, we entertain countless doubts and nondoubts about it and turn them into the indubitable fodder for the mind. But Hsuansha's expression has made it clear that our minds and bodies are the one bright pearl. And so we realize that our minds are not 'ours.'" That is, not "ours" in the sense of the self-centered dream "ours."

See, that is the point of the pounding getting dealt with by the intelligent suffering of practice and zazen. The point is not to get rid of anything but rather to transform; to transform what seems to be the difficulties and reveal them as truly the one bright pearl. It is not a matter of figuring out or being dependent upon understanding. Hsuansha says, "It is not a matter of understanding that the whole universe is one bright pearl." Practice isn't thinking about practice; practice isn't even about understanding what the universe is. Practice is being this experiencing that we are, being this bodily feeling of the totality of life.

Because it is not necessary for us to practice, because it is not necessary for us to do zazen, because it doesn't add one iota to who we are, that is why we do zazen, and that is why we must be zazen. See? If zazen and practice were about getting rid of some part of our self, then it would just be another artifice of this self-centeredness. It would just be another way that we try to get what we want, or try to get rid of what we don't want. Zazen is not so. Therefore intelligent suffering allows us to see who we are and who we have been from the beginning. Because practice is in realization, because practice is nothing but this one bright pearl that is our life, it can reveal itself by our being so, by our doing so, by our polishing. The jewel polishes the jewel; self-centeredness is eroded in this very experiencing of life that we think limits us.

See, the bright pearl is experiencing the conditions and circumstances we might ordinarily think are the problem. Whether we are energetic, joyful, upset, or in pain, in that experiencing we discover our self. This is the opposite of the self-centered way of often running away from this moment body-mind experiencing, doing something about it, doing something against it, having something else to cover it up, or having something else substitute for it. Zazen and practice are the very opposite of that self-centered way.

Dogen says, "The one bright pearl [though] from beginning to end is essentially uninvolved with cause and effect, is your original face, your enlightened nature. Therefore, no need to be anxious about being reborn in one of the six realms of cause and effect, no matter which realm you enter."

No matter which realm! Not in some magical thinking about some later realm; Dogen says no matter which realm we enter in our life today, right now. There's no need to think of the six realms as something that happens in the future in some other place after death, though we can explore that too. The six realms are what we enter now, tomorrow morning and the next morning; the six realms are what we encounter with all the different people and circumstances of the day. No matter what we enter, it is nothing but this one bright pearl, nothing but this life encounter that is the opportunity of experiencing and being who we are.

Dogen continues, "Who can be anxious as to whether birth or death, circumstances of all sorts, are or are not the bright pearl? Even if there is doubt and anxiety, suffering and upset, they are the bright pearl. There is not a single activity or thought that is not the bright pearl. And consequently, both advancing and retreating in the black mountain cave of demons."

The world of suffering results from self-centeredness. The black mountain cave of demons is pretty ferocious; this is the place where we are scared much of the time, where we experience the fears that arise in all sorts of circumstances, the fears that give rise to anger, upset, hate, and greed. This is where we experience all the human circumstances, and react in all sorts of harmful ways. All of these are nothing but the one bright pearl.

An important point here has to do with a certain confidence in who and what we are, and how we practice. We make practice effort because from the beginning, our effort is the one bright pearl; our effort is the realized life. Otherwise we might say, "Well, I've been practicing, but when am I going to really have something?" Here "something" means enlightenment or some other thing or condition. Whatever it is, you already are it.

"I don't have it."

Yes, you do.

You still say: "I don't have it, I know I don't."

Well, if you insist you "don't have it," then for you it is "don't have it." Nevertheless, it is who you are.

In a way, you could say, "Having it is not the point." But even saying "direct experiencing" is just words; these words really don't express what direct experiencing is, because we are using the dualistic language and dualistic thinking that we might mistakenly take to be accurate descriptors that will enable us to "get" who we are. Words are fine, but it is important to see that they don't express who we are.

However, if we believe we are who we think we are, if we believe the limits of our thinking, it distorts who we are. Pointing with "experiencing" is attempting to turn us from these emotion-thoughts, to open us from the held emotion-thought or have us drop below it. Pointing is so that we can see for our self what we are and who we have been all along, what our life has been all along. Many practice devices, such as intelligent suffering and experiencing, sound horrible from an ordinary point of view. Yet that is exactly this life that we are, and that is exactly the entrance to this life. Every aspect of your life is this one bright pearl.

You say: "I don't understand it." One bright pearl is not a matter of understanding or not understanding. Not understanding, one bright pearl; understanding, one bright pearl.

As Joko said, it is a matter of really dropping into this sitting. We taste for our self, in our own sitting and in our own practice. Kodo Sawaki Roshi says it nicely: "Doing your self by your self with your self." That is practice, that is zazen, that is our life. All you encounter is your self. All you are doing is your self. But we forget it so quickly, because self-centeredness intrudes and becomes mixed into all sorts of things. The holding to attachment creates and maintains self-centeredness.

Just as practice can be a mystery, self-centeredness can be a mystery. It is fine for it to be a mystery. See, all these words that we use when we talk about self-centeredness are not so that we can become experts in understanding self-centeredness. Self-centeredness isn't a matter of understanding or not understanding: it's an expression that reveals the mischief that we are doing. It reveals the ideals we hold that poison our life and poison this one bright pearl. They poison this one bright pearl by carving into it; yet carving itself is nothing but the one bright pearl. All sorts of suffering arises; suffering itself is the one bright pearl. And we have this practice opportunity of intelligently suffering.

All of you know this (some of you even acknowledge it) because you sense it in your own practice. Of course, if I said at the beginning of practice, "Zazen is intelligent suffering," then a lot of people would run away. Who wants that? And yet that is what practice is, and that is what we are thankful for. It's nicer to say, "Zazen is one bright pearl." Some people need something fancier, so we say, "Endless dimension universal life." That's just right here; it's not somewhere else. It's not far away.

See, we use all sorts of true words to encourage us, to support our ongoing life practice. Not because we need to do something other than who we are, but because we need to do something that is who we are. Otherwise we are poisoning who we are in our self-centered pursuit of ideals.

Shakyamuni Buddha said: "All beings are the wisdom and the compassion of the Tathagatha." All beings, including you, and including everyone else who you find hard to include. All beings are the enlightened life right now. It is only because of ignorance and attachment that we miss who we are. Our inability and unwillingness to suffer and experience is the barrier to our life. This inability is not because we are not able to suffer and experience but because we refuse to. We are unwilling, even though we say we are willing. We discover our unwillingness because we see that we do not do it.

So our time here in sesshin is the time to do this life of practice, this moment of experiencing; our time in zazen is the time to do this. Sitting and sesshin "work" because distractions are reduced, which supports function but most of all reminds us that because we are present, we are able to be present. This reminder is because we all forget again and again, so we have to remind our self over and over. We remind our self as we sit down and as we adjust our posture. We allow sitting still as zazen to remind us. Being still, our body reminds us. Being upright, our body reminds us. In fact, the whole room and the whole universe reminds us, even when we forget. So we forget and we remember. See, the effort in practice is always in terms of barriers, and our tolerance and willingness to be the experiencing, the physical experiencing of the moment, this moment.

Let us see one last bit of this pearl, this one bright pearl that is always in our hand, this one bright pearl that is our functioning of seeing and hearing. Round like a pearl that rolls around and around, this brilliant light, this mind. Nothing hinders it, this one bright pearl in its entirety. I recommend that when you can you go through this *Shobogenzo* fascicle phrase by phrase in order to appreciate it and appreciate our life. That is life: appreciating, experiencing, tasting with our own body, tongue, and senses. This is our opportunity of being alive. This experiencing is polishing this one bright pearl.

11

No Gap: Sesshin Guidelines in Everyday Life

Your life is the awakened life: nothing else. Having confidence in this and embodying this is the liberation of life-death.

Many of you have heard this; you may even say this yourself. And yet despite this being so, there often seems to be a gap in our life. Even saying "awakened life" is unnecessary and extra. Though this is the awakened life, this is not so for us right here now because of this gap and this barrier. Because we lack confidence, and because we do not completely believe this awakened life in our actions and reactions and in our body-mind habits, we make this gap where there is none; we make a barrier between our self and our self.

Practice clarifies this gap, this seeming barrier. Clarifying enables us to be this awakened life. Being this life we are, the gap does not appear. Being this spacious functioning that is our life, the seemingly solid barrier is revealed as "transparent." It is revealed as not a solid barrier at all; it is revealed as no-barrier. We are this seamless, boundless life.

Depending on our habits and tendencies, different means and

images can clarify our life, as well as illuminate our practice effort and opportunity. Sometimes we use the image of breaking out of a shell: really there is no shell to break out of, and yet we create and seem to be in a shell. Being in this shell is being in hell, so we speak of breaking out of the shell. Of course, while we are in hell, living in hell is our practice. In fact, being present in hell is breaking out of hell.

Another image often used is to see the Dharma as a raft to go to the other shore. We say this even though the other shore is right here: there is no other shore elsewhere, there is nowhere else to go. Nevertheless, it can be skillful and appropriate to speak of using the Dharma raft to cross from this shore to another shore, this shore of our habits of attachment and reactions. We can speak of a Dharma raft to cross from the shore of a life lived out of dualistic self-other beliefs. Nevertheless, there is no gap; there is nowhere else to go.

For this no-gap to be the truth of our life, we have to manifest no-gap in our functioning and in our life. Being this moment, there is no-gap, no-barrier. Yet in our life there appear to be barriers and gaps. Looking closely, we can see some of the ways that we make barriers and gaps. No-barrier appears as barrier for us, a barrier that seems familiar and almost natural to us. It is in the midst of this seeming barrier of habits that we have our opportunity, our practice effort. Then holes may appear in the seeming wall; there are the "pecks" in the shell, some little, some big. These pecks result in the dropping away of any gap between our life and our life.

There is never a gap, not even the thinnest of film; there is no-barrier, and yet to us it seems that there is. If we make it so, it is so, this barrier of no-barrier. Therefore, if this barrier of no-barrier is so for us, we need to pass through it; our body-mind "needs" to drop away.

How does sitting practice clarify body-mind? Some of the

things I am going to say may seem very familiar; you'll say, "Oh, I know that, it's basic." Nevertheless, please attend to this. In sitting, be attentive to your sitting bones; be sitting on your "sitting bones." We can imagine the sitting bones like the bottom of a stick; we can see them as two points at the bottom of the pelvis. Allow the body to settle on those "bones" so that that the bones bear weight. A slight inward arching of the lower back helps; this assists sitting and assists being bodily present. Being bodily present, being body-mind present, enables and supports us in practicing with body-mind habits that arise. This enables us to see these habits in the spaciousness of this moment of life, rather than being caught up in them or believing our bodily emotion-thought habits as the whole truth.

Be attentive to the head resting on the neck and on the spine, so as to not add holding tension there. Body and mind are not two different things. Even using words like "awareness" or "spaciousness" should not become an end in itself. Sitting is simply this moment, which allows the functioning that we are, and allows this responding that we are, so-called inside, so-called outside. Sitting is being present, inside, outside, this moment flowing.

When walking, we are responding to the floor, falling and being supported by the floor, taking the next step. The earth and I respond to each other: the earth is walking me, I am walked by the earth. But it can only be so if we are so, if we don't hold to habits of body-mind that blind us and maintain dualistic functioning. Body-mind presence allows body-mind dropping away. Body-mind dropping away is functioning of dropped-away body-mind; it is exactly this life. This is not something that we figure out; it is not something that we have to know about or intellectually understand.

Nontalking is a sesshin rule and guideline. Maintaining nontalking in sesshin is obviously about not talking to others, but even more important, nontalking is about not talking to self. This is important throughout every day of our life. I am referring to nontalking in thoughts, feelings, and emotions, in the sense of commenting on arising thoughts, feelings, and emotions, in the sense of elaborating on them and going on and on about them. This is charity of speech; this is giving self away. We allow mental speech to arise and pass, a mental speech that otherwise we would habitually and reactively comment about. This is giving self away so that we don't have to comment about the thought: "He did such a terrible thing" or "I don't understand it" or "It's stupid" or "Why did this happen?" You know much better than I do the speech and chatter that arises in your life.

It is important to be this charity of speech. This is also an ongoing practice guideline and an ongoing practice effort. The charity is not to anyone else; it is to our self. And this charity is to everyone else; this charity is to this boundless universe. Of course, this charity of speech also applies externally—we can maintain nontalking even in the midst of appropriate talking. A number of the Bodhisattva Precepts, such as not speaking of the faults of others, and not praising self and putting others down, are related to this charity of speech.

Maintaining nonlooking around is another sesshin guideline. This is not about closing the eyes or about not seeing. It is not even about just looking around the so-called outside. See, we look outside, we look inside. Notice the difference between what is expressed by the word "seeing" and what is expressed by the word "looking" or "looking at." "Looking" as a habit of functioning can create a gap in functioning, a gap in being. Self-centered habits are what create the gap of our life, this gap that we live out of right here.

There is no problem with talking and seeing; these are the manifestation of this true nature that we are. And yet, talking can create gaps; looking around and looking at can create gaps. Gap is just gap. And yet the consequences of this gap is that we suffer, because we are bound by the gap, we believe the gap. Charity of eyes, of inside eyes, of outside eyes, is a charity of giving away the habit of looking for something.

Again, how to work with this depends on the individual, and grows out of clarifying practice. If we look closely, all of us know how to begin working with it. Don't get stuck in particular words, but hear what is being said.

Nonlooking around leads to the next guideline, nonsocial courtesies. In formal sesshin there is no need to say "Thank you," "Please," and so forth. But even more important are the social habits of mind-body. You each know very well what the social habits of your functioning are. Do we greet someone genuinely, or do we greet them habitually without being present because we are caught up in dualistic habits? Who is greeting? Who is being greeted?

Being aware, making the effort to maintain nonsocial courtesies, encourages and supports being present right now. It allows you to notice where social habits blind and break up your life. It allows you to truly be courteous, to truly say "Good-morning," to truly bow a greeting. When you answer the phone, who is saying "Hello"? Are you? Throughout daily life, this practice reminder supports manifesting this boundless life that we are.

You may have heard much of this before, and yet this is a valuable and important reminder. For each of us, sesshin is—life is— the opportunity to be this awareness that is our life. This is what sesshin makes possible; that is, if we do what makes it possible. If we do our effort, then this is so.

Our effort is not in order to get any particular state or circumstance or experience; those might or might not occur, but that isn't what this is about. When particular states occur, even "highly prized" states, being present is the opportunity to not be caught up in them. There is no gap; there never was, and there never will be.

And yet, we seem to believe a gap; we seem to live as if there is one. At times, we can almost feel the barrier. So practice reminders are intended to support us in being this; they are intended to support our life opportunity of being what is truly so. We give self to this moment of what we like or don't like, what we think should or shouldn't be. This doesn't mean changing that thought, and this doesn't mean thinking about that or commenting on it; it means that despite your thought, you give self and you give awareness to this moment. Otherwise, that comment, this evaluation, traps us. Giving self is the opportunity of responding; it is the opportunity of manifesting this moment response.

Practice is not a mechanical process; it is nonmechanical. You can almost say it is magical. This is exactly what giving is. Giving is nonmechanical; our practice intention is to give without the act of giving being something done in order to obtain certain results. There is a mechanical way you can give, but that isn't giving. It is the intention of giving that isn't mechanical, that goes beyond the mechanical.

It is difficult going beyond the mechanical because the mechanical fits easily with beliefs such as "This is something I want; this is something I don't want; if this is something I don't want, I can fix it; if this is something I want, then here is what I need to do." If practice is mechanical and dualistic, if our life is lived dualistically, then I am calculating and trying to figure it out. But all of that thinking keeps the gap—the talking and not-talking, the looking and not-looking—as dualistic choices of yes or no. That's why I say nontalking, and that why I say charity, because practice is giving self away. Practice is being awareness.

Sometimes we can sense where we choose, and sometimes we can't. This is because our actions, habits, and choices seem natural, or seem to just happen. But the more we practice, the more we are able to sense how we are choosing and maintaining habits. In itself, this is a wonderful opportunity. It is a deepening of our practice when we see this. Sometimes we think, "Oh, this is terrible, look at what I am seeing, I don't want to see this." And yet, seeing this is a valuable and necessary step. What is it to be like a fool, functioning dumbstruck by our life? In the midst of this is nonspeaking.

Words point to our life; words express our life. Each time we sit down, we get to choose sitting. Being functioning, the bell strikes, we sit down, we stand up, we walk. We don't have to make any additional choices; we simply allow the functioning of life. Being this that we are, right now we get to make the effort. There's no need to add judgment or evaluation; everyone is doing their best practice with where they are right now. No extra choice is needed, no extra effort is needed; just give your self away to life this moment.

Practice is the moment of choice, life is the moment of choice. Giving self to practice, this is a moment of choice. Giving charity of speech, charity of eyes, charity of mouth, charity of mind, charity of functioning. Do you give choice? Only by being awareness in this moment arising-passing. There is never anything but this arising. Arising is awareness.

Practice is not a means to an end: it is the means and the end wrapped up together. Awareness is this functioning life.

PART TWO

Impermanence

12

Life of the Universe

You are the life of the universe.

There's no need to even say this. It is valuable for us to recognize that everyone and every circumstance we encounter is exactly this. Your life is living the life of the universe. Practice is supporting this life of the universe. And practice is being supported by this life of the universe. This is definitely so.

Every condition that arises is this, which is why sitting and sesshin are so simple: it's because the universe is our sitting, the universe is our sesshin, the universe is our life. And yet, at times we want to pick and choose for the universe and decide what is OK and what isn't OK. Of course, picking and choosing is nothing but the universe functioning. And yet, because we believe and attach to OK and not-OK, we get into all sorts of difficulties. Do we sit and find we are refusing to be this intimacy? Are we believing the story of me and not-me, and how me has to be and how me shouldn't be, or what me is and what me isn't? Are we believing all sorts of stories about the so-called others that we encounter, and then are we acting out of those stories?

At times we insist that the universe is wrong; we insist the circumstances of the universe are wrong. It shouldn't be so cold or it shouldn't be so hot; there is too much snow or too little snow; this tree shouldn't be here or it should be there. The snow here is our opportunity to support the universe in our shoveling. The universe as is, is our opportunity to manifest the universe in seeing, doing, and responding as needed. Your job is living the life of the universe.

All sorts of conditions arise with birth, sickness, old age, and death. We have this moment-opportunity to embrace this intimacy, to appreciate the life that we are, to skillfully respond as this life we are. Otherwise, we hold to and react from "I'm not supposed to be so achy, so weak, so forgetful, with such poor eyesight"—in other words, all the conditions that we reject or become unhappy about. Habitual reacting out of self-centeredness is especially evident with body-mind conditions. Who are you? We get into trouble if we don't see this life of the universe that we are.

Do we believe, "I shouldn't have times when my mind goes and I forget a name or an appointment"? How is it when a friend or family member does not even remember us? Do they sometimes talk what seems like nonsense (at least, it seems like nonsense to us) or do they often become angry? What is embracing this moment? This universe manifesting us, manifesting the people and conditions we are. What is this life that we are?

All sorts of conditions and circumstances manifest as this universe life that we are, which is why daily life practice and sesshin practice are so easy. They are easy because all we have to do is be right here where we are, and be the conditions that we are manifesting: be breathing, be hearing, and so on. All we have to do is be the functioning that we are, and skillfully and appropriately respond in the midst of these conditions while being this intimacy.

What is the skillful and appropriate effort? When mind-states of agitation, caught-up-ness, and "monkey mind" appear, this is nothing but the universe manifesting our life. It is cause and effect, habits and attachments—and this is exactly the opportunity to liberate the life of the universe, to be the life of the universe, to support the life of the universe, to be arising and passing. This is our life; this is zazen, this is ordinary life practice. Doing so, we are supported while we are hearing, seeing, sitting upright, breathing, and being aware. It is nothing but this; it is not some separate person inside a bag of skin—we are never so even if we believe we are a person in a body.

Always this universe is breathing us in and out. Of course it makes sense to say, "I breath, I exhale." It's fine to say this, but know that you are exhaling the universe and the universe is breathing in. So it is with the light that fills this room right now, and the chill in the early morning penetrating deeply. This is exactly our life. It is not some abstraction.

This life of the universe is this specific moment functioning, whether we are sitting or eating or walking. Always we are this life of the universe within which we swim, being supported and supporting. It is important to know what we are doing here; not because knowing these words is enough, but so that they can be a support to enable us to do the universe. It may enable us to make appropriate and skillful effort according to circumstances. In the midst of these constantly changing circumstances, we get to dance. Isn't it wonderful?

Sometimes it is not so easy to say "wonderful." Whether it's in terms of so-called internal physical or mental conditions, or in terms of social or political conditions, or in terms of familial relations and work, sometimes it is not so easy to say that our life is wonderful, and to see this life of the universe we are. This is because we twist our self up, and because we don't see that what we encounter is nothing but the face of the universe, which is our face.

It is good to clarify our effort and our practice a little bit; it is good to clarify what requires no effort, because this is who we are, and this is what allows us to be this nothing extra needed. When there is effort needed, that is exactly what is needed; it is nothing extra. This is exactly the life of the universe of ongoing change that you get to support and manifest as your life practice. Clarifying this is enabling us to practice our life together, not to get more ideas and knowledge.

Student: You mentioned that you can't just think about this stuff, that thinking about it is not enough. So what is enough?

Genmyo: [Breathes in and out] Breathe in and out; this is enough. Be breathed by the universe; this is enough. There's no need for anything else.

And yet, if you try to figure this out, right there is something to do. See what to do when you are trying to figure out "What else do I need?" See what is the skillful, appropriate practice effort right now when breathing is hindered.

Make that effort. Be right where you are; just be breathed, be sitting, be nothing extra is needed. Really! Or when driving, be driving. Be seeing the road in front of you, and allow your arms to see even as they grip the steering wheel. Then you take care of driving, and you take care of being the Bodhisattva who delivers medicine to people in need and relieves their suffering. So you are the arms and eyes of thousand-arms-and-eyes Avalokiteshvara—this is the universe functioning to support the universe, that is who you are. And when you don't believe it, see what there is to do.

Even when you are noticing being caught up in thoughts, doubts, and upset, just that very noticing is exactly the eyes of Avalokiteshvara noticing and skillfully responding. It is not something magical; it is very ordinary and simple. It is the functioning of the life that you are, all the capacities and abilities that you have at this particular moment. At this moment, we have capacities and abilities in a certain way. Who knows? Maybe next week my mental capacities will be such that I cannot make the practice effort. But right now my capacities are what they are; we make use of the capacities as we are. Does that make sense?

Student: Yes.

Genmyo: Good.

Student: I do have a little trouble with the skillful stuff because I feel like I don't have skills.

Genmyo: When do you notice that belief: "I don't have skills"?

Student: Well, it is not a belief. I do stuff, and it doesn't turn out.

Genmyo: "Not turning out" is the extent of our abilities. But it is not that it doesn't turn out, but rather that we don't get the outcome we want.

Student: Well, it's not just that. It is just like when you were mentioning about upsets and things that don't go the way I would prefer to have things go. That is the way it happens. I'm aware that this is part of life, and still I don't know; I feel like I don't have the skillful means to somehow adjust. I don't mean adjust those things, but to adjust myself, or to somehow see clearly what the truth of that is, rather than make up a bunch of stuff in my head.

Genmyo: Maybe we only get to see a little bit according to our capacity right now. Seeing a little bit enables us and encourages us, so to speak, to be here, and maybe to do a bit more or do things a bit differently at a future time. What we do is based on our capacity right now. If we hold on to the idea "I should have more capacity now," that much we aren't willing to be this capacity that we are now. If we hold the idea "I should have noticed this last week, how come it took me until today?" that much we are not here today. This creates stress and suffering.

What to do is be present, to make this effort, to do what we can now! When we see and when we make our practice effort, that's when we are able to make our practice effort. There's no need to add: "The universe was wrong last week because I wasn't such and such" or "Last week I should have been stronger, smarter, clearer." See?

If we do believe these judgments, that much we are not here now, that much we add suffering, that much we separate our self from the universe. Right here is practice. This universe isn't something else; it is exactly our life, exactly what we encounter—except if we believe we are something inside this bag of skin. If that is what we believe, if that is who and what we live, then that much we miss our self.

We are not that; we are exactly here this moment, we are exactly this body-mind universe—we are not anything else. Therefore we do our best and are supported by the universe to be able to do our best. See? You don't have to figure this out. To the extent that it makes sense, fine; to the extent that we can clarify this, good. This enables each of us to do this life that we are. That is the point; the point is not to get new ideas.

When we speak together, our job is clarifying skillful practice and clarifying what is appropriate. We are doing it to the extent that we are capable, and that's wonderful. From the beginning, you are the life of the universe; you are nothing else but that. There is no mistake, there are no errors, there is nothing lacking. Nothing lacking, and nothing extra.

13

Indestructible Nature

This life, as it is right now, is the joy that nurtures and fulfills us, the cold that chills us to the bone, the mystery that we are. Being just this is straightforward and simple.

Unfortunately, exactly this seems so difficult for us. Believing fears, we refuse this intimacy. The "icy couch," as Joko called it, is right here. All sorts of beliefs and habits, and the resulting conditions and circumstances, make it hard for us to be this very life. Refusing intimacy, we do not see this; we are confused about this. In the face of confusion, clarifying the teachings of the Ancestors can support living this moment; it can nurture and encourage our practice and this nondoing.

Dogen's Extensive Record, VOLUME 2, CASE 140, "THE INDESTRUCTIBLE NATURE IN DEEP MUDDY WATER"

I remember that a monk asked Joshu (Zhaozhou), "Before there was this world, already there was this nature. When this world is destroyed, this nature will not be destroyed. What is this indestructible nature?"

Joshu said, "The four great elements and five skandhas."

The monk said, "These still can be destroyed. What is this indestructible nature?"

Joshu said, "The four great elements and five skandhas."

This monk is no different from any of us in knowing much and having all sorts of ideas. There's nothing wrong with what he said; in fact, he was quoting Joshu: "When the world was not, there was still this. When the world is destroyed, this reality is not destroyed. Take one look at me, I am nothing other than I am."

This. We are this. In a way, the monk is sincerely asking for help: "What is this?" But notice where he goes off; he says "indestructible nature," therefore making a dream of this. Instead of being this, being nondoing, we want to know what nondoing is; even more, we think we know what this is and what this is not.

So Joshu replies, "The four great elements and five *skandhas*." This world, this body-mind. Right here, this life—here it is.

But the monk believes and knows too much about this world and this body-mind. He replies: "These still can be destroyed." In the midst of not-knowing, we are offered this, but we get caught up in believing ideas and habits of body-mind, and we believe stories about what this is. "The four great elements and five skandhas": What is this? What is indestructible nature? Do you agree with the monk's question? Will this that we are be destroyed? Are we "the five skandhas"? Ask yourself; be honest. It is important to see what we would ask in a similar situation. Can this be destroyed? Are we sure about what is and what isn't? What is this? Is indestructible nature elsewhere?

Joshu again responds, "The four great elements and five skandhas." In a way the monk's questions are fine. The monk is saying, "The five skandhas, the body-mind, is being human; this whole phenomenal world is the four great elements." He may add, "Isn't the Buddha's teaching about impermanence (and the entailed stress and suffering)? How is this indestructible nature? How does this take care of suffering?"

Right here, right now—what more is there to be sought? What is our experience? Do we believe otherwise? What do we believe? Can we open what we believe to being what is, to being what we are? We need to clarify this; we need to testify as this.

Unfortunately, to paraphrase Joshu, we turn our head or change our expression, and then this is immediately lost. Nondoing is being this true form; it is being this true form nowhere else but right here, right in the midst of conditioned circumstances, and to settle as this nondoing.

This is what Dogen Zenji says in the *Shobogenzo* fascicle "Shoaku Makusa" ("Not Doing Evil"):

> When nondoing lies behind your head, when nondoing is the base of your life, then "when you bring your own body mind to practice . . . the power of practicing with the four great elements and five heaps instantly appear in full, and your own individual self consisting of the four great elements and five heaps is not defiled. Thus you will be able to practice with today's four great elements and five heaps. The power of each moment's practice by the four great elements and five heaps causes the aforementioned four great elements and five heaps to practice. When the mountains and rivers, stars and planets, also are caused to practice, then the mountains and rivers, stars and planets, in turn cause us to practice."

This cause-and-effect moment—this moment flowing stream—is our life. Our mind-body beliefs and constructs attempt to solidify this, and so we bump into circumstances, with painful results. Being this moment is our practice opportunity. We miss this if we do not see the constructs as the source of pain, as the ignorance and beliefs they are, and we miss this if we do not open up the seemingly solid construct as this moment.

Dogen has a nice comment on Joshu's dialogue: "When the water is deep, the boat rides high. When there is much mud, the Buddha is large." Indestructible nature is exactly responding in the midst of deep water; indestructible nature, much mud, large Buddha. Do you see?

Dogen also commented on this dialogue regarding indestructible nature, saying, "I would say to the monk, fences, walls, tiles, and pebbles." For all of us, it is important to ask our question—that is practice. It is not figuring things out and asking questions from theories, but asking the question of our life practice, the question that comes out of our practice. This is our practice effort.

But what if the monk would respond to Dogen: "This is still something fabricated and perishable. What is the indestructible nature?" Doesn't that seem to be so for you? Look closely. Dogen responds, "I would say to the monk, fences, walls, tiles, and pebbles." How do you see this? Are fences, walls, tiles, and pebbles the indestructible nature?

In the *Recorded Sayings of Zen Master Joshu*, case 337, a monk asked Joshu, "What is the body of no-disease?" Some of us in this Sangha are facing serious diseases. Is there a body of no-disease? This is a very real question. Joshu says, "Four elements, five skandhas." How could that be? I have disease. How can you say "Four elements, five skandhas"? There are all sorts of suffering and violence in the world. How can you respond to "What is the body of no-disease?" with "Four elements, five skandhas"? We really need to chew on this until we can make it our own. Then we may see something, or we may say, "No, this doesn't satisfy." Good. Then our chewing practice goes on.

When we hear words like "conditioned," "cause and effect," and "impermanent," those are important and valuable ways to assist us in seeing the nature of circumstances, in seeing the nature of our life. And yet, if we are trapped in the words and ideas, then we are in trouble. Those words are just "clothes stuck on the body," as Joshu says in his *Recorded Sayings,* and if they are misused, they may become further hindrances. We can even be trapped in fancy words like "Buddha" or "Nirvana," and be "seeking for Buddha fools," says Joshu in *Recorded Sayings.* There is no conditioned except in the midst of the unconditioned; there is no unconditioned except in the midst of the conditioned. But this is explaining; it has limited utility, and at times may even hinder us. Nevertheless, live words express this very life, supporting us in being the nondoing that we are. Nondoing is practicing all good; nondoing is moment-by-moment responding to circumstances.

This is our life. Our life is not just so-called inside; our life is everyone you encounter, and everything you encounter. Our life is mind in earth and sky—exactly this. There is no indestructible anywhere else. An Ancestor says, "If you don't give rise to mind, then the ten thousand dharmas are not transgressed." There is no Buddha anywhere else.

But will we embrace this moment? Will we embrace being chilled to the bone? Unless we do so, and unless our held beliefs open, we make all sorts of Buddhas and sentient beings in our mind, and they aren't of much use. Are we caught in the midst of body-mind habit and emotion-thought belief? Look, just this— but what kind of this is this?

Original face of cause and effect is nondoing and not obscuring. To paraphrase Dogen, one's own self is neither existent nor nonexistent. Being this is nondoing; it is being functioning from morning to night, this ongoing practice.

14

Wind Bell

"Good morning" is a wonderful expression of our life. Always this is so, in the midst of conditions arising, in the midst of the seemingly easy and the seemingly hard. Our life is cause-and-effect conditions (or karma), arising right now. In the midst of this, even in the midst of illness and pain, there is no problem and there is no suffering, except when we believe and are caught up in our understanding: "I like this, I don't like this. This is good, this shouldn't be." Of course, even our way of seeing and understanding is this cause and effect.

When we hold to and believe the emotion-thoughts and the body-mind habits, there is upset, difficulty, stress, and suffering. We are unable to function as we are, particularly in the midst of health and illness, growth and dying. Instead we live as our ideas; we live from our beliefs and reactions about cause and effect, beliefs that we are sure are true and valid. Our limited vision and our limited body-mind habits keep us from being as we are, and as a result there is stress and suffering.

The words of the *Heart Sutra* clarify this life of conditions, this cause-and-effect circumstance of right now. Dogen Zenji's

Shobogenzo fascicle "Maka Hannya Haramitsu" ("Accomplishment of Great Wisdom of Buddha" or "Great Wisdom beyond Discriminatory Thought") further clarifies this matter. Studying the text is studying our life; it is studying the conditions and circumstances that nurture us.

Dogen says, "The time that Avalokiteshvara Bodhisattva practices profound prajna paramita is the total emptiness of the five skandhas, whole body seeing by illumined vision." Another translation: "When Avalokiteshvara Bodhisattva is one." This means "practices." Practice is being one; practice is being intimate as this moment. Avalokiteshvara Bodhisattva, the Bodhisattva who hears and responds compassionately to the cries of suffering, is you, is each one of us.

The word *prajna* means "wisdom," but I think it's best to leave the word as *prajna*, which here means the "wisdom beyond wisdom" or the "wisdom that is who we are." Being this prajna wisdom, and not being limited by "discriminatory thought," we see fully that the five skandhas are emptiness. In other words, this whole body-mind—which is not only this body but this whole universe and this whole being—is emptiness. We see that this whole being is as space.

What does this mean? What is emptiness? Certainly, we know what is not emptiness. We know when we bump into things, into form, into mind states, when we have trouble with the way what we bump into is, we know that is not emptiness for us. But the problem is not with form and so on. These five conditions, this whole body, are five prajna. Saying "body-mind" or "five conditions" are just different ways of describing being human. The whole of being human is prajna wisdom. The whole of each of you, each of us, each being we encounter, is nothing but wisdom.

Is that the way we act? Not when we have trouble with what other people say or do. This is even more so when we believe we know what they should or shouldn't be. For us then, how they are, this moment life, is not wisdom. We know this because we feel tension, stress, and upset about things as they are.

What does Dogen Zenji say here? When we practice, when Avalokiteshvara practices, when we are one with deep prajna paramita, then we see—you see, I see—the total emptiness of the whole body-mind, the total emptiness of everything that we encounter. We are wisdom, we are this illumined vision; seeing and functioning are wisdom, seeing and functioning are total emptiness.

Dogen states, "When this primary spirit is realized and manifested, it is expressed in words such as 'This very form is emptiness, this very emptiness is form.'" This clarifies wisdom that is emptiness; this clarifies prajna that is who we are. It's not just form is emptiness: emptiness is emptiness, and form is form. Don't get caught up in some ideas of elsewhere; don't get caught up in dualistic "either-or" formulations. Form is form. The unbounded that we are, the emptiness that we are, is this manifesting moment by moment—nothing else.

Dogen continues, "It is hundreds of grasses." This is the many circumstances that you encounter. Every encounter is emptiness, every encounter is form, every encounter is the functioning of prajna. This is hard for us to grasp and to live, because we believe all sorts of body-mind habits, and therefore we miss this. The time that Avalokiteshvara Bodhisattva—the time that she, he, you, I—practices profound prajna paramita and sees clearly that all the five skandhas are prajna, this does not depend upon our doing in order to make it so. From the beginning, every aspect of our functioning is nothing but this functioning.

Is it so for us? Or in a simple sense, does form seem like form, and not at all empty? The boss who you have trouble with comes in the room, and right away this seems like form and not empty. How do you know? You are tense, upset, and on the lookout, right here. You wake up aching, and right here: "Oh! I don't like this, it shouldn't be this way!" Right here.

We hold to the body-mind habits that see "Form is form" rather than "Form is emptiness, emptiness is form, form is form, emptiness is emptiness," which is this wisdom being, this flow of cause-effect that is this moment. This is not a matter of special "insight"; this is being this intimacy as we are.

In the "Maka Hannya Haramitsa" fascicle, Dogen cites his master Tiantong Rujing

The entire body is like a mouth hanging in air.
It does not matter from what direction the wind blows,
North, south, east, or west.
The wind bell evenly expounds wisdom for others.
Ring ring ring.

"The entire body"—the whole being, the body-mind—is a mouth hanging in air; in other words, hanging in emptiness. All sorts of karmic winds and circumstances appear to a bell-mouth that hangs in empty space, but if the bell says, "I only take wind from the east," if it holds this agenda or belief, the bell doesn't work. It would certainly be a strange bell. For the bell, it does not matter from what direction the wind blows. The bell responds appropriately to whatever wind appears.

This is the realized life we are. It also is an encouragement and a guide for how we can practice: we can hold the intention to be who we are, to voice the prajna of our life. We may not notice the ways we ask the wind to blow until we see how we are "ringing" in reaction to conditions.

Here are two different gloss/translations of the next-to-last line: "Impartial to all, it sounds wisdom for the sake of others." Another translation: "Always makes the sound of prajna." By not holding to "my agenda," responding is the expression of the wisdom of this bell of emptiness, this empty body-mind. We are this ability functioning, we are this prajna. This is the functioning of hearing and speaking. Practice is allowing; prajna is being in the midst of forms, voicing and expounding the prajna that we are.

In *Dogen's Extensive Record* 9:58, Dogen adds his own version of this poem:

The whole body is just a mouth defining empty space.
Ever arousing the winds from north, south, east, and west,
Equally crystalline speaking your own words.
Ring ring ring.

"The whole body is just a mouth defining empty space." He does not say "is like a mouth"; he says "is just a mouth."

"Ever arousing [playing host to] the winds from north, south, east, and west." In place of "it does not matter," he says "ever arousing"—this ever arousing is our ongoing Bodhisattva practice. This is the practice effort required of us, which we must discover for ourself.

"Equally crystalline [expressing eloquently] speaking your own words. Ring ring ring." "Speaking your own words" is your ongoing practice in the midst of the realized life that you are.

To hear the image the poem is invoking is to sense functioning this way. The whole body is just a mouth. See, it is never anything else. Not only like a mouth, but our body is just defining empty space, right now. It is the articulation of emptiness, the defining of emptiness. Emptiness is this manifesting right now, according to circumstances and conditions, according to the wind—in fact, ever arousing the winds. All sorts of winds appear inside, appear outside. We use the winds to express, to speak our words, to express for others, to express the profound prajna of life.

Please hear what Dogen says, because this is how we are. This is a guideline for what it is to sit, to be this sitting here, to be open as this form-condition, this body-mind. This is not just when we sit, but when we step out of the zendo and meet people and circumstances and all sorts of conditions. What is it to function as this wisdom that we are, this wisdom that is exactly who we are? Fivefold manifestations of wisdom; it can't be anything else. It is simply this manifestation of wisdom.

Dogen says, "When Avalokiteshvara Bodhisattva is one with deepest prajna." This includes whatever belief, thought, body condition, and feeling arises. This is nothing but the expression of wisdom, and yet our ongoing practice effort is living as this prajna. Though it is so right now, "when" is our effortless effort. It's interesting: when you practice prajna, you are prajna. But you are able to practice because you are prajna. What is this?

Often our functioning is out of form as form, out of habits as habits, out of habits that deny prajna, out of habits that state, "This habit isn't prajna, this habit isn't empty." We see form is form, but we do not see form is empty, and so we do not truly see form is form. Only if we see form is empty, emptiness is form, then form is exactly form. This depends on making it so for us, and this depends on our practice, otherwise it is not so for us.

As I have said, we know this is not so when there is stress and suffering. If we feel reactive anger, then we know this is not so. This is a practice signal and support; this tells us, "Somewhere I'm missing the prajna right here." Our human ability is practice, practicing the wisdom that we are, being sitting, being this nondoing, being in the midst of the winds of cause and effect that are constantly blowing from inside, from outside, from others, from myself. All these things are just opportunities for us to speak this profound prajna that we are.

This is what Dogen Zenji is encouraging us to see. How does Avalokiteshvara Bodhisattva respond to this and speak this? How can I articulate Avalokiteshvara's wisdom, which is my wisdom? When chanting the *Heart Sutra,* allow yourself to articulate the

Heart Sutra; allow yourself to be speaking for the *Heart Sutra* that is who you are. As we state in the "Gatha on Opening the Sutra,"[5] "Now we see this, hear this, receive and maintain this": allow this to be your articulation of what is so.

You may think, "Well, that's not the way it is. No, no, this is not true!" But believing "That's not the way it is" is the articulation of usual body-mind habits. All you have to do is speak what is so, to speak from this prajna that is always so and that is always your life. Being the Bodhisattva that you are, responding as the Bodhisattva that you are, is a wonderful ongoing practice, a lifetime koan. Right here, this whole body is articulating empty space. Ring ring ring.

15

Boundless Rushing Waters

Our practice is being who we are. It is not something extra, not something added on. As Dogen Zenji says, "From the beginning, practice is in realization."

This is what we are throughout sesshin: sitting, walking, and eating. We are being who we are. And yet, we find ways to go off, so to speak; we find ways to get caught up in what we think and believe. Attachment and getting caught up blind us, but noticing being caught up is a wonderful practice opportunity; it is one of the supports for being as we are.

I would like to discuss the koan "Joshu's Newborn Baby," which is case 80 of the *Blue Cliff Record.*

A monk asked Joshu, "Does a newborn infant have six consciousnesses?"

Joshu said, "A ball tossed on rushing water."

The monk went on to ask Toshi, "What is the meaning of a ball tossed on rushing water?"

Toshi said, "Moment to moment, nonstop flowing."

The verse:

Sixth consciousness inactive, he puts forth a question.
The adepts both discern where it comes from.
A ball tossed on boundless rushing water.
It doesn't stay where it lands. Who can watch?

Joshu's exquisite verbal expressions led to his being described as having "golden lips" or a "golden tongue." "Six consciousnesses" comes from various forms of Buddhist teachings that describe mind functioning. Often the sixth consciousness is connected to conceptual thinking. The monk is speaking about practice and attainment, and comparing it to a baby.

This monk is good but slightly off. He equates practice with mindlessness, as if the six senses should be cut off; he uses that as a way to understand a phrase like "no-mind." He is saying that practice has something to do with annihilating, with getting rid of emotion-thought. He is not asking about some newborn baby somewhere else.

Is he saying, "This is how I am?" Maybe he has had certain insight in his practice and now he is asking, "What do I do here? Or is he challenging Joshu: "How can you, Joshu, express this to me? How can you show me this state?"

Hakuin Zenji says of Joshu's response: "He has lots of breasts producing sweet and sour at will. . . . It is verbal samadhi." Hakuin is praising Joshu's immediate response, saying it is directly appropriate to the monk. Although the monk may have been looking for a conceptual answer and may have been holding some idea about nonactivity, Joshu's response shows and expresses for the monk what he is asking.

"A ball tossed on rushing water." Joshu's response is just that—a ball tossed on rushing water—which demonstrates the Buddha Way very directly in functioning. This is the compassionate answer that Joshu gives; this is breast milk produced to nurture our life. Where is there room to attach and spin with "A ball tossed on rushing water"? It is not a matter of traces from the past, it is not a matter of planning for the future, and it is not a matter of trying to copy something else.

The monk goes on to ask Toshi, "What is the meaning of a ball tossed on rushing water?" Again, he wants to understand it. How do you see this? Is the monk testing and challenging Toshi, or is this more conceptual thinking about the phrase? Toshi's answer fits exactly with Joshu: "Moment to moment, nonstop flowing." Toshi comes right out and expresses this directly: "Moment to moment, nonstop flowing." Do not be trapped by the words. He is cutting off everything that this monk is sticking to. Not only this monk; he is also talking to us. Moment to moment, nonstop flowing—this is our life. This is what we are doing: we sit here, the period ends, the timekeeper rings the bell. "Ching!" we stand up, we walk. In the midst of this stream of flowing where there is no trace, traces of all sorts arise. In the midst of all the streams of our life, which seemingly bring us here and seemingly carry us from here, our practice is being exactly this functioning now. Life activity is in the midst of this traceless universe. Sitting here, we are in the midst of traffic, bustle, light, cold. Responding in the midst of circumstances and freely functioning is exactly our life.

Let us look at this verse: "Sixth consciousness inactive, he puts forth a question." In a way, the monk is trying to test Joshu, yet he is also showing his own state; he is showing where he is stuck, and where the words of the sutras and commentaries have become more ideas. The monk's thoughts about how other people practice and understand this may be strongly held ideas.

We all have heard and seen many things in books and in Dharma talks. These things may be wonderful, but only if they support us in doing what we need to do. What do we need to do? To be exactly right here now. Always. We need to be exactly this life-functioning that we are. We don't need anything else. We don't need my words, we don't need this new phrase, we don't need to know anything. You don't need any of that. Do you believe it? You don't need anything.

The stream presents right here, in this rushing water. Here. The ball bounces one way, the ball bounces another way. That is our life. The stream, the ball, the water, all of it is nothing but our life. That is what they are talking about. "The adepts both discern where it [the question] comes from. / A ball tossed on boundless rushing water. / It doesn't stay where it lands. Who can watch?" As soon as we try to grab life and figure it out, that much we miss our life. Our life, our practice, is not to figure out. It's not to figure out life and it's not to figure out practice, much less to figure out and compare our practice with someone else's. To paraphrase something Joko once said, "Your life is not your business." That is why it can be so poisonous when someone explains, much less brags, about their practice and understanding. It does not serve you.

"If you want to see it right now," Tenkei Zenji says, "focus your eyes quickly and look! Arising, passing. Starting, stopping. See it right now." If you get any ideas about starting and stopping, then ask yourself: Who is starting? Who is stopping? It doesn't stay where it lands, right here, right now. Right here, right now is exactly our life. Not sixth consciousness, seventh consciousness, eighth consciousness. All these different ways of explaining are just guides and supports to be exactly who you are. By being exactly who you are, it all takes care of itself very well. Then you get to taste it, and you get to appreciate who you are.

When you're asked for sweet milk, you produce sweet milk. When you're asked for sour milk, you produce sour milk. That's what Hakuin is saying about Joshu: "Lots of breasts producing sweet and sour at will"—they are responding to circumstances. Responding is exactly our opportunity. And yet, we are caught up in ideas about how I am and how I am not, how I should be and how I should not be. That much we miss this ball bouncing on water, that much we miss this life that we are.

In a way, this is a very simple case. It is very simple and straight-forward, and not much needs to be said about it. And yet, in its simplicity, the point is very direct. Over and over we jump into this rushing water; over and over we are thrown into this rushing water, and we find our self in the midst of it. The more we stick and hold to the water and the more we try to go in a certain way, then the more we are bumped around by the water current. This is not even moment to moment, nonstop flowing; it's: moment, moment, nonstop flowing, be this that you are. This sesshin is the opportunity to enjoy the wonderful milk of our life.

16

Fundamental Endowment

Keizan Zenji says, "Zazen just lets people illumine Mind and rest at ease in their fundamental endowment. This is called showing the original face and revealing the scenery of the basic ground."

How is zazen being at ease—in other words, how is zazen relieving suffering—in the midst of difficulties? Because it is being this functioning that we truly are, because it is being this illuminating Mind. In seeing and being this life that we are, then ignorance, fear, greed, and anger have no basis.

"The Buddhas and all sentient beings are only One Mind. There are no other dharmas besides One Mind. Since beginningless time, this Mind is without arising, without extinction, without attributes. . . . This, right here now, this is it. Once one tries to get hold of it by thinking about it, one goes against it. It is like empty space which is without any limit and beyond measure."[2]

Practice is illuminating Mind; it is illuminating who and what we are. It is not that I illumine Mind; it is not that there is a separate Mind that I clarify and illumine. Our very functioning is this illuminating Mind.

Is this really so? People are suffering, and circumstances are difficult—we know this. In the midst of this, Huangbo says,

"This, right here now, this is it." This is not a theoretical text; it is a way to relieve suffering.

Unfortunately, because the word "mind" in Western tradition is often connected with and limited to thoughts or conscious understanding, including awareness, feelings, and emotions, Huangbo's and Keizan's comments are not easy to see. But no need to be limited by this understanding of "mind." In fact, practice includes working with the difficulties that arise when we believe thoughts and feelings, and with the unskillful ways that we use beliefs to try to resolve difficulties or to clarify life.

"Endowment" is what you are or have. When we believe we are emotion-thoughts within a body, or when we believe that this body-mind is separate from the changing conditions of the universe and separate from "other" beings, we miss this endowment. We make assumptions about birth and death and about gain and loss of this separate self, and we operate out of these assumptions—and we do so without being aware of these assumptions or examining them. We react and suffer when circumstances and conditions are not what "I" want. Then, in place of responding as ever-changing circumstances, our reactions grow from our fear and anger; they grow from "I don't like" or "I'm threatened."

If we know our fundamental endowment and if we live as this fundamental endowment, then there is no basis for fear. This is the same as a university with a large financial endowment: when making faculty or programs decisions, the university can respond on the merits of the issues without the added fears of financial gain and loss. (Of course, finances may be part of the circumstances being responded to, and so they do need to be considered.)

"The Buddhas ["the unconditioned" or "the nonarising, the nonceasing"] and all sentient beings [in other words, what seemingly arises and passes] are only One Mind." One Mind isn't a nominative; it is not one as opposed to two, but here "one" is an adjective. This One Mind is just the same Mind. There are no other dharmas besides One Mind; there are no outside things, no conditions, and no phenomena. One Mind is not a thing or a condition, and yet, besides One Mind, there is no other. This is our life right here now. Hakuin Zenji says, "Sentient beings are primarily all Buddhas. It is like ice and water. Outside of water, where can you find ice? Outside of sentient beings, where do you find Buddhas?" This Mind is our encounter from morning to night. If we say self, there is only self. Self and other are a fiction that we can use, but they are still a fiction. Everyone we encounter is only self meeting self. Provisionally, we can say sentient being meeting sentient being. Nevertheless, "Buddha" is everyone and everything I encounter. There is only Buddha in here, only Buddha out there. This! Is this so for us?

Zazen is illuminating and allowing the light of Mind to come forth. Illuminating means this functioning is being apparent. We are illuminated by being present, and by the presence of being human; we are illuminated by not being the limits that we may put on this Mind by attributes, names, and so forth. Being illuminated is circumstances arising, being illuminated is responding, being illuminated is everything changing all the time, being illuminated is our functioning.

Our practice and zazen are being present as we are in the midst of everything changing; our practice is to be present despite and beyond the limits of the ideas and thoughts that we keep holding on to and that we habitually believe: thoughts of gaining and losing, or thoughts such as "That isn't fair," and so on. There are no dharmas besides this Mind, besides this illumination that is always functioning: hearing, seeing, thinking, even believing thought. This is why when we are upset, when we are believing and holding upset, our practice effort is to be the very upset, to be even the pain—and in a way, to turn it back on itself, to turn it to the very source. It's not that the source is other than what this is; yet by doing this, by being this, we can "go beyond" the way we usually think of it and believe about it. This is to respond compassionately to circumstances. Unfortunately, if we don't do our part, it is easy to believe the shapes and characteristics, the gaining and losing. As Huangbo says, "Once one tries to get a hold of it by thinking, one goes against it."

What is this? We don't lose by not feeling well, despite the fact that we think we do. We don't gain by feeling well. We don't even gain by "having" a great insight. We don't lose even if we believe thoughts and even if we suffer in the midst of reactions based on our beliefs. Suffering is based on believing thoughts and feelings as truth, and believing the resulting body-mind habits. Despite suffering and despite the pain, we don't "lose" anything. And yet because of suffering, there is a need and importance to practice. Practicing this and clarifying this enables us to be "all the more" who we are, to use such inaccurate language. To function as we are, responding in the midst of our life—this is illuminating mind, being this.

Our usual body-mind habits blind us to no-birth and no-death, "since beginningless time." Literally, Huangbo's text is "This Mind no beginning finish arriving." When we say "Since beginningless time," this is beyond past, present, and future. "Past" and "future" may be useful terms, but when we live in the fiction rather than simply using the terms, we miss who and what we are. This is why when we are sitting and practicing whatever comes up is always the opportunity to be and to enter this present moment that we are. Entering this present moment, we are able to live the fundamental endowment that we are. We are not limited and bound by worries, upsets, and difficulties, and we are able to take care of what arises right here.

If we are used by self-centered thinking and feeling and therefore do not see or function as who we are, then trouble is guaranteed. Self-centered thinking is narrow; it is based on "me versus others," which is the dualistic fiction that we live out of. Look at your life: Does this happen? If so, when this happens, look: What is going on beyond this self-centered limitation? What is being this functioning that you are? Despite nothing lacking, this moment calls for ongoing practice. Always, this body-mind functioning, even this self-centered thinking, is an entry point into what we always are. Provisionally, I may say "entry point into"; this makes it seem as if this is something else, but it never is anything else. Being this, here, is "opening up enlightenment," as Dogen Zenji says.

Truly, who and what we are right now doesn't lack a single thing; it is only that we may believe that we lack something. You lack nothing. Even if you "had" a great awakening and "became" Buddha, you did not gain a thing. From the very beginning, this is One Mind. Lifting your hand, moving your feet, breathing, is this. Sitting is being this fundamental endowment that you are. And this fundamental endowment hears chirping, is chirping, is sitting. Nothing lacking, nothing to gain, nothing to change. Opportunities of practice arise, so we do our part, giving self away to self, being who we are.

Zazen allows us to illuminate Mind. Practicing, we discover that zazen is not limited to the form of sitting, but zazen is all the forms of being human. It is invaluable to do sitting Zen, or zazen, because due to various reasons and various body-mind habits, it is so hard to be who we are in the midst of many forms of functioning. Practicing, sitting, zazen support us in being at ease, in being who and what we are, in being the original face coming forth.

17

Alive? Dead? Part I

The Sixth Ancestor said, "Impermanence is Buddha Nature." Impermanence "is the Tathagata's great and perfect enlightenment," says Master Yongjia. How is impermanence enlightenment? How is the suffering of myself and others, how is what I do not like and even what I hate, the Buddha's great and perfect enlightenment? Clarifying impermanence is clarifying our life; living this is to live the cause-and-effect change that we are. Easy to say, not so easy to do.

We encounter dependent arising moment by moment. No-self "inside" here; no-self "outside" there. Things, people, concepts, cause and effect are right here now; they are all devoid of self. Despite acknowledging impermanence, even to recognize this is rare; to embody this is living the ongoing practice life that we are.

In Buddha-dharma, we don't say "life or death": life is completely this great matter, death is completely this great matter. "This great matter"—but what is this? If we believe such words, it becomes nonsense.

Blue Cliff Record, CASE 55, "DOGO'S CONDOLENCE VISIT"

Dogo and Zengen went to a home to make a condolence call. Zengen hit the coffin and asked, "Alive? Dead?"

Dogo said, "Alive, I won't say. Dead, I won't say, either."

Zengen said, "Why won't you say?"

Dogo said, "I won't say, I won't say."

As they were returning, halfway back Zengen said, "Master tell me at once, or I'll hit you."

Dogo said, "Hit me all you want, but still I won't say."

Zengen then hit him.

After that Dogo passed on. Zengen went to Sekiso and related the foregoing story.

Sekiso said, "Alive, I won't say; dead, I won't say either."

Zengen said, "Why won't you say?"

Sekiso said, "I won't say, I won't say."

At these words Zengen had an insight.

One day Zengen went to the teaching hall carrying a hoe and crossed back and forth east to west and west to east.

Sekiso said, "What are you doing?"

Zengen said, "I'm looking for relics of our late teacher."

Sekiso said, "Enormous waves roll far and wide, foaming billows flood the skies—what relics of the late teacher are you looking for?"

Setcho commented, "Heavens! Heavens!"

Zengen said, "This is just what to work out."

Taigen Fu said, "The late teacher's relics are still there."

"Alive? Dead?" What kind of question is this? Is it a silly question to ask? It is a coffin, so we assume there is a body inside. This question is not about anyone else; this question is not about theory. We need to see Zengen's urgency and courage in asking directly. What is this—not saying born, not saying dying, not saying unborn, not saying deathless? What is this—not something else like a coffin, not someone else? It is this fundamental matter right here: Alive? Dead? The question reflects the practice this moment of whole being impermanence.

Unfortunately we often live all sorts of selves and all sorts of permanence, and we suffer accordingly. Not only do we have ideas about being alive right now, but we have ideas about all sorts of pasts and futures. We see this in our habits of body-mind that are right now reacting to thoughts and feelings that arise, and reacting to stories about other people, events, and conditions. Impermanence is the condition right now. If we are able to see, is it fine? If we are blind, is it fine? If we are sick, is it fine? If we are alive, is it fine? If we are dead, is it fine? We get caught up in all sorts of ideas, and we make a solid, fixed, permanent self. Dogen says, "Life is life of the Buddha, death is life of the Buddha." This is not some Buddha out there, not some Buddha who is someone else, but the Buddha that you are.

But what is this? "Buddha" is just another word, a very stinking word if we get caught in it. We can see this problem clearly when we hold to a story about our so-called past or our so-called feelings right now. Feelings seem true as the whole reality; they even seem permanent. We make feelings into a self; we give conditions selfhood.

Impermanence is fundamental; dependent arising is this fundamental matter, and yet it is most difficult. So this "Alive? Dead?" is a vital question. Nevertheless, by asking this way, already we are in trouble. Some of us visited Valjean before she died, some visited after she died. Alive? Dead? What is this?

Dogo responded to Zengen's question: "Alive, I won't say. Dead, I won't say." This is the key to this koan. Not only is it the key, it is the vital presentation of this matter. Do you see this? Hakuin, praising Dogo's kindness to Zengen, says of Dogo: "He presents a pearl that lights the night, along with a tray and all. This is a good saying. If it were up to me, I'd say to Zengen, are you alive or dead?"

Zengen then asks Dogo, "Why won't you say?" Though Zengen hears Dogo's words "I won't say," he does not hear Dogo.

This isn't some esoteric matter; this is immediate. When we are with someone who is dying, right here is immediacy. Do we see what this is? Or are we caught up in a self of living, a self of dying? Can we embrace this moment of impermanence?

Dogen says, "Birth is a phase that is an entire period of itself. Death is a phase that is an entire period of itself." We need to clarify further that because they are each an entire period of themselves, "Birth is understood as no-birth, death is understood as no-death."

Being alive, then embrace, actualize, and manifest this moment alive. Being dead, then embrace, actualize, and manifest this moment death.

Let us look at this case again. Dogo responds to the initial question "Alive? Dead?" with "Alive, I won't say. Dead, I won't say." Is this revealing or is it not revealing? Is it answering or not answering?

Zengen asks, "Why won't you say?"

His teacher responds, "I won't say, I won't say." Zengen wants him to say, and we want him to say. We hope that his saying will clarify this matter for us; we hope that he will take care of this and enable us to be at peace, to live freely in the midst of changes, to relieve our suffering over the changing impermanence. Does "I won't say" clarify this matter?

As they return to the monastery, Zengen, who does not see what his teacher Dogo is showing him, is still struggling with this matter. How wonderful that he is doing this! He says, "Master, tell me at once or I'll hit you." Think of that—how audacious, especially in China!

Dogo says, "Hit me all you want, but still I won't say." "Hit me all you want"—listen to that great kindness. Our urgency and determination to clarify right now should be like Zengen's.

The truth is that you can't say. Anything you call it is extra, even beside the point. So Dogo can present the pearl directly: "won't say." Death, complete as it is. Life, complete as it is.

Though Zengen hears it, he still doesn't get it, so he says "I'll hit you. Please, help me with this." And despite Dogo's "won't say" kindness, Zengen does not see this, and he hits Dogo.

Impermanence is sitting, it is practice, it is this no-self. Being this empty, impermanent, body-mind life is our practice. And that is what encountering death reminds us, and how it encourages our practice effort. Death reminds us how we take impermanence as permanence, how we take no-self as self; it reminds us how we attribute permanence to things, people, and conditions, and how we attribute self to things, people, and conditions—and then we act out of that, missing who and what we are.

When we have a funeral, what is a funeral? When we have a memorial, what is a memorial? Alive? Dead? A wonderful koan. And remember, the word "koan" means something to gather together our practice, something to gather together this great matter that is our life. This is what we are doing here when we sit, when we walk, when we are well, when we are sick. If we break it up into our stories and reactions, that much we miss what we are doing. That much we miss what our life is.

My late teacher Maezumi Roshi said, "Mind and all the different interpretations of mind is altogether Buddha-nature." In other words, each of us is altogether nothing but Buddha-nature. Buddha-nature is nothing but the great perfect enlightenment of Tathagata Buddha. "Altogether" means not only us, but everything: walls, tiles, mountains, rivers, shit stick, trash. So everything that arises is our wonderful opportunity to be intimate as this that we are, no matter how hard it seems sometimes. Intimacy is being, intimacy is responding. Illness and cancer are intimate friends when they arise; sight, no sight, pain, no pain, are all friends to be intimate with. They are all the life of this moment that we are.

This may be hard to see and it may be hard to penetrate, but this is our opportunity, the opportunity that we are—living this intimacy, functioning and responding intimately.

18

Alive? Dead? Part II

Right now, this life that you are is fully revealed. Just be natural open awareness; nothing special needed. Everyday activity is polishing this gleaming pearl, this life-death practice. Awareness enables practice; by practicing skillfully, we are manifesting this. Right now, no-self reveals and manifests this life-death impermanence.

We may think we know what life is, and we may think we know what death is: "I'm alive," "She is dead." At such times, when we are believing "what I want" and "what I don't want," a practice-effort shift may be required to open as this moment universe, this endless dimension life, this face. Whenever holding to body-mind habits makes us miss this gleaming pearl, a skillful practice right here is to turn the body-mind habit and look: "Who?"

Are we sure we know what is so? "I am going, he is coming, I have lost, he has gained." The practice opportunity that is revealed in the judgments we believe and the reactions we hold calls for us to give self away to this moment. Otherwise, not only are we not polishing this gleaming pearl, but we are completely missing the pearl. We are insisting that there is no pearl, insisting that this life is the way our habits describe and exclude, the various either-or categories that we believe. We believe self and others, likes and dislikes, life or death. We may even insist that the universe does not provide enough or is not right. What are the consequences of this?

Being who you are is exactly this life, this opportunity, this practice. Just this. Body-mind habits are this wonderful functioning life. Unfortunately, not seeing clearly this life that we are, we often funnel who we are through habits, and we become caught in them and the resulting reactiveness. This life that we are becomes limited and distorted. Not aware that this is happening, we live an almost fictional life based on delusions and attachments—and as a result, as we sadly know very well, we suffer and cause harm. Conversely, suffering and harm are indications that we are caught in attachments and beliefs. Rather than freely using circumstances and arising habits, we are often used by them.

Believing and maintaining fundamental ignorance keeps us missing who we are. Despite missing it, this is who you are right now. Dogen encourages our practice of forgetting self. Forgetting self, this Dharma that we are reveals our life. Giving self away is just this: just sitting, just walking, just working, just listening, just speaking. This is practice, this is being present, whether we call it *shikantaza,* koan practice or breathing. This body-mind moment, the whole universe is breathing us, the whole universe is aware-ing us. Awareness is being human, so there is no need to "stay aware," nor is it a particular state that we need to add. Likewise, it is not a matter of making "effort at awareness." Awareness as is: foreground, background, narrow, broad.

Nevertheless, when there is a "narrowing" of awareness to a "particular state of mind-body," which we see in attachments to, for, or against particular conditions, there is the practice effort as response to the circumstances of the moment. This is skillful

action: opening this—not pushing away or changing—so that the narrowing does not cut off awareness, does not make the particular state more fixed, separate, or solid. Thus we can function skillfully, manifesting and responding in circumstances and conditions as this universal life that we are.

Now, with a Sangha death two weeks ago and a funeral coming up, we can't avoid this; we can't miss this. See, this matter of life-death is right here; we can see this especially easily when the confronting circumstances open our life. When we face grief, reacting habits may be opened and become transparent. We are supported in being present in the midst of the arising circumstances and conditions. The Ancestors' teachings and our practice remind us that life is life of the Buddha, death is life of the Buddha—life of who and what you are. Do not miss this.

So Dogen encourages us, "When life comes, face and actualize life; when death comes, face and actualize death." Manifest death, manifest life. All of us have this opportunity, despite being caught in dualism and fear at times. Manifesting life-death is manifesting this moment, the whole universe that is right here; it's no problem.

In saying and believing "This is alive" and "This is dead," trouble is created in many ways; not just through the ideas of "alive" or "dead" but through the underlying fears and other beliefs that we put on top of the very life that we are. Seeing these beliefs is our opportunity; it calls for a courageous practice effort. Seeing clearly, being who we are, we can act skillfully. How do you answer right now? Are you alive?

Death is some place we may not want to be, dying is some place we may not want to be, illness is some place we may not want to be. Yet when this is here, embrace it, because this is our opportunity; this is impermanent no-self life revealed this moment. We don't need special occasions for this. This moment, please take advantage of this—otherwise you miss this.

19

Gardening with Weeds

Being who you are is Zen practice. Unsatisfactory and difficult circumstances arise when we limit reality to a self-centered perspective, to beliefs of mine and not-mine. The entrance of essential nature is this mind-body-moment.

Actually, to say "entrance" is not quite right, because there is nowhere to go, nowhere else to be. Even to say "essential nature" or "true nature" is not correct, because this is not different from ordinary nature. There is no such thing as true nature, no such thing as ordinary nature.

Nevertheless, practice is being intimate and "opening to" this body-mind moment. Being so, we live, function, and respond to the circumstances that we encounter this moment. Sitting is the opportunity to clarify this, not as theory but as the reality of this breath now. Instead of bargaining with the so-called reality of thoughts and feelings, and trying to make them fit what we want, practice life is being this moment as is, taking care of this moment. What are difficult and unsatisfactory circumstances for you? Clarifying these, you may discover all sorts of bargaining, and also discover the practice effort opportunities these present.

The Song of Enlightenment by Yongjia Xuanjue begins, "Can

you see the leisurely person of the Way, beyond learning of the Tao, beyond the pursuit of knowledge; neither trying to avoid deluded thoughts nor seeking truth? The true nature of ignorance is Buddha-nature itself; this empty body of illusory transformation is the very body of the Dharma. Once we have realized what the Dharma-body is [once we have awakened to essential nature], not a single thing exists that we can call our own."

Do you see this Buddha of things as is? Remember, not a single thing exists that we can call our own, neither mine nor not-mine. Essential nature is right now.

"The conditions of life"—the five skandhas, the circumstances of body-mind functioning right now—"come and go like floating clouds in empty space. The three poisons of greed, anger, and ignorance appear and disappear like water bubbles, appear and disappear without purpose."

What of our seeming difficulties and problems? They are not other than bubbles, arising and passing. Nevertheless, believing difficulties and problems makes them so; yet this is also the opportunity of practice effort. Why make effort? Because when we miss this functioning, there is suffering. We manage to miss being at ease, and we miss this which is neither avoiding delusions nor seeking truth.

We intimately know the three poisons of greed, anger, and delusion; they seem to have a power of their own. Sometimes we justify them: "I should be angry, he should do what I want." Or "I felt great when I got that" or "I felt great when I told him off." Look! What is going on when greed, anger, or confusion arise? What keeps you from this moment? What keeps you from being present? What words about mine and not-mine and what beliefs are connected to that? Always, this Dharma-body is this body-mind world.

Entering body-mind is not a special effort; true nature is right now, right here. It can't be anywhere else. If it could be anywhere else, then it would not be true nature; it would not be who you are. This is exactly hearing, sitting, breathing, birds chirping, exactly right now. Is it so? Can you attest to this? When anger arises, what is assumed? What should or should not happen? Seeing assumptions can be a useful tool to make the needed effort when we miss the truth of reality.

With greed, anger, and ignorance, there is grasping and attachment. Not out of anything malicious but simply a result of body-mind habits. And just as attachment and grasping arise, there is also the opportunity to see them, the opportunity to make an effort. We can make our practice effort with the so-called difficulty, upset, or anger; these are just different names of me and not-me, should and should not, that I impose on circumstances.

I like to garden and grow a few vegetables. If I pull up weeds or cut grass, as long as they are not noxious, I put them back on the ground where I have tomatoes or other vegetables growing. In a way, this is exactly our practice. The very energy of anger, difficulty, or confusion is the energy of our practice. Truly, there are no weeds! According to our capacity, according to what we are capable of working with, according to what is not-noxious, we turn the weeds right back to this moment, this body-mind-world.

Practice is not about getting rid of weeds; it is not about getting rid of deluded thoughts and going out to find truth elsewhere. It is this very energy, this greed, anger, and ignorance as is, which is the practice-effort opportunity of being this moment. There is no need to avoid illusion. Weeds are weeds! Tomatoes are tomatoes! Though it is important to see that weeds and tomatoes are exactly this life functioning, this can be mere theory, and not much use. I will pull up weeds; I will grow and eat the tomatoes, not weeds. Dogen Zenji clarifies this in "Genjokoan": "Nevertheless, flowers fall amid attachment, weeds spring up amid antipathy."

The problem with weeds is that as they multiply, they take nourishment and moisture from the garden. The seeming weeds

in our life—call them self-centered beliefs or delusions—are not anything else but true nature. Unfortunately, when we are caught up in beliefs and attached to them, they take nourishment and keep us from functioning as we are. Life becomes caught up in greed, anger, and ignorance, and in self-centered views. Problems, suffering, and difficulties arise when body-mind habits take nourishment, when they take our ability to be present and to respond; when this happens, they turn into so-called weeds. Our grasping, holding, and confusion come from believing that the weed is who we are; they come from being caught up in and reacting from emotion-thoughts.

When this happens, practice effort is appropriate. It is important to see the necessity to weed, to turn the weeds right back into the earth. What seems difficult or painful in your life? Look: What keeps your life from being nurturing? What practice effort allows "grasping" to open into being this moment? What is your specific practice effort that allows the weeds to nurture this reality moment?

"Elements of self come and go like clouds, without purpose." And yet, we make them solid by assuming all sorts of purposes, causes, and conclusions about circumstances inside and outside, like "I shouldn't feel this way." Can we take this weed and use it to support being this? "I'm so angry at him; I'm going to get him." What is the weed that gets in the way of functioning? How do I take that weed and allow it to nurture this functioning moment?

There's no need to look for essential nature; this is your life. And yet if we are confused by the elements of self that come and go, life becomes the confusion because we make assumptions about coming and going, me and not-me, should and should not. Practice is always in noticing our believed emotion-thoughts and being bodily present.

How do you garden life? Not bargain with reality, but garden in it and embrace this. What is the believed weed right now? What is the purpose and goal added on to this moment? What is the assumption added on to this moment? The way that you assume persons and things to be may actually be what keeps them from nurturing this garden. Though circumstances seem to keep us from being this functioning, nothing can keep us from who we are. Nothing.

Unfortunately, somehow we manage to fool our self. When you say "purpose," "feeling," "difficulty," or "pain," these are good practice opportunities. They can nurture entering this moment if you garden with them, if you see and make the practice effort. Allow this to serve; it makes no difference who is served, because serving others is serving our self.

Life is the leisure walk of the Way. Yet it is only so if we realize and actualize this life that is without a single thing we can call our own. This is nothing but our own original self-nature, nothing but circumstances that come and go. Walking leisurely, you say, "Oh, is there something to do here?" And you do it. The plants grow, the sun shines, all things work naturally and manifest essential nature, Buddha-nature. But these words are stinky words if we are caught in them: "Nothing but right now." So walk at leisure in your garden. Not trying to get rid of anything, not trying to gain anything. Step-by-step, garden growing, you see exactly what you need to do.

We come and go according to circumstances. Upset, anger, and confusion are nothing but breezes and rain falling in the garden, appearing and disappearing. The weather changes, the amount of rain changes, the condition of the plants change. See where and if concepts and attachments solidify and get in the way of being in the garden, and then respond accordingly. Being present, being intimate, take good care of this moment. Enjoy your garden.

20

Mazu Is Ill

I often say, "Be who you are." Practice is being who you are. Cause-and-effect conditions and arising moment-by-moment circumstances—what is this?

Unfortunately, often who we think we are, who we act as if we are, what we believe this is, is made up of ideas, beliefs, and habits—some that are so-called our own, some from so-called others, some from the so-called past. These things seem "natural"; we believe and feel they are natural. If we hold on to them, if we react from them and react to them, we get into all sorts of trouble. We miss who we truly are. Buddha is never anywhere else, never anything special or extra. So, this Buddha life is always being who you are in the midst of these circumstances and conditions, and responding to circumstances and conditions.

A few years before she died, I visited Joko for a few days. She was ninety-two, and she was recovering from some medical difficulties so she was weak and in some ways physically frail and limited. At the same time, she was present; she was teaching and working with people within the conditions and circumstances of body-mind that she found herself.

Within the conditions of body-mind-world that we find ourselves is our practice, our practice opportunity. But we have to see
clearly what this life of the universe is so as to manifest this; Buddha-
nature is never anywhere else, and yet it is not our ideas and attachments about the conditions and circumstances. Those habits, ideas,
and attachments get us into all sorts of trouble and disturbances.

Joko was teaching at ninety-two; another Zen teacher, Joshu
Sasaki Roshi, is presently over a hundred years old. He is guided
into the zendo in a wheelchair and helped up to his platform seat
for talks. Half-blind, unable to walk, dependent on all sorts of
supports—these things are just the conditions and circumstances
of this body-mind, these things are just how we are. Being our conditions includes states of mental functioning, such as forgetting
things and having limited abilities. However, we are only limited in
the sense that we are comparing our current state to some ideal or
"previous" state. An ideal is what we make up; practice is being in
the midst of conditions as is, manifesting who and what we are.

So we have all these wonderful opportunities to be aging
Buddha, half-crippled Buddha, suffering Buddha, dying Buddha,
forgetful Buddha. Can we be half-senile Buddha? Of course,
there's no need to hold on to the word "Buddha."

Case 3 in the *Blue Cliff Record* and case 36 in the *Book of
Equanimity* is "Mazu Is Ill."

The abbot asked: "Master, how is your health today?"
Mazu said: "Sun-faced Buddha, Moon-faced Buddha."

An earlier text in *The Record of Mazu*, which is probably the
source of the koan text, reads:

The master was going to pass away the next day. That evening the abbot asked: "The reverend's health has not been
good. How is the reverend feeling today?"
"Sun-faced Buddha, Moon-faced Buddha."

Mazu had been sick for a while. This is the eve of his death. Really see this: "Sun-faced Buddha, Moon-faced Buddha" is our life. It is our life all the time; we don't have to wait until before we die. How do we live this? Do we see it clearly? Coughing and wheezing, we are sickness Buddha. How are you doing this morning? Feeling better from last night? Sun-faced Buddha, Moon-faced Buddha. What is this?

Scholars inform us that in the *Buddha Names Sutra*, Sun-faced Buddha is said to have lived for eighteen hundred years, and Moon-faced Buddha entered pari nirvana after one day and one night. Some Buddhas live for a long time, some live for a short time. Be that as it may, it has nothing to do with this koan. Some explain this koan by saying that sickness is a condition, that Buddha is who you are. But truly, there is no Buddha other than sickness, no sickness other than Buddha. So not sickness, not Buddha.

The introduction to the case states that Mazu's aim is to make a place for people to enter, but nevertheless this is still gouging a wound in healthy flesh. See? If you believe you need this, you get in trouble; if you are attached to this, you get in trouble. Because healthy flesh is this: Sun-faced Buddha, Moon-faced Buddha. Nevertheless we need to gouge a wound: What does that mean? We need to be clear on what our practice is, otherwise we think our practice is to get us somewhere else because we think we are lacking something, we think we are in bondage. If we believe that, then we are creating trouble. Though we create trouble, it could be necessary and useful—but it still is creating trouble.

Hakuin says, "Just exclude nonentry, that is enough; there is nothing else." Nothing else, just this intimacy. Tenkei Denson comments that although fundamentally this koan is gouging a wound, "This dialogue between teacher and student is an activity intended to show a learner a way to enter." Is Sun-faced long? Is Moon-faced short? Sun-faced Buddha, Moon-faced Buddha: Is it two? Is it the same? Is it different? Please enter here.

Our practice is being this condition we are, which is why I brought up Joko and Joshu Sasaki Roshi. Our practice is not dependent upon the condition of body-mind-universe. Conditions are always changing; we are all in the midst of changing conditions and cause and effect. If we don't see that, we are going to be in trouble, because we may think that our practice is going to make us better. We may even believe that there is something wrong with the way we are, and that there is something wrong with the way things are.

Yes, conditions change—and effort and intention create change. Our practice effort, presence, concentration, *samadhi,* create changes in body-mind functioning, and they create changes in this universe. No doubt about it. But if our practice is in order to change conditions, rather than a change of conditions being a by-product of practice and responding, then even as we are "improving" conditions, we are trapping our self. This is because we are reinforcing a belief that conditions determine who and how we are. We react to conditions, attaching to or rejecting them, rather than responding to them as this practice opportunity, as manifesting the wisdom and compassion we are.

Every one of us, at some point, will be a day before our death— every one of us. We don't know when; I might die this evening, who knows? None of us knows. We may think we know, but we don't. Some of us might die with no pain; we might just go to sleep and not wake up. Some of us might die with long illness and long pain.

Suzuki Roshi went through a lot of pain before he died; he was practicing cancer. If we allow the conditions of body-mind, of others, or of the world, to determine our life, then we are driven by conditions and circumstances and trapped by them. Our practice life is not to create some place where we can avoid those things; doing that is another daydream. Our practice, our life, is being in midst of the circumstances and functioning according to circumstances.

Hakuin says, "Real students are as careful and attentive as if they were carrying an open jar of oil so as to prevent any spilling, or like pounding rice cakes in a crystal jar." Some might complain about pounding in a crystal jar, and they might even try to change the container. If you have a choice, pound the rice cakes elsewhere. But when there is no choice, then we pound in a crystal jar. And the truth of each moment of our life, no matter what we try to control with our choices, is that as it is, our life calls for us to function as if pounding in a crystal jar. Can you imagine what it is it like to pound rice cakes in a crystal jar? Of course you don't want to break the crystal jar—and yet, what is this? See what Hakuin is saying.

I bring this up to share that Joko was teaching even when she was ill and frail. I spent a day and a half with her. Not continuously, because at ninety-two she became tired; those were her conditions and circumstances. Conditions: whether you can get up by yourself or you need help to get up; whether you can walk or need a cane, a walker, or a wheelchair. Whether you can hear or need hearing aids; whether you see with two eyes, one eye, or not at all. These are all conditions and circumstances. Being blind, we are a blind practitioner; we are practicing in the midst of blindness. See? There are all sorts of mental, physical, and social circumstances that we live—how do you practice in the midst of this? Manifesting Sun-faced Buddha, Moon-faced Buddha is our task.

A poem by Dogen (*Eihei Koroku*, 10.7):

Sun-face and Moon-face are the way;
Buddha face and Ancestral face are also the way.
Face-to-face meeting is expressing the way.

Expressing the way is face-to-face meeting.
Right here, directly confronting reality is the crown
   of creation.
The way is completed with the same red clay,
verifying the unique realization in the dawn sky.
Who speaks of the great round mind?
Simply say, this is it.

See these words of Dogen: this is it. When motorcycle noise appears [sound in background of motorcycle], it appears as motorcycle noise [makes motorcycle sound]. To paraphrase Dogen, When a Chinese person comes, he appears as a Chinese person. When an American person comes, she appears as an American person.

There is a nice koan in *The Gateless Gate* called "Shakyamuni and Maitreya Are Servants of Another" (case 45):

Our Ancestor Master Hoen of Tozan said, "Shakyamuni and Maitreya are servants of another; who is he?"

You are not supposed to be like someone else; you are not even supposed to be like Shakyamuni. Shakyamuni Buddha is the servant of another; Maitreya, the future Buddha, is the servant of another. Who is she?

In the Chasidic tradition, there is a story that relates to this idea. Reb Zusha said, "When I die and go to heaven they are not going to ask me 'Why weren't you like our teacher Moses?' [an exemplar of humility and closeness with God] They will ask, 'Why weren't you like Zusha?'"

Your opportunity is being who you are. This is Sun-faced Buddha, Moon-faced Buddha. Who are you? This is always our task.

Another poem by Dogen (*Eihei Koroku*, 10:121):

Within the eye of the sun-face is a round moon-face;
Getting a sutra to put over the eyes, your eyes become a
    sutra;
With practice and mastery, ultimately nothing is outside;
Clouds in the blue sky, water in a jar.

Sun-face, Moon-face, eyes wide open, is our practice; it is our life. Your life is this intimacy opportunity to manifest who you are in the midst of the conditions arising and passing.

21

Entangling Not-Knowing

Sitting is being not-knowing; practice is being not-knowing. All the supports and forms of practice, all the supports and forms of our life, enable us to be this and to manifest this. Our whole life is the entanglement of not-knowing.

Not-knowing is the Dharma, the teaching of the Buddha that reveals what is so and shows us how to be who we are. Not-knowing is not the opposite of knowing; do not be fooled by words. Not-knowing is not a negative state; it is not about lacking. Knowing and not-knowing are not separate, never two. Being entangled, knowing is completely wiped out, and not-knowing is completely wiped out. Be careful: as soon as you say "not-knowing," it is not so; saying "not-knowing" is not being "not-knowing."

This term "entanglement" is analogous with the quantum physics idea that two particles can be entangled, despite being at seemingly great distances. This entanglement means that the actions of one particle are reflected and manifested in the actions of the other; distance and time do not exist for these two particles, or at least not the way distance and time exist for us. Of course this is simplifying entanglement, while at the same time conceptualizing it into two distant particles. We are the entanglement of this unknown, we are the entanglement of the unconditioned. This is the truth, this is the reality, this is the nature of our life.

Often we don't see this and we don't manifest this, because through holding to knowing and through self-centeredness, we have cut off this entangling unconditioned. Much of the time, we lead with knowing; our functioning grows out of a knowing that misses the "backside" of unknowing. Then knowing complicates functioning; it complicates being who we are by creating suffering and stress. Or to say it differently, we are holding on to and are attached to the condition and the form; we hold on to and are attached to what we think we know, what we think we see, who we think we are.

So when we bow, we sometimes think, "I'm bowing here and I'm doing it well" or "I'm not bowing as good as I could." That much we do not bow the whole universe, we are not the whole universe, past, present, and future. If we allow self and give self away to bowing, to chanting, to walking, to sitting, then we can discover right here the entanglement of not-knowing, being not-knowing right here.

The more we open to the Dharma, the more the Dharma opens to us. The more we open this moment of life to life as it is, the more we open up what we know. The more we are the truth, the seemingly bigger truth that we are. Not something else, but right here. And yet, unless we do our part to allow it, unless we manifest this to be right here, this is not right here for us. But despite the fact that this is here and has nothing to do with our doing, we can still do something. Do you see this?

Often, we think and act as if we live in an either / or universe. By that, I mean we think either "This is me" or "This is not me." When doing zazen, we either think "I'm sitting still" or "I'm off caught up in thoughts, figuring things out, planning things out." An important aspect of practice, of just sitting—of not doing any particular thing, of doing no-thing, of being present—is to discover in the midst of doing nothing that there is all sorts of arising and passing, all sorts of thoughts, feelings, and sounds. And then in the midst of this arising and passing, we discover nondoing.

I am the universe that I call "not-me." Not as something opposite, even though we tend to think in that way. We tend to think that this life is either form or empty. We miss that in the midst of form is emptiness. So the *Heart Sutra* states, "Form is emptiness, emptiness is form." It is important to see that form is empty; it's important to clarify that emptiness is exactly form.

Form and empty are not two. When we chant, when we do service, we are not doing service just by our self, just here; we are joining with all others doing service, with the service of the whole universe, which is just here now. "Endless dimension universal life" is not just a fancy phrase; it is the truth of this moment. Our acknowledging this allows us to taste this, and it allows us to manifest this through our actions.

Of course, the more I explain this, the further from the truth of life it is; we get ideas that the explanation is what this is. We have ideas about form, we have ideas about emptiness, and we know too much. This is nowhere else; just this.

The conditions and circumstances of life offer us life koans for us to resolve. Being not-knowing is getting out of the way, which enables resolving this life koan moment. Being not-knowing allows us to see and manifest the reality that without our efforts isn't clear for us. Knowing arises and disappears. Our specific practice effort varies according to life and circumstance, whether we are sitting, bowing, walking, speaking, eating, or working. Our practice effort is giving self away to this moment, being right here. Though we are so from the beginning, it is our practice effort, including the conditions and actions, such as bowing as we enter into the zendo, which allows us to be this each moment. This is what allows us to give knowing away, to give not-knowing away. Being not-knowing supports us in giving away while we are in the midst of trying to know how to be not-knowing. Not-knowing is not dependent upon knowing, even if we use words like the "mystery" and the "unknown." Not-knowing takes away everything. So not-knowing is most intimate. See?

This is the entanglement of form and emptiness; this is the entanglement of this conditioned life "with" the unconditioned, with our life of unborn intimacy. This is the deathless that we are from the beginning, the form of form, the emptiness of emptiness. Not-knowing through and through, there is no not-knowing; so knowing through and through, there is no knowing. Just this here-now.

Student: As soon as you started talking about "not-knowing and knowing," I thought, "Oh, I bet I know what he's going to say next." [Laughter.] I've been really having a problem with thinking that I know things and getting in trouble.

Genmyo: Good for you to see this. It is a wonderful opportunity, because "knowing" that you know things now can be a practice support to enable you to open knowing. The more you see it, the more it is an opportunity this moment to be this, to go "beyond" the knowing. Knowing is just another human habit, another habit of thought—except if we clutch it, except if we build on it and miss our life.

Student: Yes, it is a practice opportunity, because I am a student and there is not much point in being a student if you know what you're supposed to know already.

Genmyo: Yes.

Student: When I was finishing up medical school, I was very insecure about my abilities and so I did an extra year of internship. During that time, I was with a lot of people who were so into medicine that they loved knowing things. I was coming from a position of insecurity and feeling like it was a mistake that I was doing this, so I was kind of always standing in the background, wide-eyed and wondering why these people were so into this, and thinking, "OK, let's just make it through." That was the best training that I ever had in medicine. Because standing in the background and feeling like I didn't know what the heck I was doing led me to see that it was my not-knowing, my feeling that I didn't know what was going on, that very often led me to know before they did. They were jumping to know; they had a frenetic kind of "I know what's going on," but it was actually through my not-knowing that I would take much more information in, because I wasn't jumping in and deciding what was going on. In the long run it taught me, even during my practice as a doctor today, how much I am able to feel secure even when I don't know something. It taught me that I can still take things in; my not-knowing is fine.

Genmyo: This is important. Being not-knowing, that is our choice, that is our opportunity. It is hard sometimes, but being sitting and entering into this moment not-knowing rather than sitting and knowing what is now and what is going to be, that much we can be what is. Not-knowing is embracing suffering, not-knowing is embracing arising-passing, not-knowing is embracing this moment cause and effect—embracing just this.

22

Nonabiding

Nonabiding is Buddha Dharma. Nonabiding is exactly our life. Yet in the midst of nonabiding, there are all sorts of abiding that we attempt, that we insist on. So we fight our own life. Being just this moment is nonabiding. In fact, we can't be abiding and "be this moment." And yet we try, we attempt it; we say, "Oh, yes, I am just being this moment," while we cling and we abide in all sorts of ways.

Nonabiding is how it is, how you are and what you are. Doesn't matter if you agree or not. Doesn't matter if you insist that this is not the way it is. We may insist physically, we may insist mentally with emotions and thoughts, but our insistence doesn't matter. This is nonabiding. Nonabiding is ongoing change; it is nonself.

If we heal into the moment, we can only do this "in" nonabiding. If we abide, we often find that we hold to regrets about the past and insistences about the future. That much we can't heal into this moment, that much we can't be this that we are. The practice of nonabiding is how our effort and our practice allows us to come together to penetrate exactly who and what we are.

Of course, there is nothing to penetrate because we are this. It is nonabiding that nonabides. And yet, there are all sorts of ways that we attempt to avoid this nonabiding reality that is the truth of our life, whether we call it personal life or the so-called bigger life of the universe.

What does abiding mean? It is simple and straightforward: abiding means holding on to thoughts, feelings, and ideas; abiding means to want something to be a certain way, to insist that this is the way an idea, feeling, or bodily condition—our own or that of others—is, should, or should not be. Nonabiding is the sense of not holding on to this; nonabiding is not being reactive to this physical, emotional, body-mind state of wanting things to be a certain way, and not believing and suffering over how this is supposed to be.

Can we be, practice, and enter this nonabiding that we are? That is our task. It is not some special skill that you have to develop, because it is what you have been from the moment you were born. It is your very functioning, from birth until death. Nonabiding is birth-death. Birth-death is nonabiding, so it is not born, and it is not destroyed. It really is this. It doesn't matter if you believe me or not, and it doesn't matter if you believe it for yourself. This doesn't require me to tell you, or tell myself, or tell anyone, because this is how it is.

We can choose to be congruent with this, to be congruent with who and what we are—and therefore we can be the joy of our life, be nurtured by life, and be healed by life. Healed from what? Healed from acting incongruent, healed from when we go against our own life, and healed from the habits of reactiveness and the various consequences of these habits.

Nonabiding isn't abiding, nor is it not abiding. Those are dualities that further misdirect us. Unfortunately, many human habits are based on abiding. They are based on an abiding that we think will give us safety and security in the midst of this nonabiding reality. So even as we have an intimation of this nonabiding nature that we are, we attempt in various ways to avoid it.   ·

In zazen, even though it seems we are being still, upright, and stable, even though someone would say, "Oh, that looks like you're abiding," in that very abiding is nonabiding. Just sitting, being just this moment. Zazen is the coming together of the whole of being human, the whole of this life. It is being human in all different aspects of human functioning; being wholeness, being unified. We breathe, the heart beats, we hear sound, we see light—this ongoing human moment. We manifest this nonabiding wisdom in naturally compassionate responses to this ongoing change.

When we break up the whole that we are and when we believe this or that story about this fractured, dualistic life, we end up abiding in little pieces of this. We abide in feelings, in thoughts, in fear, in misunderstanding, in anger, and even in physical and mental pain. Right there, we can't heal. Much of our actions then grow out of a fog, where we are not even clear on what our intentions are. We can say, "My intention was such and such," but then at some point we discover, "Well, there were other intentions there, I just didn't realize that I also was this and this, and I was also that and that." So even our very intentions are simply cause-and-effect habits that manifest.

To some extent we are so-called conscious of our intentions, and to some extent we are not conscious. So there is no blame involved, and that is why we can atone. Even blame is abiding; even blame is holding on to blaming. That much we hold on to regrets and that much we carry along blame or judgments—"I should have, I could have"—then that much we can't be. Does that make sense?

Intentions are an important part of our practice effort and opportunity. Buddha emphasized the importance of intentions in terms of cause-and-effect consequences. Intention is important, and yet unless we are clear about the very nonabiding of intentions, intention can become another excuse, a way of trying to break up this very life by justifying my intentions and my not-intentions.

Whose intentions are these? Some things we see, and some things we don't. Sometimes we see clearly, and sometimes we do not see clearly. There is no blame involved in our practice and our life. And yet, we often use intention to blame and to attribute self and not-self: "These are my intentions, those aren't my intentions. He intended that, she did not intend that." As if we really know who we are, and as if we really know that we and others only do things that are "intentions."

What is yours? What is not yours? What is somewhere else? Where else is there? You are the whole universe; it is your whole life. What else is there? What is mine? If the universe is nonabiding, where is there any "mine" that you can hold on to? Any "my" that I attempt to grasp is actually nonabiding. It is like trying to grasp a flowing stream. Even more, it is a flowing stream trying to grasp a flowing stream.

And yet, as you see, we believe mine and not-mine, and then we get into trouble. Why? Because reality doesn't go along with mine and not-mine. It just doesn't. We have an example right in front of us on a very simple level: the leaves are changing colors, and then falling off the trees. Are the trees insisting, "Oh, those are my green leaves, what's happening to them? Why are they changing colors?" Are the trees trying to grasp the leaves, saying, "Where are my leaves going?"

The universe doesn't recognize laws of property. It doesn't even recognize laws of property of our so-called body. Your hair used to be a different color. What happened? It has changed to gray and white, and some day it may all be gone. The universe didn't recognize "your," despite your insistence that your hair should be brown, or whatever color it was. Notice how much in our society we try to fight the universe. There is a huge hair-coloring industry. That's fine, changing hair color is an option for us, no problem with that, but we need to know when we are fighting the universe in all sorts of ways, physically, mentally, and emotionally. And the only thing that happens when we fight the universe is that we lose. This is all that happens. We can fight the universe, but we will lose. Fighting is different from skillfully and appropriately responding in the midst of the ongoing change in conditions and circumstances.

The Buddha taught about impermanence, about cause-and-effect dependent arising, and yet even twenty-six hundred years ago in India, people resisted that teaching. We humans don't like impermanence; we don't like ongoing change. We often act out of, and sometimes justify, this beginningless greed, anger, and ignorance. These are our self-centered habits, which is what fighting reality is. We either hold on to reality, trying to push it away or stop it, or we are just confused about what is going on. We act out this greed, anger, and ignorance, and we refuse to see this cause-and-effect impermanence for how it is. This is part of what comes with human habits, with our human DNA that is this body-mind, and as a result we experience stress, suffering, and dissatisfaction.

And yet, we have the capacity to go beyond. This is the important thing. We have the capacity to live out of this nonabiding that is who we are. We have the capacity to be congruent, to tap into and enter into the nonabiding stream, and then live out of that wisdom and compassion.

PART THREE

Nonself

23

Who?

Right now, who reads? Being who we are is our life; clarifying is our practice.

There is a koan in *The Gateless Gate*, case 23, "Think Neither Good nor Evil," which is often condensed into the following:

What is your original face before your parents were born?

Be careful: "original" isn't something else somewhere else that you have to go searching for. "Before your parents were born": this is not the genetic, biological, much less the sociological and psychological inheritance from "parents." It is not being stuck in the specific conditions and circumstances, stuck in the reactive habits—all the self-centered names and ideas we have for who and what we call our self. But do not look elsewhere. This is not anywhere else, this is not anything else.

So what is this? Being this that we are is our practice. Do not be caught and limited by conditions, by thoughts about the conditions, about the feelings and circumstances that arise and pass. "When Guanyin manifests, what sort of person can it be?[1] / Even if you peeled away the skin it would be no avail," writes Ch'an nun

Jingang.² Be most ordinary; be this moment as is. Be human, be this moment conditions and circumstances, be these five skandhas, this form-empty, this empty-form, this wholeheartedness. Flowers appearing, buds blowing in the wind, the traffic passing by right now, the person with whom you are speaking—it's not something elsewhere.

So who hears? You know this very well. Not something extra, not something extraordinary; in fact it's most ordinary. Practice is being most ordinary—nothing special, nothing extra. Unfortunately, we like to pile on extra and the extra special. Then maybe we feel better, knowledgeable, important, significant, or safe. The ideas and habits of a fixed, separate self blind us.

Abilities and skills make it possible for us to function. And yet, if we talk of practice, it is being dull, "a rusty, dull needle." Not a sharp, shiny needle. Of course, there is a time for sharp and shiny. But as practice deepens and—if I may use the word—as practice matures, then it is this rusty, dull, ordinary moment, this most rich moment of hearing, seeing, tasting, breathing. Yes, being born this moment. And yes, being original face before parents are born.

Who is this? You all know. No need to say "know." We all are so; we can't be otherwise. And yet, we need to be what we are. We need to taste who we are, we need to testify to what is so. This is what our practice calls for from us. And we testify in sitting, breathing, walking, working, and eating. Being born includes being dying. Being dying means being nothing extra needed, nothing extra held on to right now.

When we are upset, depressed, or sad, that is exactly the time to look: Who is upset? Who is sad? When "I am so angry," that is the energy to turn and look: "Who is angry?" This is most difficult if we are caught in the throes of the anger, righteousness, and upset. Yet this is exactly the best practice opportunity, to turn this body-mind anger or upset, and look directly: "Who?"

We might want to use our particular skills of figuring it out, thinking it out, sensing it out—whatever our own particular style is. We each have our own style, and these styles are wonderfully useful, but those skills are not necessary for this most fundamental intimacy that is who we are. Yet our particulars are not anything else. This is our life, our sitting, our practice. Even those words are extra, but I say them.

So being born doesn't take anything extra; it doesn't take an effort to be born. You are born. So who is born? Who is it that declares, "Above the heavens, below the earth, I alone am the World-Honored One"? Who is this? Who is this most intimate that you are? Who is this that you can't miss? If you find anything, that is extra.

Our practice together is "filling a well with snow." Does the well need the snow? Will the snow fill the well? And yet, we do our part. You will get nothing extra. You need nothing extra. And yet, be born this moment. You are here—and yet, be born right now. That is why when we celebrate Buddha's birthday, we are not celebrating something that occurred twenty-six hundred years ago. That is why when we sit zazen, we are not doing something we ever did before. Always original face, always original practice.

We are supported by practicing with others, by giving self away body-mind to this moment, this zazen, this walking, this eating. And in spite of being supported by others, by the structure of a practice center, by the schedule, it is our opportunity and our effort that allows us to be our self, to forget our self, to be this intimacy that no one else can give us. And this is not dependent on adding anything or getting rid of anything.

Student: You said, "Who is hearing?" And you also said, "We all know." It doesn't seem describable in words.

Genmyo: Show me.

It is certainly expressible. Knowing isn't dependent on thinking it out, except that many people limit themselves and their knowing to what they think out. Many of us limit life to what we think out. Yes, there are all sorts of words we could use, but descriptions are just that.

If I limit this tea to what I think about it, then this tea becomes very limited. I may know about the tea's wetness, texture, and taste, but those are all thoughts. Without holding to thinking about the tea, such as "This tea is too expensive" or "I wish I had more of this," just drink. Similarly, feelings are limited. So if we limit our self to what we think and feel about our self and about this universe that is our self—much less live in this universe as "me" versus "not-me" versus "people" versus "trees" versus "wood" and "sounds"—then that much the world that we are becomes only a pale imitation of what our life is and a pale imitation of who we are.

Talking about practice can be useful, but we have to do it for our self, just as we have to taste the tea our self. We can be encouraged and supported; certainly, the form of the teacup enables me to drink the tea. Here in the zendo, the form of practice supports us in being able to be our life. The form of your life supports you. But the tea isn't dependent on the teacup; our life isn't dependent on particular forms.

See what an analogy is and see what an expression is, but don't be stuck by them, and don't be limited by them. And yet, express the whole of the truth in this form, just as the teacup contains the whole tea in this form right here.

Student: So what is a person's life if they are in a coma?

Genmyo: Be in a coma. Then see.

Student: What if they are in a coma, then they die?

Genmyo: Then die.

You want to figure it out, and then try to make something from that, comparing and evaluating "coma" and "dying." Coma is functioning of being. Dying is functioning of being. "Life is life of the Buddha, death is life of the Buddha," says Dogen.

What is it? Good question. Who dies? Don't look outside. If you know who hears right now, then you know who dies. So take care of right now, then you can take of dying as well.

Student: There is just hearing and then not-hearing.

Genmyo: So who hears, who not-hears? You, with your own tongue, with your own body, with your ears, eyes, mind, you have the opportunity to see this from the inside out. So don't limit your life to thinking out what it must be, but just do this moment, and then see what this life is. That is why when you say, "I hear this, I feel this, and I see this," I encourage you: look who hears, look who feels, look who sees. Your practice effort is to clarify this "I hear"; it will become clear at some point. The clarifying is the process of life practice.

Our effort is to live this life. What comes of that is not up to us. But we are this functioning right now. We are this right now, whether we "know it" or not, whether we realize it or not. To the extent that we realize it, to that extent that it is clear, to that extent we manifest this.

This is not dependent on creating, just like hearing is not dependent on creating, just like our being born is not dependent on us—and yet we can miss being born this moment. Practice is not to miss what is so; practice is to enable us not to miss what is so. Be intimate as you are. Trust yourself; nothing extra is needed. Our practice is to trust our self. Trusting, we allow forgetting self. Trust this ordinary life that we are. Be this very Buddha life that we are. Of course, there's no need to use such fancy words.

24

Not-Self, Not-Two

Being just this. We need nothing extra, nothing special. This is simple and straightforward. There is no particular thing to concern your self with; still, this seems difficult.

Yasutani Roshi said, "Buddha wisdom: cause and effect with no one at its core." Cause and effect: you can say impermanence, you can say constant change, you can even say emptiness. No one at its core; truly, no self to forget. And yet, we all are sure of self, sure of constancy of self. Not as a theory, but as the way we function in the world, the way we function with so-called others, the habits and reactions we live. We are sure of the constancy of who and what we are, and the constancy of who and what they are.

Exactly this results in problems and suffering: problems in the midst of being this moment, problems in the midst of responding to this moment. We have a practice expression: "Forget the self." This is the practice life of "walking in the void," as Master Dongshan says.

Book of Equanimity, CASE 94, "DONGSHAN IS UNWELL"

When Dongshan was unwell, a monk asked, "Master, you are not well. Is there anyone who does not get sick?"

Dongshan said, "There is."

The monk said, "Does the one who doesn't get sick take care of you?"

Dongshan said, "I take care of him."

The monk said, "How is it when you look after him?"

Dongshan said, "When I do that no illness is seen."

This practice isn't something fancy; this practice is exactly this moment. Being nothing, doing nothing—just this. There is no void somewhere else.

Reacting out of confusion about this life that we are will result in all sorts of suffering and harm. There is suffering and harm because we see what is impermanent as permanent. Noticing "wanting permanence" is itself practice, an aspect of seeing the belief of a separate, fixed self.

Dogen Zenji said, "Just understand that life and death are nothing other than nirvana." There is nothing to try to get away from. In fact, you are completely free in the midst of life and death. And yet, we are not free. To walk in the void is diligently practicing not holding on to beliefs and ideas, not holding on to physical form. The more we know, the more we insist on what is so; the less we forget, the less we are the intimacy of not knowing, of forgotten self.

So Dongshan says, "Forget physical form and obliterate tracks." "Obliterate tracks" means doing just this: forgetting tracks, forgetting habits of attachments, body-mind, emotion-thought, and karmic dispositions. This is forgetting self. Doing just what we are doing is doing nothing. This is being present. Not inside here as opposed to outside there; not outside there as opposed to inside here. Just doing the whole universe of this moment, with no one doing. Just complete doing. Being nothing, we can be anything. This is our practice: intimacy being, giving self away.

So much of how we live and what we do is based on beliefs, thoughts, and judgments, and based on a life of self and other. I am in here, everything else is out there; things are something separate, the sounds of the universe come to me. We have judgments of how I should and shouldn't be; this includes a pernicious attitude and belief of duality, which unfortunately we often don't notice. So our functioning is about me going out in the world and doing things, and about the things in the world and what they do to me. This separation includes judgments about whether I am the way I should be, whether the world is as it should be, and so forth.

Not-two reminds us of what is so. Not-two supports practice. Not-two is the way it is, the truth of our life. And yet when we act out of our habits, when we believe our habits and judgments, we miss what is so. Sometimes we do this very consciously, and sometimes we do this very subtly. To use Dogen's expression, when we carry the self forward and function in the midst of the ten thousand things, right here we perpetuate delusion. We perpetuate circumstances that create difficulties, because it is me doing to others, and me doing to circumstances. Or vice versa.

When we hold the belief and the attitude of self going forward, it goes the other way, too. We think the ten thousand things are doing things to me; this is still duality. Only if we forget the self are the ten thousand things functioning as me, only then am I functioning as the ten thousand things. There is no holding to a separate me, there is no creating and maintaining dualism; therefore we can say the ten thousand things function as me.

Please, forget about the ten thousand things. This moment, be this sound. This moment, drink, eat, talk, listen, sit. Giving self away as the present moment. Forgetting the self in the midst of daily functioning, in the midst of the universe functioning. This is not knowing.

Master Fazang says, "The mysterious pointing of the prajna, is it not to be found exactly here?" Nowhere else. This is Dongshan encouraging his disciples before he died: "Work hard to diligently walk in the void." This is exactly what we are doing right here; we can't be anyplace else. Whether sitting or standing, we can't be anyplace else. And yet, we try to be elsewhere.

Don't be trapped by the words "permanent" and "impermanent." You want to use the word "permanent," fine. The whole universe is permanent right this moment. If you want to say "impermanence," just say impermanence. But permanence is not apart from impermanence; impermanence is not separate from permanence.

So Buddha says, "All dharmas are the true mark. The self permanently abides in nirvana." Have I switched all of a sudden? Remember Dongshan saying, "I take care of him." "When I do that, no illness is seen." No illness is seen. So Dongshan talks about the one who isn't ill, the one who doesn't die, the one who is not born, the one who is not destroyed, the one who is "unborn."

We even think that this so-called body-mind has permanence. We think that there is a continuous life we are living. And the same for others; we think, "He is, she is not." We get into all sorts of trouble because of judgments and should-haves and could-haves: "If only I did such and such, I wouldn't be such and such." Those are more of these poisonous words of permanence that we hold to.

I don't say not to use these words, but when you see these words arising out of tracks, arising out of habits of body-mind, take them as practice reminders. There are a number of different ways to practice with this. A simple way is to look: "Who shouldn't? Who couldn't?" Or simply: "Who says this?" Just turn it around and look. Or simply just be present; be exactly this moment.

How is it to frolic in the midst of sickness? How is it to frolic in the midst of dying and death? This is the fundamental matter. Life doesn't turn into death, despite the fact that we insist it does.

It is only we who insist on constancy and continuity. Insisting on constancy and continuity, we miss this fundamental matter. All of us are sick in different ways, and yet we don't want to frolic in the midst of this. We complain about sickness and others, because we believe sickness. We believe the "should-haves, could-haves" that make sickness. We don't see, much less be, this "one who isn't sick." We find it hard to forget the self, despite the simple encouragement of being just this moment.

Of course, the truth is that we can never be other than this moment, never. Despite this, we manage to suffer because of what we insist is so. To encourage us, Hakuin Zenji says, "Don't try to enter, just don't exclude." Don't remove yourself. Right here is where you are; you can't be anyplace else.

Student: Is "free will" a poisonous term? It seems to me that if anybody had any choice, they wouldn't suffer.

Genmyo: You always have choice, right now. See, the problem is that you insist that "I" am having the "free" choice, "I" am "suffering." There is pain, and yet no one has to suffer. Things, conditions, arising circumstances, are essentially unable to satisfy us. Self-centeredness inherently can't be satisfied by the nature of reality because self-centeredness wants permanence. So free will is the practice opportunity to be this moment, to make whatever is the appropriate practice effort of this moment. This is free will.

You can choose to be caught up and attached, with all the consequences that come from that—though you might not "know" you are doing this because it is a familiar habit, a track. If I choose to let go of this stick [releases stick] it drops; that is a guaranteed consequence. Or I can choose to hold on to the stick; then it doesn't fall, and it doesn't make a sound. Choosing habits, choosing reactions, results in suffering. That is free will.

Sometimes we only see a sliver of choice in the midst of circumstances and conditions. Then the only practice effort that we can make is that sliver-practice choice effort. But if we make that sliver effort, then we see more slivers, bigger slivers, of opportunities for skillful practice effort, for the practice of being just this.

When we say "free will," we assume self that has free will or doesn't have free will. We are giving away the game without even noticing it. Another aspect is cause and effect; our life is nothing but cause and effect being manifested right here, right now, as is. It is not a matter of theory; it is walking this life diligently. This is our free will.

Bringing up various points as encouragements for you, for me, is practicing together. As Hakuin encourages us, just exclude non-entry, then right here is where you are. You can't be elsewhere. Nothing else is needed, the whole universe is just right here. Everything that is needed is just right here.

25

Amid Conditions and Circumstances

We seemingly live in a world of conditions and circumstances. Because it seems that way to us, we often become confused about conditions and circumstances, about this arising and passing. We are not conditions and circumstances, and we are not other than conditions and circumstances.

So what is our life? Who are you? What is being who you truly are?

There are different ways that Buddhas and ancestors have tried to clarify this life. They have supported us in clarifying this so that we can be who we are and see who we are; they have supported us so that we can live without being caught up in stress and suffering as a result of being muddled up about things.

The Buddha says, "Do not sorrow over the past, neither hanker for the future. Maintain with what is present" (*Samyutta Nikaya* 1:18). This is a good place to start. Sorrowing over the past or being angry over the past; being fearful of the future or thinking the future will take care of what we think is not OK right now—those are reactive habits that arise, very human habits.

Unfortunately, we often take these habits as truth when they arise, and because we don't know what and who we are, we react to circumstances and conditions out of these habits. So it is important for us to notice. Just sitting, and throughout our practice life, we can notice where sorrowing over the past occurs. And right there is a wonderful opportunity to maintain our self in what is present, in this body-mind moment. Maintaining the present is being this conditioned circumstance, this moment, inside-outside. Because we are free; truly, we are free of conditions and circumstances, and we can therefore be conditions and circumstances.

When we are muddled about things, we can't be serene. Muddled means we believe that what is not so is in fact so. We believe that conditions and circumstances determine who and what we are. We believe that the name and form of the things that we do or don't have, the things that we do or don't call our self, the things that we do or don't call others, are what determine who we are.

We sorrow or are angry over the past, and we fear the future. These are just habits of mind that arise—and yet they are a wonderful opportunity to see these habits when they are here, and see that we don't need to reactively live out of them, and don't need to hold to them.

We get tangled up because we are unclear about self and conditions. Our practice, our life, is to see that we are truly free. Therefore, conditions and circumstances don't tangle us up, because we don't believe that conditions and circumstances are what our habits "encourage us" to believe they are. We aren't muddled about things.

In one sense, the Four Practice Principles remind us over and over what we need to do, and they remind us over and over what is so. Conditions and circumstances are not a problem. The desire for them or the fear of them, as well as the belief that they limit who we are, is the source of our stress or problem. If we identify our self as conditions and circumstances, they limit us. There's nothing wrong with conditions and circumstances, except when we identify our self with our idea of them, and when we identify our self with our conceits about them.

So identifying with "conceits" and ideas is what we need to notice. And the way to notice this is not by thinking about identifying but by being present. And that is what we have the opportunity to do, to simply be present. Of itself, identifying melts away. Because in being present, we can see for our self and we can taste for our self how we are free in the midst of conditions and circumstances. We are free because we can, as the Buddha said, maintain our self with what is. "Maintain our self with what is" means to maintain our self in the present moment of conditions and circumstances. And we do so without adding on self-centeredness, and without adding on ideas of self and others, which would hinder us. Or at least we can notice where these things come up to blind us. To blind us from what? From this present moment that we are. We do this so that we can be exactly who and where we are.

"No sufferings torment one who has nothing, who does not adhere to name and form" (*Samyutta Nikaya*, 1:104). It's this adhering that we get to notice. Adhering is sorrowing over the past, hankering over the future; angering over the past, fearful of the future. So when anger arises, right there is an opportunity to see. At some point, bodily inhabit the feeling of being angry over the past. And see in that anger how we hold to both the identity of our self and hold to our view of things, our view of conditions and circumstances being as we think they are. Right there is the formula that leads to tormenting.

These phrases in the *Samyutta Nikaya* are verses that the Buddha recited to help those who were practicing with him remember how to practice. These aren't a substitute for practice, but they are reminders: How can I be and do what will enable me to be who I am? To be liberated? To be serene? To be awakened? To be untangled? It is not that there is any problem with the circumstances of our life. Even the "pretty things" that appear are fine. And yet, it is our desire and our hankering for them, or our fear of losing them (or even having them) that gets us in trouble.

What is living in the midst of conditions and circumstances, and yet not being tormented by them? This is our real task. I ask what it is to live in the midst of conditions and circumstances, because we all do! Conditions and circumstances, you understand, are bodily conditions, mental states, everything that appears and disappears. Inside and outside are conditions and circumstances. They arise, they pass. We live in a world of ongoing change, and yet we live truly in a world of only this moment. We only have this present; the rest is a story, and it is a story with which we can create all sorts of difficulties.

Being the present in the midst of ongoing change, in the midst of conditions and circumstances, can we freely enter into conditions and circumstances? Can we not fear them, not sorrow over them, not hanker for them, not be angry about them? Or alternatively, can we notice when sorrow, anger, fear, and all the other things appear? And can we see what the appropriate practice of this moment is for us?

The point of my writing is not for you to remember anything that I write, unless it assists you and supports you to be who you are, to be in the midst of conditions and circumstances and be free. The way to be free is because you are free; because you are free, you can be—and you must be—conditions and circumstances. And because you are conditions and circumstances, you are free of the conditions and circumstances. Because you are willing and able to be the conditions and circumstances, you are free.

We only think we are not free, which is why we sorrow, or why we are angry, fearful, hankering, or greedy. We only think we are not free because we are confused or muddled about things, inside and outside. Because we don't know who we are, we have this idea of who we are: "I am such and such," "You are such and such." When we believe that identity and that view of who we are, it automatically and inevitably brings in this sorrowing about the past, this anger about the past, this fear of the future. Because we are not clear on who we are right now, the past and the future can do that.

How do we practice skillfully and appropriately when these emotion-thoughts arise? We need to consider this question because it is guaranteed that these habits will arise for some of us. Maybe these habits don't arise for you; but if they do arise, it is important to be able to practice skillfully when we become caught in them. Of course, if they doesn't arise, wonderful!

26

Possessed

Zazen is experiencing our self moment after moment. Of course this "self" isn't "inside" this skin; it is this moment opportunity throughout life. Experiencing moment-moment is not limited to formal zazen. Experiencing is so common, and yet it is so uncommon for us to live life as we are, as this experiencing moment. So zazen, this practice, is most important. Not as a means to get anywhere, and not as a means to get somewhere else, but just being who we always are.

Our ideas of what we possess or don't possess are a way we refuse to be who we are. Even the idea that there is someone possessing and something to possess is a way of refusing to be who we are. Look for a moment: we feel strongly that we possess all sorts of "things." Gain and loss grow from this. Not just things: we "possess" feelings, we "possess" memories, we "possess" attitudes. We believe "I'm such and such, I know such and such, I have such and such skills." These are all the things that I possess.

Whether it's money, people, or circumstances in the world, believing in possessions flows into reactions when these "possessions" aren't the way we want them to be. And with these reactions, we can get in trouble and cause trouble. But it is not the things that are the problem; this is just this. The trouble is that I believe I possess this, I believe this permanence that should be so, and then when this thing starts wearing out, I start having problems. Take this thing away, and right there we see reactions. Instead of possessing, this possesses me. Possessions possess me. Not only do they possess me, they create and perpetuate me.

So I miss this moment; I miss this moment right now that is my life. This moment is this moment. We miss our life when we believe possessions and when we hold on to possessions with self, with satisfaction, with permanence. These possessions might be "I'm smart," "He is such and such" or "She is such and such," "This is my son, daughter, husband, wife, lover, friend, mother, father." We believe these kind of possessions, and all that goes along with them. Not that we don't love various people, or feel connected with them. But this aspect of possessions, of wanting things to be a certain way in order to give us satisfaction, is the potential for suffering.

Throughout our life, we have never possessed anything. There is a phrase: "Naked you are born and naked you die." At best, we have borrowed many things. Even this so-called body that we think we possess is just a daydream—and the daydream uses us to separate self and other and circumstances. We dream birth, we dream death. We miss this moment, the universe that we wake up into. Instead, we compare how it is with how it should be and could be.

Not possessing anything and not being possessed by anything, we can possess anything and we can possess everything. Sitting zazen is allowing self, giving self away to the present moment, experiencing this life that we are. Very simple: we are sitting down and being exactly this moment as is. Forget self; discover this moment life. Be free.

All of us practice, whether this is the first time we have sat, whether we have been sitting for thirty years, or whether we never sit. Our whole life is the practice of encountering this universe that we are, the practice of encountering this moment opportunity. As we say in the "Gatha on Opening the Sutra": "Now we see this, hear this, receive and maintain this." This.

Student: When I hear you talk like this, part of me feels relieved. There is a certain burden that is relieved in not possessing. For example, I don't know who will be elected president, but the fact is that there is a certain belief system that some people have, and that belief system affects me. I think I have to take certain steps.

For example, I feel that I have to renew my passport, because if a person of my sexuality is going to be discriminated against, I might have to leave. Not that I want to leave, but I don't want to be in a concentration camp. That is where my story goes. And I understand that it is a story, but how much of it is really a story when you see policies that will affect us? That is where I have an issue.

Genmyo: "My fear"—and even "my profile"—is another possession I have. That need not hinder being present and skillfully seeing what to do right now. In seeing clearly what is so, we can act skillfully. If "my story" is a possession, that possesses me; we are possessed by it. We are fearful, we become angry, we live a fearful life; maybe we become depressed, suffer, or even cause harm. These possessions and reactions blind us; they keep us from seeing what is so, and then acting appropriately and skillfully. All because we are possessed by something, as opposed to being present this moment.

Being present this moment is the whole universe seeing what there is to do skillfully, right now. But often, as you say, we become possessed. The term "being possessed" is usually reserved for strange circumstances, like when someone is possessed by a strange spirit. Being possessed, they cannot see reality as it is.

The truth is that much of the time we are possessed by strange spirits, but we just have an agreement with lots of people that this is the normal way to be. It can be simple things like getting angry when someone cancels a meeting, to being upset when traffic isn't going the way I want, to more "extreme" circumstances, when someone reacts violently to something said or an event. "Road rage" is a form of being possessed. There are all sorts of ways we become possessed by self-centeredness in the midst of this universal life that we are. These possessions blind us, and they keep us from being who we are. This is our practice opportunity.

The choices we make depend on the circumstances that we can see clearly right now. But when we are possessed, we can't see clearly right now. Therefore, to aid our practice in the midst of this, we have various practice supports and guidelines to help us see and act clearly. For example, the Precepts are a way not to be blinded by the reactive habits, by the spirits of craziness, the "spirits of the dream life.

Student: I was just thinking of the earlier question and your response. The upcoming presidential election especially creates all kinds of identifications for me: "I'm this party, I'm this person, and blah blah blah."

Genmyo: "I'm not this, and I'm not that."

Student: That's right. And it's strong. And I notice that. But I like my identifications much of the time.

Genmyo: Are you possessed by them?

Student: Sure.

Genmyo: OK, then they're not yours. They have you.

Student: But I wonder sometimes about all these identifications, and this is particularly strong right now with the election. Without them, as you say, you're free to act. But because the habits of mind have created who I think I am, who would I be without these?

Genmyo: Good! Explore! Discover! This is practice. Not to

discover who "would you be," but who you are, even in the midst of all these so-called possessions, all these so-called identifications.

Some of our identifications have to do with "I'm the person that so-and-so is supposed to be nice to because they are my brother, my daughter, my friend." So when they don't do the expected thing, what happens?" "How could you!" or "Oh, it's so terrible! They didn't talk to me when they came by!" Often, these reactions are daydreams. The person might not have even noticed what they did, but we suffer because of it. We poison our life, and we poison the lives of others.

Zazen is to be the life that we are: all the ongoing practice opportunities of our daily life, all the supports in the midst of the seeming possessions that possess us, support us to be the life that we are. This is ongoing practice.

Student: How do you undo sixty years?

Genmyo: This moment! This moment! There is no sixty years.

If you start talking about it, not only do you have sixty years, you have thousands of years. We all have this so-called baggage, but it is only right now. The baggage in the stories, in the culture, in the habits, is endless. But it doesn't make a difference. Just take care of right now. In zazen, there is no such past.

Precepts are one way to support this zazen life; they are one way to work with the baggage. For instance, we can work with the seventh precept, which is not elevating myself (or anyone I can connect with myself) and not putting others down. There, right there, we can work with that for a month, even for a lifetime.

Each precept contains all the other precepts. So you know very well that even though I bring up this particular precept, it contains the precept of nonkilling and all the other precepts. Because as soon as we get caught up in self and others, we have killed this universal life that we are. But we just have to pick up the corner, the edge of this life that we are working with, and everything else is connected.

This is always this moment, this being present. Zazen is not being something extra; it is being exactly this moment as is.

27

The Seamless Moment

A Zen meal verse begins, "First, seventy-two labors brought us this food; we should know how it comes to us." This is the interconnectedness of all of life, of all the activities and beings that are our life. Zen practice encourages and supports us to be this interconnectedness, this interbeing, this interdependence.

But if interdependence remains just another good idea, then it is not much, because our actions continue to be based on our beliefs of separateness, and therefore they result in suffering. To practice is to experience our actions, and to notice when they grow out of separation.

Even as we explore connectedness and separation, there are areas of life we try to avoid. I encourage you to explore the interbeingness of "our self" and those "beings" we see as outside the pale of the acceptable, even including extremes such as the murderer in Rwanda and the torturer in Bosnia. How do we act appropriately in terms of unacceptable behavior (even horrific actions) and interbeing? And not only in terms of individuals who are difficult to accept "out there," but also "in" our thoughts, the murderer and torturer "in" what we think of as our self. What experiencing do we avoid?

As we become aware of making self and other out of life, as we become aware of separating our self from our self, the effort needed is to stay as this bodily-sensory awareness. There are activities and things we exclude from our experience and awareness. What are these?

You may want Zen practice to make you calmer, more relaxed, and more peaceful. But though these things may occur, they are not what practice is about. In fact, Zen practice is learning how to live in hell, the hell of suffering and the hell of creating suffering. Practice is experiencing life and responding to whatever arises in the midst of hellishness.

Here, it is valuable to discover our preferences and our requirements. What is the difference between the two? Do we react when our preferences are not met, and then justify our anger, fear, sadness, or depression? Can we make choices, and yet not discriminate? As we practice, we notice and experience how we discriminate.

Memorial Day is a day to remember past persons and events. In this life of arising and passing, what is a "memorial" that is not in the realm of past, present, and future? There is a pertinent case in the *Blue Cliff Record* called "National Teacher Chung's Seamless Monument" (case 18).

Emperor Su Tsung asked National Teacher Hui Chung, "After you die, what will you need?"

The National Teacher said, "Build me a seamless monument."

The emperor said, "Please tell me, master, what the monument would look like."

The National Teacher was silent for a long time; then he asked, "Do you understand?"

The emperor said, "I don't understand."

The National Teacher said, "I have a disciple to whom I have transmitted the Dharma, Tan Yuan, who is well versed in this matter. Please summon him and ask him about it."

After the National Teacher passed on, the emperor summoned Tan Yuan and asked him the meaning of a seamless monument. Tan Yuan said:

South of Hsiang, north of T'an,
Within there's gold sufficient to a nation.
Beneath the shadowless tree, the community ferryboat.
Within the crystal palace, there's no one who knows.

These events occurred in the late eighth century, but it is no other than right now. The emperor asks, "After you die, what will you need?" In other words, "Do you have any last wishes, any last requests?" The National Teacher responds, "Build me a seamless monument." Actually, this monument isn't for him. The emperor must comprehend the teaching of Hui Chung to know the seamless monument. Who is the National Teacher? Who are you?

The emperor said, "Please tell me, master, what the monument would look like." Tell me more, give me some last instructions; I need more help in clarifying this matter of life and death.

"The National Teacher was silent for a long time." Some people think that being silent is a special Zen answer, but silence has nothing to do with it. Silence or not silence isn't it. What is the National Teacher showing clearly? What is the seamless monument he is revealing?

The National Teacher asked the emperor, "Do you understand?" The emperor answered, "I don't understand." We may say that life is seamless, seamless in the sense of no break, no division. Is it true for us? What is our seamless life? Conversely, what are our seams? Life is an opportunity to appreciate our interconnectedness and to appreciate our separation; this is ongoing practice.

The National Teacher, seeing that the emperor needed more help, said, "OK, since you need more, go see my Dharma successor." Tan Yuan recites his verse to help the emperor: "South of Hsiang and north of T'an." That might be a province, since at that time there was a province with those two areas as the borders. So he is referring to this whole piece of land. "Within there's gold sufficient to a nation. / Beneath the shadowless tree, the community ferryboat. / Within the crystal palace, there's no one who knows."

When asked about Buddha's teaching, a Chinese Zen teacher said, "Not-knowing is the most intimate." What is not-knowing? Step one is becoming aware of all the ways we think we "know," and facing and experiencing our life, our bodily-sensory presence.

All is revealed. All is realized. Yet, it is hard to see. The capping phrase is: "It is not something eyes can see." Yet the appended verse states, "Forever and ever it is shown to the people." What is it?

Is life seamless? It is!

How?

How and when do you experience life as not seamless?

28

Dogen Hides Buddha

"Ascending to the Dharma seat," Master Dogen said, "When the dawn star appeared, Shakyamuni Buddha said, 'I and all sentient beings on the great Earth simultaneously attain the Way.' Now tell me, what is the way that he attained? If one realizes it, even Shakyamuni will have no place to hide his face. Why is it so? Speak quickly! Speak quickly!"[3]

Upon enlightenment, Buddha realized this unconditioned that we all are from the beginning: "I and all beings on the great Earth simultaneously attain the Way." Now Dogen asks his disciples—right now, he asks us—what is the way Shakyamuni attained?

Do you realize what Shakyamuni attained? "I and all sentient beings" includes every one of us, everyone that Dogen Zenji was addressing, everyone here, everyone we encounter. All beings of the great Earth. If we realize this, even Shakyamuni will have no place to hide his face.

How is this? How would he have no place to hide? Reflect on this. What is Buddha's face? What is it to see Buddha's face? What is it to hide? How is there no place to hide?

We believe that beings and circumstances, and even states of mind, create difficulties for us. We believe that they are not OK; we believe they are a problem, and they are separate. If we do something about those "things" and this "problem," then all will be OK. Alternatively, we think, "Oh, I have got to do something about myself." An aspect of sitting is noticing the comments, judgments, and beliefs that we hold. We notice these things not in order to fix them, but as an opportunity to be this life that we are. This is sitting, being this, being open bodily awareness. Stated conceptually, experiencing is being this Attained Way of Shakyamuni. Dogen Zenji is revealing this.

Joko said, "Everything in life is to be appreciated." This is our practice life; this is not-two. Appreciating whatever we encounter; allowing appreciation. Or notice how you are not appreciating. Just to notice, not to fix. This is "not-two," as the Third Ancestor Jianzhi Sengcan states in *On Believing in Mind* (also known as the *Faith Mind Sutra*).

Of course, sometimes we say, "Be one." But be careful! Though Sengcan also says, "One is no other than all," we may too easily say, "Everything is one." This can become something conceptual, and then it does not penetrate the many ways that we believe judgments, separate self and others, and duality. Even if we rephrase this as "All is one," it may become another matter. "One" can become a transformed self-centeredness: "Yes, everything is one, but it's got to be one the way I want it to be." So this can be a trap.

"Not-two" springs the trap. Not-two is not a belief but a useful pointer. Notice what you believe is two; notice when you say, "Oh, that's not me" or "It's not OK for him to act like that, it's not OK for this to happen." Practice is functioning, being this functioning that we are, responding to this circumstance of life.

Look: "How do I appreciate this?" When we sit, functioning

is sitting, functioning is being alive. As a training device, in sesshin we sit from morning till night. But at other times in life, we sit, we work, we speak to people, we do many things, and yet there is nothing other than this "not-two," this functioning Attained Way. Where can anything hide? Is Buddha hiding? Is Dogen hiding? Are you hiding?

Everything in life is to be appreciated. Maezumi Roshi has a book titled *Appreciate Your Life,* because he often used this phrase to encourage practice.[4] Many traditions have nice expressions that point in this way; the words support us in being this awareness that we are. The sixteenth-century Catholic thinker Nicholas of Cusa's expression was "Not other." Even God is not other, and yet we get trapped with all sorts of ideas about "other." There is a Chasidic tune called "Du," which means "you" in the most intimate form, like Martin Buber's I-Thou God: "Where I stand, Du. / Where I sit, Du. / Where I go, Du. / East, Du. / West, Du. / North, Du. / South, Du. / Du. / Du. Du." These are expressions that we can appreciate in order to clarify practice, especially if we are caught up in self-centeredness and reacting to so-called internal or external circumstances.

How do we welcome life? Appreciating is welcoming, appreciating is being present. Do you believe there is a special way to be present? Do you hold to thoughts, reacting from them, and therefore miss this aliveness, this body-mind presence? Sitting is the opportunity of being this body-mind. Being this, body-mind drops away. Body-mind drops away, and all encounters are revealed as this, the Attained Way.

At times, we want to parse the word "appreciating." Being this, being as life is, is appreciating. This is zazen. A useful image for being caught up in self-centered emotion-thought is being stuck on and attentive only to the surface of a vast ocean. Living on a small piece of the surface, feeling, believing, and reacting to the ever-changing surface conditions, to likes and dislikes, you suffer, you harm, and you are harmed. Practice is noticing how we hold to self-centeredness. Practice is to lift that up for a moment, and see the surface and ocean as it is, the self-centered dream of emotion-thought that we are holding.

Zazen, practice, is diving in right in here. Open awareness is zazen, open awareness is being the ocean that we are. Being so, the self-centered perspective is not solid, and it is not the truth of our life. Being the ocean is being this particular moment, this surface that is the whole of the ocean. Being so enables us to enjoy the seemingly pleasant things that are the whole ocean right now, and to embrace the seemingly unpleasant and even painful things that are the whole ocean right now.

But beware! Do not get stuck in an analogy: there is no ocean, no surface, no diving! It is right where you are, right as you are, being body-mind presence. This is bodily-sensory experiencing, appreciating life, life embracing life. Being so, we respond to circumstances as needed: we fix, we change, we put up an umbrella, or we do whatever is appropriate.

Day by day especially in sesshin, sitting is richer. As self-centeredness becomes transparent and the self is forgotten, everything in life is to be appreciated; everything in life is the original face of your Shakyamuni. So where is there to hide?

Yet we find lots of places where the universe doesn't suit us, so we hide from our self. Therefore practice is noticing how and when we believe life is two, three, four. How do we believe that? How is this manifested physically and bodily, as reactions and as emotional feelings spinning off? Simply noticing is the opportunity to appreciate our life. We can even appreciate that we do not want to appreciate our life. You say, "Appreciate everything in life? Come on, there are lots of things I don't like to appreciate." OK, fine. Then notice that you do not want to appreciate them, and experience this.

You do not have to believe any of these words. Anything here that resonates, fine; if you don't find anything useful for your practice, throw it away. You don't need anything extra; just be exactly as you are. Anything extra, throw it away like a used-up piece of toilet paper. All is revealed as it is. Please appreciate this wonderful life.

29

Awakening of Faith in the Mahayana

Nothing lacking, nothing extra. Of course, saying this is extra, and yet not at all extra; exactly this. This very clear matter becomes unclear with self-addiction. Self-addiction is seeing this life in terms of me and not-me, in terms of what I want and what I don't want. This ignorance and the fearful reactions that grow from it seem to be the truth for us; we live in a "me and not-me" universe. Our life transforms into reactions of likes and dislikes, sadness and happiness.

Being self-addicted is ignorance and delusion. As in a twelve-step program, acknowledging self-addiction is to see the arising of ignorance, to see when and how this universal life we are is transformed into self and not-self. Though we are powerless over the arising of self-centeredness, ongoing practice in the midst of arising self is zazen; it is forgetting the self, turning self over to being this moment. This ongoing practice of Bodhi mind is the seeing and functioning right now as is; it is the skillful means of ongoing practice effort.

Let's look at the text called *Awakening of Faith in the Mahayana*.

This text is attributed to Ashvaghosha, but as there is no extant Sanskrit version and the earliest version we have is Chinese, some scholars think it was written by Paramartha, the Chinese translator. The text, as translated by Alexander Mayer, states:

> It is like the water of a vast ocean. When it is stirred into waves by the wind, the motion of the water and the activity of the wind are not separate from one another. Yet water is not mobile by nature. If wind ceases, its motion will also cease. But the wetness of the water will not thereby be annulled. In the same way, when the intrinsically pure mind of sentient beings is stirred into motion by the wind of ignorance, mind and ignorance, not having distinct characteristics of their own, are not separate from one another. Yet the mind is not mobile [clinging, attached] by nature. If ignorance ceases, its continuance will also cease. But the insight nature of the mind will not thereby be annulled.

Awakening is being awake as who and what we are, which is this awakened nature. Of course, when you are awake, it is nonsense to be told that you are awake! And yet when you are not awake, when self-centered ignorance arises, sometimes it is useful to talk about being awakened. The word "Mahayana" literally means great vehicle, the great vehicle that is our life. Our life is being awake; by its very nature, our life is the great awakened vehicle. "Awakening of faith" is zazen, being this moment, this body-mind koan right here. Being so, we taste, we see, we manifest this awakening.

The text clarifies who and what we are. Using analogies enables us to see and be who we are, because in not seeing and not being who we are, we live out of fear and we live out of all the reactions of suffering and harm that grow out of this fear. We can speak of this in terms of the intrinsic and the experiential. If you see a snake you might react with fear, and then live out of inaccurate beliefs that create a basis for fear. But if you know that what appears to be a snake is really a rope, then there is no reaction of fear; you know it is not a snake and will not harm you.

See, if we appreciate who we are and if we can be who we are, there is no fear. Conversely, we can be who we are because fear doesn't get in the way. Doing zazen, being who we are, there is no place for ignorance and fear to arise; we can then respond and make skillful use of circumstances that arise, which is the arising of our life, the arising and functioning of wisdom and compassion.

The analogy of waves and water is our life, this life in the midst of a great ocean. All around us is nothing but this ocean. The ocean is subject to cause and effect, to the winds coming and going, yet it's only ocean—no problem. The winds of ignorance, our attachments and reactions, change the great ocean into a threatening, fearful place. This analogy can help us see what we don't see when we believe our misconceptions and our fear. And this analogy can clarify our practice of zazen, this doing nothing of being present, this not-knowing of forgotten self.

You are driving, and all of a sudden you see the high price of gas. You may think, "How dare they?" Cause and effect is the price of gas, and ignorance is my upset about it; the ocean and waves are being stirred by the wind of ignorance. Yes, in one sense the water is always being stirred; this is cause and effect. And even so-called ignorance is cause and effect. Our attachments, our instincts, our habits of body-mind are cause and effect. And yet, this is the opportunity of practice, to be the ocean as it is, to reveal and appreciate what is so. See? Then even the stirred-up ocean is the great calm ocean; it is wetness all the way through and through.

All sorts of winds are raising the ocean waves, the ocean of our life, the ocean of this moment. We are ocean appearing as this body, appearing as sounds, appearing as feelings. All is this ocean appearing right here. In the midst of the inherent purity of mind of all beings, which is the mind of our life, in the midst of the inherent unmoving, unconditioned nature, there seem to be conditions arising and passing.

More significantly, there are conditions that I like and conditions I don't like; there are conditions that I use to judge myself and others, which results in suffering and harm. Always our practice is being who we truly are; and yet, unless we see it for our self, it is so easy not to be this.It is important and significant to realize that intrinsically we are all awakened, and it is also important for us to make the zazen effort to support being awake, to help us experience and taste our awakened nature, our Buddha-nature. Because then we can practice in winds appearing and disappearing, we can practice in winds arising. Doing this, those very winds are transformed, and instead of keeping us suffering in fear, the winds enable us to ride the waves, to be the waves. Rough waves, this; calm sea, this.

In riding the waves, we get to taste the wetness of the water, to feel and embody the wetness of the water. How do we ride the waves of life? There's no need to go looking for any waves to ride, because you have them right here; you are them in this breath. You are them in standing up, in sitting down, in chewing food.

Zazen, practice, sesshin, our whole life, are all so that we can wake up, right here. Wake up but not to something else—don't think there is some other wetness somewhere else that you are lacking. You right now are the ocean. You are the wetness of the water. Sometimes the waves are small, sometimes the waves are big; that is cause and effect. And in the midst of this cause and effect big and small waves, we have a wonderful ability at this moment of being who we truly are.

The text states, "Mind and ignorance, not having distinct characteristics of their own, are not separate from one another." In some ways, this is hard to see. Mind and ignorance are not separate from each other; otherwise we tend to differentiate what we think is awakening, what we think is good, and what we think is so-called bad or the so-called problem. Whatever arises in life is the practice opportunity of the moment; it's only our belief that the rope is a snake that makes the rope troublesome for us. When we believe the rope is a snake, we react, we run. When we see it is a rope, we can take care of it. Otherwise, rope and snake don't change.

It is more difficult when we don't see the winds of ignorance at the moment we are looking at another person and commenting and judging; or at the moment we are looking at our own condition and believing our judgments about our self. See, comments stir the water; they stir our life. Even in the midst of waves, even in the midst of seeming turmoil and messy, gray, cloudy water, there is what we add to that. To us it may appear like there is water / life here, and thoughts and reactions are something else. But it is all this vast ocean, although it appears to be so-called me in here and so-called other things out there. This is our self-addiction ignorance that we fail to see. We don't know who and what we are. So there is awakening.

Of course, it is extra to talk about awakening this way, but I do it. It's extra in that analogies are not quite true. However, they can be encouragements and supports. The image is to remind us of what we know for our self—because the very nature of water, the very wetness of water, is insight. The very wetness of water is compassion and wisdom. It is up to us to manifest this. It is up to us not to be limited by the habits, beliefs, instincts, and ideas of what seems to be so, of what we are sure is so—all of these things are ignorance, the winds that stir the water.

How do we do that? How do we take care of that? Zazen, sitting, walking, eating, your work, your family, and all beings. Calm sea, this; low waves, this; high waves, this.

30

Blank Slate

If we see practice and various skillful supports from the point of view of ordinary functioning, which is self-centered functioning, this often creates difficulties rather than nurturing our practice and our life. I remember hearing encouraging words like "Be a blank slate," "Be like a blank piece of paper," or "Be a perfectly clean slate." And I thought, "I've got to have a certain state of mind, maybe stop my thoughts, or stop something." If we read that "Sitting is doing nothing," we might think, "OK, how am I going to do nothing?" So we try to do nothing. Of course, we have "I'm doing" and the "nothing" that I'm trying to do. So piled on top of the usual habits, we add more ideas such as "blank" or "nothing."

Sitting zazen, we see thoughts and emotions, which are arising and disappearing. We might become caught up in them, and we might follow along and build upon them. While sitting and practicing, we notice what occurs, including self-centered thinking; we sense the times and ways that "my doing" comes forth in the midst of functioning. While sitting still, we also sense our bodily "doing"; we may discover "doing" something with our tongue, our mouth, or our eyes, not to mention other bodily tensing and movement.

Sitting enables and forces us to discover all the ways "I'm" doing the universe, or "I'm" believing thoughts about the universe. We see all the ways that thinking and feeling are interfering, all the ways they are getting in the way of this blank slate that we always are right now, this original face that is functioning, responding, and manifesting morning to night. Because I believe thoughts, feelings, and emotions, this original face seems not at all this life. Holding on to body-mind habits, we miss this that we are from the beginning—just this.

Sometimes it takes bumping into reality over and over again for us to see what is occurring. We see the believed thoughts bumping into the reality of what is, into this actual manifesting. We see the stress and suffering that is multiplied by believing emotion-thought, by holding to it and building on it. "It's not supposed to be this way!" Oh! And it is this way. "It's not supposed to be this way!" And it is still this way. No matter how many times we think how it is supposed to be, it is as is.

Sitting is being this moment that you are. To quote Dogen in "Shoaku Makusa," "One must practice through good and evil, causes and effects. This is not, as commonly said, a case of altering causes and effects, nor a case of creating them. Causes and effects on occasion cause us to practice. This occurs because the original face of causes and effects is already clearly discerned: it is non-doing, it is uncreated, it is impermanent, it is not obscuring, it is not falling, it is sloughing off [dropping away]."

This original face of cause and effect, this original face of our life. See, we are each of us exactly cause-and-effect manifesting. We can't be anything else; just ordinary. You don't have to take or make anything special or fancy. As we are, we are so; this condition right now is cause and effect. The causes manifest right now: call them genetic, biological, psychological, environmental, and so forth—they are this body-mind circumstance. This cause-and-effect moment is not limited or determined by how we think and feel this moment is; in fact, thinking and feeling are cause and effect. This is the whole of the original face; this nondoing is our life.

What is this nondoing? To say it another way, this clean slate is who and what we are. That is why we can have an instruction like "Be a clean slate," because this is who and what we are. And yet because we so strongly hold to body-mind habits and beliefs and because we attach to emotion-thought, we need this practice to encourage us to be who and what we are. If I can use crude words, our practice is being bodily present and opening up to being this very moment that we are. So the instruction is to be: not be what we think and believe, not cut our life off through holding to believed emotion-thought, but be this that we are. This, this that we are, is the original face right here coming forth.

And yet, if we don't see it for our self, it is of no use. So whatever the specific form of our practice is—whether breathing, being present, shikantaza, being listening, looking at "who" is thinking, or a koan such as Mu or the sound of one hand—over and over, our practice is being altogether this moment. Of course, as soon as we believe our thoughts about any practice or about this listening, we miss this listening that we are. We miss this nondoing, this cause-and-effect listening right here. This clean slate is no longer the clean slate that this is.

This practice intent and effort is what all teachers are encouraging. The particular form doesn't make a difference. Particular forms are particular forms; for various cause-and-effect reasons, each of us resonates with particular skillful means and are encouraged to use particular skillful means. But the point is always to enable us to be who we are, because who we are from the beginning is nondoing.

As we sit and practice we discover this nondoing—to the extent that we do discover it. Or we may discover the doing in the midst of zazen, whether our bodily habits are doing or whether we are caught up in thoughts and emotions. We are in the midst of being listening, and right here we believe: "Too much traffic," "Too little traffic," "Ah, it's good traffic now"; or "Those birds aren't doing it right," "Ah, the birds are so wonderful this morning." Or we might be believing the thought, "I've got to do this, I've got to sit correctly."

See, cause and effect enables us to practice. Cause and effect is the condition each of us are, exactly as we are; there is not a thing lacking for any of us. We are the ability to respond. And what is this ability to respond? This is Buddha ability.

Ch'an master Caoshan says, "The Buddha's true Dharma body resembles empty space. Responding to creatures, it appears in physical form like the moon reflected in water." It's not some Buddha out there; it is the Buddha sitting on your cushion. Responding as the listening [chirp, chirp]. So Dogen says, "Because there is the nondoing of responding to creatures, there is the nondoing of appearing in physical form."

Moon reflected in water; this is our functioning. So "Be an empty slate" is not to squash your mind, and it is not to force yourself to be something else. That is a misunderstanding; we are adding mud to the mud that already confuses us. There is nothing lacking. Right this moment, your functioning is the functioning of this nondoing.

That is why each of us can and has to testify to this; we testify to the original face that is our life. "Testify" means manifest what is so. When you give testimony in court, you swear to tell the truth, the whole truth, and nothing but the truth. Testimony in court is testifying to what is so. Practice is testifying to what is so, not because we have figured it out, or because we know it as some sort of knowledge, but because this is our life. We testify by being who we are, by manifesting the original face we are. This is what bows, who bows, who sits. Right now, this is who is listening.

Of course, it is useless to merely tell someone this. That is just repeating words. We need to testify as life. Our practice is doing so, over and over, moment by moment, being exactly who and what we are. Being exactly this nondoing. This is not about abstractions, and it is not about some added knowledge or even insight. To quote Dogen: "One's own self is neither existent nor nonexistent. It is nondoing."

31

True Person

Cold, snowy day; perfect for January sesshin. *Rohatsu* sesshin in December, which commemorates the enlightenment of Shakyamuni Buddha, is often a cold sesshin as well, with long, dark nights of sitting and ongoing practice effort. We practice in a zendo with many windows on three of the four walls and limited insulation so we sense the elements.

This sesshin in January is often connected with Master Linji. It's even colder and snowier this time of year in Illinois, when practice and being present are supported by the elements. Of course, practice is supported in warm weather, too. Nevertheless, body-mind habits and attachments that arise are pushed and exposed by the snowy cold. Body-mind habits are just body-mind habits. Unfortunately, we miss this life when we are caught in body-mind habits, when we hold to them and react to them. This is the practice opportunity of the manifested koan of our life.

Here is a koan from the *The Record of Master Linji* (Linji-lu). Linji died in the ninth century when he was in his fifties.

> Master Linji took the high seat in the hall. He said, "On your lump of red flesh is a True Person of No Rank who is

always going in and out of the face of every one of you. Those who have not yet proved him, look, look!"

Then a monk came forward and asked, "What about the True Person of No Rank?"

The master got down from his seat, seized the monk, and said "Speak! Speak!"

The monk faltered. Shoving him away, the master said, "The True Person of No Rank, what kind of shit-wiping stick is he!" Then he returned to his quarters.

Linji was addressing monks, so he said, "True Man of No Rank." Nevertheless, "True Person" is not limited to "man," and it is not limited to "woman." So although Linji says "True Man," I say "True Person."

True Person of No Rank on this lump of red flesh is exactly this lump here, "just this face"—just each of us, just each of you. Going in and out of face, going in and out of whole body, is this functioning True Person, your functioning right now!

Don't be distracted by the phrase "No Rank." In one sense, "No Rank" means no status. If we think of Chinese society during the Tang dynasty, where everyone had some status, whether high or low, not having any status was very unusual. Even more, "No Rank" means no boundaries: not bound by any particular status, not bound by rules of society, and not bound by ideas and concepts. So True Person of No Rank is this person of emancipation.

Look at all the ranks that you believe and hold! We may even turn Linji's phrase into some idea: "Practice is finding this No Rank, which is different from rank." No! Dogen Zenji comments, "What is the True Person of Rank?" No problem with rank. One of you is a doctor, one an engineer, one a professor, another a student—you have various ranks. If we interpret "No Rank" as something other than this right here now, then we do not see No Rank.

Being exactly the rank we are is rankless, statusless. But although it is so, "rankless rank" or "statusless status" are stinky words. Sometimes we lead people around the zendo, sometimes we are led around the zendo. This True Person of No Rank is freely any rank; we are this rankless rank right now. Being No Rank right now, we are this rank of our life right here. Linji reveals this True Person for each of us right now. Dogen shows this for us right now.

Unfortunately, there are all sorts of ways that we are not willing to be as we are. "He can't say that to me, I'm his boss" or "She can't do that to me; after all, I'm her father, mother, sister, and so on." All the rank ranks. "Well, I don't do that, that's someone else's to do." When my son was a teenager, he was willing to walk the dog, but he was not willing to pick up the dog shit. Even with a plastic bag, he said, "Phew, I don't do that." There are lots of ranks that we hold to, ranks that blind us right-here-now; even rankless can blind us. We don't want to be, to see, to respond.

Unfortunately, when we spin off, when we imagine things the way we want them, then we never see and we never are this right-here-now, this very moment. This is what Master Linji is saying. If I explain this conceptually, this True Person is this very functioning, hearing (reading) this, always going in and out of this body; this True Person is every one of you. Not something else. Do not think there is some "True Person" coming in and out other than this; that is nonsense. This is exactly your functioning! Not a hairbreadth of separation! And yet if we do not see this and we do not live this, then it is not so. Then even a hairbreadth of separation blinds us.

Truly, we can be every rank, and every position—and yet we hold back. What is the boundary of ranks in your life? What are the rank boundaries right now? Where is this True Person? See, this is what the monk is talking about.

What is the problem? In the *Record of Master Linji*, he says,

"Bring to rest the thoughts of the ceaselessly seeking mind; allow the mind to rest." Allow this open awareness. The constantly spinning mind is trying to create life in a way that will be pleasant, that will make us feel safe, secure, and good. It is grabbing on to every emotion-thought that arises. So allow thought, emotion, and feeling to arise and pass; be this open awareness that you are, and as Linji says, "you will not differ from the ancestor Buddha."

Linji continues, "Do you want to know the ancestor Buddha? He is none other than you who stands before me listening to my discourse." In many Chinese and Japanese monasteries, the tradition is to stand while the discourse is being given by the master in a high seat. All of you listening are none other than the ancestor Buddha! [Hits stick on floor.] That is what he is talking about, this True Person of No Rank right now listening.

According to Linji, "Since you students lack faith in yourself, you run around seeking something outside." Or seeking something inside. "Even if through your seeking you find something, that something will be nothing more than elaborate descriptions and written words. In the end you will fail to gain the Mind of the living ancestor. Make no mistake, worthy Ch'an practitioners, if you don't meet it here now, you'll go on transmigrating through the three realms for myriads of kalpas and thousands of lives, and, held in the clutch of agreeable circumstances, be born in the womb of an ass or a cow." This is very direct and descriptive language.

So what is going on when this monk comes forward: "What about the True Person of No Rank?" Whatever the state of the monk, he is making the effort to clarify! "The master got down from his seat, seized the monk, and said, 'Speak! Speak!' The monk faltered. Shoving him away, the master said 'The True Person of No Rank, what kind of shit-wiping stick is he!'"

Is a shit-wiping stick different from the True Person of No Rank? Do not be fooled! My teacher Soen Nakagawa Roshi said, "I, too, am such a shit-wiping-stick fellow, but also, this True

Person of No Rank." This True Person is exactly our life. Not anywhere else, and not something other than the exact life we are now. This True Person transcends life, death, good, bad, delusion, enlightenment. True Person even transcends shit-wiping stick and True Person. It is not that, and yet not anything else; this is exactly who we are.

Linji says it right here: "The True Person of No Rank, what kind of shit-wiping stick is he!" This is not a question. Look! What kind of shit-wiping stick he is! Only if we are not so, only if we are not clear, then this is not enough. It is our practice opportunity to be the shit-wiping-stick fellow, though it may be hard or painful to be so in the midst of body-mind habits and attachments.

What is this ceaselessly seeking mind? Look! Only this seeking mind gets in the way of this True Person functioning. Bringing this ceaseless seeking to rest is allowing thoughts to come and go freely; then they are at rest. And "you will not differ from the ancestor Buddha." When the Second Ancestor requests, "My mind is not at rest, please put it at rest," Bodhidharma responds, "Bring me this restless mind." Finally, the Second Ancestor sees for himself the ungraspableness of this seeking; he tells Bodhidharma that this mind is "nowhere to be found." Realizing this, ceaseless seeking is therefore at rest.

Right here now is not other than this True Person that we call ancestor Buddha. It's none other than you who are listening right now, you who are breathing and sitting. Even by saying that, we make it into something. So Linji says, "We don't have any Buddhas here. If you meet the Buddha, kill the Buddha. If you meet the Ancestors, kill the Ancestors." If you seek for Buddha, Buddha is merely a name. Buddha is exactly our life: anything else we seek is only a name, only something extra, an obstacle, a hindrance.

Have faith in this awareness that you are, this functioning that you are. Joko used the expression: "Create a shift from this spinning world we've got in our heads to right-here-now." I have talked of: "A gap between the world that we are and the world that we are caught up in and live in." There is not actually a gap; and yet we create a gap with this ceaseless seeking inside and out.

So we must look, we must prove, we must testify for our self. "Those who have not yet proved him, ["proved" means to testify] look, look!" Look right now! This is exactly what we are doing here in sesshin on this cold morning. It is nothing but this going and coming on this lump of red flesh. This going and coming is nothing but this lump of red flesh functioning, it is nothing but this True Person.

This True Person and our life are not two different things, yet they are not the same for us. Otherwise, we get satisfied with what is not satisfactory. And we can see the unsatisfactory right away when we are spinning off, where we falter as the monk does, where we "cloud." Master Linji speaks this way, as all teachers do, in order to encourage us: "Bring to rest the thoughts of the ceaselessly seeking mind." Be this awareness functioning. Zazen is this open awareness functioning. Our practice effort allows this gap to disappear, allows us to taste and testify as this True Person that is sitting right here.

"Followers of the Way," says Master Linji, "as I see it we are not different from Shakyamuni the Buddha. What do we lack of our manifold activities today?" You don't have to remember any of Master Linji's words or anyone else's words. Just take them like the monk took them: allow them to encourage practice, and allow them to remind you of who and what you are. It doesn't matter what rank you are; our rank doesn't make us better or worse, our rank is the rank of No Rank.

Zazen is manifesting who and what you are, this True Person functioning right-here-now, sitting, standing up, walking. Being so, then this gap, this spinning off, is gone of itself. We make the choice and we make the effort, and of itself, moment by moment, this is taken care of. When it is time to testify, we testify.

This endless functioning is exactly our life, whether we know it or not. It is not a matter of words. Faith in words, ideas, and thoughts, faith in what we get from others from outside, or even what we get from so-called inside, is what ails us. "Lack of faith in yourself" is what ails you. So please allow your practice to practice you; be lived by your life, allow zazen to zazen. Then sitting and standing, you are exactly this True Person, you are nothing but this True Person.

32

Light

Our life is revealed moment by moment. This life right now is manifesting who and what we are. This very life is exactly what we need in order to see, to learn, to function.

"Objects" change, "others" change, the conditions of this mind and this body change. In the midst of changing circumstances, body-mind habits and reactions to conditions may result in fear and anger, pain and suffering. Zazen is inhabiting this moment; zazen is manifesting this very life we are and clarifying this ongoing practice life. Being so, this moment we are not blinded by self-centered beliefs, attachments, and reactions to changes; we are not trapped by the form of life.

Inhabiting this impermanence that is the form of our life, our ongoing practice-exertion in the midst of conditions supports this very life. Thus we live freely as this, not because we get some idea about emptiness but by being this very life, by being this emptiness that is exactly this life. Each form as form is exactly this life that we are, and it is the opportunity to manifest this. As we examine Ancestral words, we can clarify this life and see how and where we might be blinded, so we can function as we truly are. Let us illuminate this moment, this functioning life.

The following koan is "Yunmen's Bright Light," case 86 in the *Blue Cliff Record:*

Yunmen states "Everyone has light. When you look for it, you don't see it, and it is dark. What is your light?"

He answered on behalf of the assembled, "The kitchen pantry and the main gate."

He later said, "A good thing is not as good as nothing."

Everyone is in the midst of light. This is our life; our life is always this brightness. Everyone is light. Unfortunately, looking for light as something separate limits us; in trying to understand and interpret this life brightness, we don't see it. This life functioning is always our opportunity, and yet what we do and our ideas about what we are doing may dualistically cut up this life.

In the introduction to this case, Yuanwu comments about Yunmen: "He holds the world fast without the slightest leak, he holds the myriad flows without keeping a drop." Myriad ways of manifesting this, myriad ways of expressing this—yet not keeping a drop, not sticking to even a drop. Usually we hold on to all sorts of things in our beliefs and habits of body-mind; we hold on to to various flows, and in holding on we miss this: "My way is right, her way is wrong, his way is inadequate, this should not happen, that is unfair," and so on.

Tenkei Denson comments: "Simply not eating with your nose is everyone's light." Isn't that a nice phrase? "Not eating with your nose is everyone's light." We all are so! This is not something special or extra; yet so often we miss this very life that we are. What Yunmen is saying is very straightforward. This is what Shakyamuni Buddha said: "All beings are the wisdom and the perfection of the Buddha." "Everyone has light," every one of us. Not because we are doing something special like sitting and practicing. This is not limited to people; this is each moment.

But when you look for light, when you make it one thing and not another thing, then you are in trouble. Then you miss what cannot be missed. Our practice, this ongoing exertion, is being this functioning and responding to conditions. To paraphrase Dogen: because practice is in the midst of realization, our ongoing practice effort is exactly this realization. When we are in accord with circumstances, we see this clearly.

Being this moment is taking care of this moment, whether we are eating, cleaning, or resting. Thinking and analyzing are also this wonderful functioning. All of being is so, life and death. In this very life we are seemingly bound, and in this very life we are seemingly liberated. Getting caught up in analyzing, thinking about things like, "Am I brushing my teeth right?" that much teeth are not being brushed and we are not brushing teeth. When we look to make something of this very life, even to make it be just light and not darkness, it is dark and dim. We use these wonderful abilities as humans to hold on to some things and to push away others: "I'm correct" and "He's mistaken," "He's right" and "I'm wrong," or all sorts of other beliefs. When we hold to body-mind habits of functioning, and when we hold on to explanations, that much we miss this.

Changsha says, "The whole universe in the ten directions is the eye of a practitioner. The whole universe in the ten directions is everyday speech of a practitioner. The whole universe in the ten directions is the whole body of a practitioner. The whole universe in the ten directions is the brightness of self. The whole universe in the ten directions exists within the brightness of self. In the whole universe in the ten directions, there is no one who is not themselves."

This is nice; is it so for you? The phrases are not much good if this is not so for us. Reflect for a moment on conditions and functioning: What do you see that you are sure is not the brightness of self? Are there individuals and circumstances that you are sure are not this functioning of brightness? Notice what you believe. Is our functioning this brightness of self? What are you believing? In the midst of suffering, we must respond.

Yunmen says that everyone and every circumstance is this brightness of self. "Everyone has light." What is this? This is not a matter of words; it is not a matter of interpretation. What is Yunmen doing? Yes, intrinsically everyone is light, the wisdom of Buddha-nature—but although these words and explanations are true, they are of little use of themselves. They are of little use the next time you get angry about what someone said, or the next time you are afraid when someone walks in the room. This life is in the midst of many "difficult" conditions. In the midst of suffering, upset, anger, and fear, the phrase "Everyone has light" may not be of much use. After all, this is where the rubber of our practice meets the road; this is where our practice meets the the reactions that get us in trouble, such as the reactions of greed and hatred that give rise to and support suffering.

So Yunmen asks those practicing with him, "What is the light?" Hakuin comments that this "case is a crucial pass within the *Blue Cliff Record,* no explanation is needed." Practice is really inhabiting our life. What is this life? Yunmen wants something that is alive, that we can spit out—our own clarity, our own light—so that it will shine forth in our speech, in our actions, in who and what we are. Yunmen doesn't want an intellectual answer, he doesn't want a conceptual answer; he wants something that is alive and bright.

This is what is important for our practice; what is important is what is alive. Chew on this! What is this light? Trying to see it, you don't see it, you can't see it. You can't see the brightness; only brightness sees brightness! Only light sees light! Being light, it is easy to respond. Or being darkness, it is easy to respond. Darkness isn't "bad"; darkness is light, too. Just be this light darkness; this responsive functioning is our practice exertion.

Yunmen's response is: "The kitchen pantry and the main gate." How is that a response to "What is the light?" Please reflect on this. Yuanwu states that this sentence opens a road for you. But fearing that people would get stuck here, Yunmen also said, "A good thing is not as good as nothing." In other words, he grabs away whatever you see in the kitchen pantry, he grabs away however you understand the main gate. Otherwise you might make something of his words and be stuck in beliefs and ideas—and once stuck, you will act based on this stuckness.

What is everybody's light? What is your light? Another comment asks, "If you cut off light and darkness, what is it then?"

Our practice is being this light. According to circumstances, we awaken to this light that we are. But don't think that this light is something out there, or something special, or something different from dark. What is your light? Nothing but the functioning of our life. This is zazen, this is sitting and being present. Our light: not my light, not your light—this is exactly light. No one else's light. This is the opportunity we have sitting here together and practicing together. The point is simple but difficult to actualize.

Dogen says, "Practicing and experiencing this brightness, we become Buddhas, sit as Buddhas, experience as Buddhas." He also says, "The brightness of the hundred weeds is already their roots, stem, twigs, leaves, fruit, flowers, light, color; never something added on or taken away."

This is our life, living and dying. In our services, we dedicate our practice to people who are sick, to some of those who have died, and to others who are dying—like all of us. All of us are dying; the only question is when. And all of us are living. All of us are living dying. Living and dying is the going and coming of this brightness, not more or less. Being the brightness life, whether we "know it" or not, enables us to taste, see, and realize this. The more that we do so, the more we function as this.

Of course, saying it like this may make it seem like a matter of more and less. To paraphrase Dogen, practice and experience are not nonexistent; they are the brightness being tainted. This is the whole of our life. Practice is always exactly where you are. It is important to know that exactly where you are is the whole of the brightness. Yet this requires practice; it requires ongoing exertion, including seeing where you are refusing to be brightness. Doing so right here in the midst of our ordinary functioning, right here the brightness reveals itself, right here the brightness reveals our self.

33

You Are Light

This is a wonderful practice chant in Pali:

Attha dipa
Viharatha
Attha sarana
Annana sarana
Dhamma dipa
Dhamma sarana

You are light itself,
Do not doubt.
You are haven itself,
There is no other haven.
You are light of Dharma,
You are haven of Dharma.

"You are light itself" reveals and reminds us of who and what we are, clarifying how and where we might misunderstand. Most of us think we know who we are and who we are not; unfortunately we often suffer because of these beliefs, such as whenever our misunderstanding creates difficulties and stress. The *Heart Sutra* clarifies this matter; this life is boundless. This life—this form, sensation, conception, discrimination, awareness, the five aggregates that are this human life—is the wisdom of reality, the perfection of wisdom, prajna paramita. It is only the seemingly "natural" beliefs about particulars that create suffering and harm. We are not limited by the one-sided particulars we attribute to conditions and to this life. So *Attha dipa:* you are light itself.

What is light? Though we might think light is some particular thing, it is not so. At the end of the nineteenth century, scientists asked, "Is light waves? Is light particles?" They thought it was an either / or matter; light was either waves or particles, and they were mutually exclusive. But we discovered that light behaves as waves and as particles, despite the fact that these seem to be mutually exclusive ways of behaving. In addition, we now know that there are many aspects of light that humans do not see or sense; there are wavelengths that humans don't see despite their presence right here. However, there are other beings that can see these different wavelengths and different aspects of light. Bees see ultraviolet wavelengths (300–400 nanometers), which humans cannot see. Other insects and many birds can see in this range. For some birds, the ultraviolet vision helps them find food and make mating choices.

Although we think that this life is either form or emptiness, and although we suffer over "how" we are or are not, the *Heart Sutra* reminds us that form is shunyata: it is empty of fixed separate self, and it is boundless. Form is emptiness, emptiness is exactly form; so form is form, form is always prajna being exactly form. Our life is not limited by our ideas of this form, this life. We are light.

Often we say no to this; we say, "I am not light, I am solidly this. I'm these particular thoughts, and these thoughts exclude other thoughts. If these thoughts and feelings are sad feelings that are painful, that is who and what I am." In many ways we act as if life, the five aggregates, are either / or.

Practice is going beyond either / or, going beyond knowing and not-knowing. Going beyond is being this, including the wavelengths that do not fit self-centered thinking and attachments. This is something we discover in practice by realizing this for ourselves, clarifying this for our self, and being this. This is Buddha Dharma: it enables us to manifest this prajna paramita and be this light that we are. Despite the fact that we hold a narrow vision, we are not limited to a narrow vision, and we are never limited to what we hold onto. This very form is light.

How does light extend across the universe? How do we go beyond ideas of who and what we are? Zazen, practice, is being light. You are light itself, the light of the Dharma. Dharma is the nature of reality. Dharma is this: Dharma is cause and effect, right now; Dharma is no fixed, permanent, separate self. Dharma is the teachings of the Buddha that express wisdom and compassion that is our life, the joy and bliss that we truly are. You are the light of the Dharma.

Some waves penetrate what seems solid to us. Is this moment life solid? Is this circumstance either / or? Are you inside the skin? Do you end at the skin? Who are you? How does your action extend? We have discovered aspects of light, but there are aspects that we do not understand and do not see. What is dark energy? What is dark matter? Zazen is being this; being zazen clarifies this, practice reveals and manifests this. Do not be trapped by either / or. What is this? Be light; be dark; be the universe right here. As Dogen Zenji says, "When one side is realized, the other side is dark."

You are light itself. Do not doubt. Be doubtless. There's no need to hold on to or believe doubts that arise. Doubts are habits of cause-and-effect self and body-mind reactiveness. Originally, we are light. From the beginning, we are light—and "from the beginning" means this now. Despite thinking otherwise, this here now is intrinsic realized subtle practice.

Looking closely, we see that life does not fit any categories. We generate all sorts of waves; light is our functioning. We are expressing and expanding light. Light is not elsewhere; light is not out there.

Do not believe that you have to know what is so in order to be what is so! We do not have to figure out what to be and why to be, in order to be. Not-knowing is the opportunity to be so. Be what is so; be this body-mind universe, be this zazen.

Sometimes this seems most difficult. It seems like just what we do not want to do: be present and body-mind intimate this moment. It seems easier to follow attachment and reject habits, easier to follow our seemingly natural reactiveness—except that we see the consequences of doing this, the harm and suffering that result. Zazen is the hardest thing to do; the only thing harder is not to do it. So we make the effort, sometimes most difficult effort, to do what is most simple, to do zazen; to be this moment, to be intimate as this. Being so, according to conditions we realize what is so. Manifesting what is so, realization clarifies. Actualizing what is so, Dharma reveals itself.

The use of radios was not discovered and developed until the beginning of the twentieth century. But it is not as if radio waves did not exist until then; we just didn't have any instrument to tune to them, to sense them, to generate them. The same with X-rays and other forms of light, other forms of this life that we are. There are so-called solid forms and so-called not-solid forms. We know the forms of life in different ways. Mass and energy are not two; the formula $E=mc^2$ shows this (the energy aspect of something is exactly equal to its mass multiplied by the constant c^2; the c^2 is speed of light squared). Form and emptiness are not two.

Yasutani Roshi said, "Ordinary individuals handle Buddha-nature as ignorance, and suffer. Buddhas handle ignorance as

Buddha-nature, and experience great peace and happiness." This is our life. Do we only see form as form, not seeing that form is empty? Do we see that emptiness is form? Of course, because form is empty, therefore form is exactly form; there isn't something somewhere else called emptiness, boundlessness, shunyata, prajna paramita. There isn't some other thing. You are light itself, all the time; from the beginning, it can't be otherwise.

So you are the haven itself. There is no other haven. The Pali word *sarana*, here translated as haven, can also be translated as refuge, as in the phrases "taking refuge in the Buddha," "taking refuge in the Dharma," "taking refuge in the Sangha." Nowhere else are we going to find a haven, a refuge, from ignorance and self-centeredness. If we hold to ignorance and self-centeredness, then unconditioned Buddha-nature appears as ignorance and self-centeredness. By its very nature, ignorance generates suffering. This is because we do not see much of the spectrum; craving and attachment create misunderstandings that limit the ways we manifest. So when someone does something we don't like, the ignorance habit that we believe is to get angry and maybe violent. We believe this reactive habit because it is the only form we see, and this is because we are living through habits of self-centeredness. We may think the solution to suffering is outside; we may look for all sorts of things to fix other people, to fix our self, to get away from the pain, because we don't see that exactly this life is the haven.

You are light of the Dharma. To say too much limits this. You, your life, are the manifestation of Buddha-nature reality. Inherently, we can only say a little bit about the waves, the light of the universe; truly, we don't know. The mystery of our life is exactly like this. The more we practice, and the deeper our practice and clarification, the more we see that we only see a little bit. But we can be clear. Being the light of Dharma, right here is the haven. We can manifest and actualize this, rather than being blinded by the reactive habits of attachment, grasping, and rejecting. Right here is the haven from handling Buddha-nature as ignorance: the haven is our Dharma encounters and exchanges with Buddhas right now, from morning to night.

It once seemed natural to say, "You can't have communication with people at a distance. Sound going over wires? A telephone? A radio? That is nonsense. A cell phone? Come on, that doesn't make sense." Holding to thoughts and reactive habits may make life seem to fit them, but this is never so. You are light. Ongoing practice is available because this is being life—ongoing clarifying, ongoing realization, ongoing actualization. This is Buddha's teaching from the beginning.

Practice is sending prajna waves throughout the universe without wires, without connections, without limitations of past, present, or future. Always, being right here now, the great mystery of our life. We know a little, and it is wonderful to keep discovering more. But if we don't see how fundamental suffering is generated, then we are playing on the edges and missing the fundamental point. We are "ordinary people handling Buddha-nature as ignorance," and thereby we are suffering and creating suffering. Our practice is being Buddhas handling ignorance as Buddha-nature. Then we experience peace and happiness, and then we can offer liberation.

We may think we know who we are and who we are not. Please reconsider; please reconsider so that what you know does not perpetuate suffering and harm, and does not limit or hinder manifesting wisdom and compassion. This is the practice choice we have this moment; this is original realization subtle practice.

Being intimate is our practice. This is being "bigger" than the anxiety or fear, the narrow picture we have of this present-moment situation. It is being intimate beyond the limits of ideas of this moment life, and jumping into life just this moment. We do this despite thoughts like, "I don't know how to do that." We are the functioning of prajna and the manifesting of prajna, despite the fact that we deny this and doubt it. And the way to be so is to do so. This is practice. This is sitting. This is bowing. All the ways of manifesting this prajna we are.

It is hard to see those we love suffer, and it's even harder to see them doing what we think is causing their suffering. We may think that they would stop suffering if they would only stop doing it their way and instead do it our way. And despite the fact that we offer our way, they seem to continue to do it their way. What to do? It is often unclear what skillful compassion is. Is our idea of how things should be something we are stuck on? How do we face impermanence? How do we face cause and effect, which is Buddha-nature? Do we add on a fixed, separate self that justifies criticizing our self or others? What is a bigger picture? What includes "more" wavelengths of life?

Practice is manifesting this. Then we see what to do. There is really no more or less; this is empty and boundless. We do as best we can right now, as skillfully as we can. The extent of our ability and vision is cause and effect of this moment. Form is exactly form, form is exactly emptiness, emptiness is exactly form.

When we have a narrow vision, reality somehow doesn't fit. There are states of mind and body—in other words, there are forms of light—that we might think aren't acceptable. We don't see how to appreciate and how to be intimate if we are holding to habits of self and habits of self-centeredness that seem natural. We doubt the boundless light that is our life. Skillful practice is opening all the ways that we want to close around our particular self-centered habits—because who we truly are is open from the beginning. Buddhas are not just "out there"; Buddhas suffuse our life.

In the *Shobogenzo* fascicle "Maka Hannya Haramitsu," Dogen comments: "There is a single piece of prajna paramita, which has been manifested right now. It is *anuttara samyak sambodhi* [unexcelled perfect enlightenment]. Three prajna paramita: past, present, future. Six prajna: earth, water, fire, wind, air, mind. Four prajna, which are ordinary activities in life: going, staying, sitting, lying."

Our life from morning to night, everything we encounter, inside, outside, the whole universe. Be intimate as this light you are; manifest this light!

34

Ordinary

Our life is the life of Buddha. Somehow we manage to miss and forget this Buddha life that we are. In facing difficulties, confusion, and suffering, we have the opportunity to notice that we are missing our life. In making and clarifying our practice effort, we are opening to exactly this life that we are.

The Ancestors have said, "Ordinary mind is the Way" and "Mind is Buddha." (And very directly, they have said, "Not Buddha, not mind, not thing" even though this may seem contradictory.) "Ordinary mind" is exactly this; "Mind is Buddha" is exactly the truth. These are not merely utilitarian sayings. At the same time, these phrases clarify what we do that keeps us from being who we are; they point to how we hold to a concoction of habits of emotion, feeling, and thinking. We usually call these habits ordinary and natural, although they are not. We do not see these habits for what they are because we are so used to them.

More significantly, we do not see that in holding to habits, reacting from them, and living out of them, we hinder and limit this ordinary functioning that we are, and so we suffer and experience all sorts of difficulties. Living out of habits and out of self-centered views, we turn activities into something that serves our expectations and conditions. And we usually blame the difficulties and suffering that arise on people and things "out there." Even hearing the phrase "ordinary mind," we limit the word "mind" to thinking and concepts, and get stuck in this misunderstanding.

Similarly, we connect the word "ordinary" to particular activities, as if practice has to do with so-called ordinary activities. When carrying along our so-called past or bringing up a so-called future, ideas or expectations can get in the way of even ordinary activities being ordinary activities. If we are dreaming, even ordinary activity is no longer ordinary.

Ordinary is being ordinary functioning, whether sitting, working, talking, or performing a fancy ceremony. It is being the ordinary intimacy of whatever we are doing. Don't believe that ordinary mind is cognitive; ordinary functioning is not a particular state of mind. In each and every aspect of our life, this is exactly who we are. To restate Nagarjuna's declaration "Because of emptiness, all things are possible": being ordinary, everything is possible. Being plain water, we take on any form, taste, shape, or color. This is because we are ordinary, because we enter intimately into the moment, because we give self away to the arising circumstance moment.

This is the simplicity and the richness of sitting, of entering the moment. This is the emptiness that responds to suffering; this is the emptiness that clarifies how self-centered habits of body-mind create and perpetuate suffering. The character that gets translated as "mind" (*hsin* in Chinese, or *shin* in Japanese) can be translated as "mind," "heart," or "heart-mind," none of which are completely accurate. Mind is ordinary, simple, exactly this functioning that we are; nothing else. As Huangbo said, "Buddhas and all sentient beings are only one-mind—there are no other dharmas (phenomena) besides that one mind." So, practice is being ordinary.

Our life from morning to night is nothing but ordinary. It is sitting still, it is walking and eating and speaking and thinking, and all the other ways that we are alive—and that we are not alive. Dogen gives the instructions on how to sit upright, and then states, "Do not think." Dogen then poses the question, "How do you not think?" "Nonthinking." He then say this is "the art of zazen, the Dharma gate of ease and joy." This is not some special state of functioning; it is being ordinary. But as soon we make something of "being ordinary," it is far from it, as Nanquan states in case 19 of the *Gateless Gate*, "If you try to direct yourself toward it, you go away from it." Attempting to be simple is not simple anymore.

So in our practice, we need to make the effort to notice what is added on to the ordinary moment—if need be, to see over and over again the words and ideas that we try to squeeze reality into. Our practice effort is not to create something ordinary; when necessary, it is to see what seems to be blocking or limiting us. "Nothing special" means just that: no special thing. This, always this. Being completely what we are, doing each thing, each functioning moment as it is.

Of course, thinking "Am I doing this completely?" or "How do I be complete, simple, or ordinary?" is an added drama. Wholeheartedness is our practice; not-knowing is the Way, not-knowing is ordinary.

If you try to be ordinary, then ordinary is something extra. And going along in our usual way is not ordinary, even though we say it is ordinary. Our usual way is a particular collection of habits of body-mind and emotion-thoughts, which are often far from this moment. Seeing exactly what we are up to allows this ordinary functioning that we always are.

From morning to night, all we encounter are forms of emptiness; all we encounter is our original face. Forms of emptiness are emptiness, forms of emptiness are exactly form; clarifying form is emptiness. So we see that form is form, emptiness is emptiness. And yet if we stick to this form, we miss it; unfortunately that is one of our habits. Similarly, if we get caught in emptiness, we are caught there.

Being ordinary means being the functioning we are, being the bodily sensing, being as we are. Reacting to circumstances is an indication that there is something we are holding and believing, right here; these beliefs are the basis of our reactions. Noticing is to sense where and when we say, "But this is not enough," "This should not be," "This is too boring," or thinking about the thousand things that are OK or not OK about the so-called past, so-called future, and so-called others. No matter which of these is the moment that we are caught in, right here is our practice opportunity of opening as this ordinary functioning that is our life, that is exactly this condition.

So whichever dharma we encounter, whichever form of emptiness, whether so-called inside or so-called outside, whether so-called body or so-called mind, exactly this is ordinary. This is the whole of our life. Whatever arises is taken care of. Being clear how to take care of this is the functioning of being ordinary. Being ordinary is ordinary mind. Every one of us as we are is ordinary; not when you attain some other skill, but as you are. Not as anyone else is, not as any picture you have that is based on what other people have told you, but exactly as you are. There is not a single thing you lack in being this ordinary functioning, this ordinary mind—ordinary Buddha, ordinary no-Buddha. Nevertheless, it requires wholehearted practice, because you are the only one who can take care of what needs to be taken care of. You are the only one who can see exactly what needs to be taken care of in this moment.

Student: So basically ordinary mind is awareness?

Genmyo: Already there is an added word. See, ordinary mind and awareness are not different things. Yes, being ordinary is awareness, yet this is not a special state called awareness; it is no particular mind. So no-mind, no-Buddha, no-awareness, being ordinary. This is exactly your functioning this moment.

Part of what we discover as we sit, as we are being present, is all the ways we spin off or get caught up. Noticing this, we can see and make the appropriate practice effort. This is a support of zazen, of practicing with others, and of our intention to practice, all of which enable us to be this. On the other hand, we sometimes slip off into not trusting what is ordinary; we may slip into "Oh, it's just ordinary," and call it dullness. As noted, often what we call "ordinary" is continuing the chatter of habits in various forms. None of these habits serve this ordinary functioning that we are; they blind us, even though we can't be blinded. Though we cannot be hindered, we are hindered.

This is the opportunity of appropriate practice effort, noticing and being this moment that doesn't exclude thoughts and dreams, and yet is not at all that. When you are working in the kitchen, the job is to respond; the response is this functioning of ordinary, this ordinary functioning. Ordinary mind is the Way.

When using the word "mind," it is valuable, as I mentioned, to note the tendency to narrow this ordinary functioning into thinking, into a human psychological or emotional state. Since we are human, ordinary functioning of course includes emotion-thought; this moment being alive as we are, this exact body-mind-world multiplicity, this moment. Of course, saying this is too much, and gets in the way. Simply doing this, there is no extra thing needed.

Let us all make good use of these few days of sitting together. Let us all make good use of this life, and let us do our part and make our effort. Intention enables us to truly taste and savor the life we are, to see our life to the extent of our vision and clarity. Being who and what we are is this opportunity, this ordinary functioning, this ordinary life, which is nothing other than the life of the universe, the life of the Buddha.

PART FOUR

On Being Transparency

35

Some Notes

How do we encounter the truth of our life? Buddha's teaching is the truth of this life that we live, the reality we encounter each day, each moment. Despite being this, despite encountering this, we miss this—and yet we do not miss this. We see these truths of existence, we see this life that we are. And when we are fortunate at some point to meet the Dharma teaching, then we have the opportunity for what we have seen throughout our life to click, and we are able to sense, each in our own way, the Dharma truth that our life has been and is.

For me, this has resulted in a thread of my life being clearer. The seeming past is more clearly present now. Often in my life, there was no sense of what was what. Concern and confusion about the future, dissatisfaction about the present, misunderstanding of the past were the dominant notes. Now these aspects of my life are clearer; I might say it is a flowing stream, with all sorts of boulders and rough water, and yet no separation.

Memory floats to the surface, sometimes clear, sometimes fragments of darkness. An early memory arising: lying on the couch, the world heavy and still. Very full. Not moving. I was six. My father had died. No one told me, but I knew. Being there—

not a thing I could do, and maybe not a thing I wanted to do. Sadness would come, tears, loss, and lacking. But not just then. Lying on the couch, no one else in the room, sounds from a distance. Peaceful, present, alive; not quite enough to do anything, to be part of anything. Holding back what was hard to bear, but not holding anything. Holding still, so nothing would move, nothing would happen, nothing further would occur. No change! But despite trying to hold back change, slowly the world seeps in, the reality of change and then the rush of sadness, grief.

My father had been sick for several years. He was often weak, and at times he was hospitalized for long periods. Not being told what was wrong, my two younger brothers and I were sent to live, often individually, with cousins and friends. Sometimes we stayed for a few weeks, sometimes for months. Not much of an explanation about why we were there, not much contact with each other, or with my mother or my father.

A very deep sense of impermanence. And that gave rise to loss and grief, loss and grief. And maybe a feeling that there is, there was, there had to be something I could have done, should have done, should have been able to do, so that it would not happen. Of course, this is not true, because I could not change the past—but feelings do not make sense, especially to a small child. Even as adults we often act out of the small child that appears. I did.

Later in life in other circumstances, I would find this very deep feeling of what I should have done, could have done, to make things different, to take care of the unsatisfactory right now, to stop the changes. Eventually, coming to practice in my twenties, I began to see this practice realm when it arose. Did I notice it? Did I practice skillfully when it arose? In the beginning, no; practice was another form of self-centeredly trying to get what I thought would take care of unsatisfactory feelings and fears of loss.

Eventually, some of the time I could see a bit of these blind habits and reactions when they appeared, and hopefully act skillfully. Especially interesting was seeing the ways I tried to take care of things so that reality worked the way I wanted it, and then discovering that impermanence, arising conditions and circumstances, the nonsubstantiality of conditions, was such that reality worked the way it did—sometimes in accord with my plans and strategies, and often not. The link between the appearance of self-centeredness and the resulting stress and suffering was only dimly seen; even practice and sitting were at first another aspect of self-centeredness, despite my seeing that there was a bigger reality, that going beyond "me" and "my" was what was called for.

Over and over as a child, in the year after my father's death, I found myself on the couch for long periods. Doing nothing, being present. Not trying to stop or fight thoughts, emotions, and feelings but sinking into the silence that seemed to suspend them, the dim autumn and winter northern light of the late afternoon. The quiet back window opening on to rows of windows at the back of tenements across the way. No one home, no one out in the days that got colder and colder.

What was happening? I do not know. A sense of life, yet the hurt of lack, the grief of loss, feeling dulled, slowly seeping in, coming in tolerable measures rather than the feared overwhelming pain. In fact, at home it seemed that there was an effort not to tell us about my father's death, but instead something was said about his going away—and yet we chanted the prayer for the dead three times a day for almost a year.

A six-year-old attempting to rest in the moment of overwhelming loss. Too much all at once. Nevertheless little by little, as I could tolerate it, in living life I was being forced to allow the moment to open in my daily activity.

I remember other times when I had tried to deal with change in this same way. As a three-year-old being in a barn, the doors closed somehow, heavy and stuck. The rotting boards on the floor kept breaking when I stepped on them, and there seemed no way out. I was too afraid to search thoroughly for a way out. Lost and cut off. Staying still, even when the door was stuck and I was locked in, seemed like a way to stay safe.

My mother screamed and cried often after my father's death. I remember her being upset during his long illness, and it seemed to get worse and worse. Looking back, I can see how overwhelmed she was by being left alone with three little boys (when I was six, my two younger brothers were five and three). She had not been employed for a long time, and was left with little money; my father's business partners and family gave her only minimal support. I later learned that when she was about seven years old, her father left the family in Jerusalem and went to America to find work to support the family. She had felt abandoned. She did not see him again until she was seventeen. Throughout her life, she was often angry and upset about feelings of abandonment.

Though my father's brother lived a block away from us and even attended the same synagogue as we did, he paid little attention to me or my brothers, rarely showing any care or love that I could feel. I know there was occasional financial help and hand-me-down clothes. My mother's brother lived a little farther away, and though he called regularly, there was little active mentoring or help, especially when three small boys growing up without a father became difficult.

So, in addition to my experience of the loss and abandonment of my father's death, what my mother taught in her being, her behavior, and her attitude, was what she knew well: the sense that abandonment was going to occur. Abandonment by what? Abandonment by conditions that would, or at least seemed to, make life safe, that would at least give the sense that circumstances could be worked with, could offer joy and richness.

I also learned this from her emotional abandonment of my brothers and me in her anger and criticism. I learned this even though she made a heroic effort to raise the three of us by working

full-time and caring for the house, ensuring that despite our pov-
erty we had the basics. Yet an underlying theme that I often felt,
though could not articulate, was this sense of separation and
abandonment, with no clear sense of what was going on, and no
clear sense where or how to look for a response. My mother knew
no more, or maybe even less, than my brothers and I; we did not
know much at this age, especially after years of my father's illness
and being individually "farmed out" to relatives and friends for
weeks at a time, without much explanation. Feeling this, all sorts
of unskillful coping habits developed.

After my father's death, I was at a father-son ceremony in the
shul (synagogue) for Simchat Torah, feeling utterly alone in the
world. Others have a father, why not me? Why am I abandoned,
alone? Going down to the basement near the *mikvah* (ritual bath)
and hiding, so at least I wouldn't have to be there when other kids
dance with their dads.

Two years later. Late on a Sabbath afternoon. Not yet night,
not yet over. Outside the shul, before evening prayers. A day of
prayers and ritual meals, but somehow God has not touched the
pain. A gray twilight sky. So I cry out for him to do something.
"What do you want? What can you do?"

Loss, extinction, was so hard to face, so painful. An aloneness
that was not touched by contact with others, not touched by
events. Why not touched? It does not make a difference; just that
it was not touched. And the sense of not touched, of separation,
was raw and present.

In pain and at a loss, I did all sorts of stupid things. Things to
fill the loss, to get away from the pain. Stupid because of not seeing the results, stupid because of not seeing the source of what was
missing, stupid because it only made more discomfort and suffering for myself, for others. Not knowing what would touch the
pain, not knowing where to turn, and finding no one who knew,
even when they claimed to.

Sitting for the first time when I was twenty-one, I thought, "This is it, this is the Way!" But it was just a flash in the pan, nothing that extended beyond the sitting. And very quickly, even the sitting became another way to continue (self-centered) stupidity. But despite blind alleys, continued self-centered habits, and inadequacies, sitting is, was, the Way. How to walk the Way was unclear, unknown. In fact, at first the Way was to get away—or at least to get somewhere else. It was not to see, be, life as is.

Little by little, very slowly, only after smacking into it so many painful times, there is the dawning sense that sitting is not limited to a physical posture or a mental posture. Though body-mind sitting was and is vital, what is revealed is the life that is always right here, not just when sitting.

We are transparent. From the beginning, life is transparent. Circumstances and events arise and pass. Nothing remains, nothing abides. In the midst of this nonabiding is created all sorts of solid and fixed positions. Solid and fixed transparency. Failing to see transparency, failing to be transparency, the solid is solid, the fixed is fixed. So naturally when solid bumps against solid, there is stress, there is difficulty, there is suffering. It is only holding to fixed solidity (self-centeredness) that keeps the transparent from being transparent for us. It is transparent, and yet we are quite sure that it is not. We bet our life, over and over, on it not being transparent, on our refusal to be transparency and to be nonabiding. And we ensure that we win the bet; and in winning the bet, we are losing our life. Being broken over and over by this loss. And if we are fortunate, we are broken open so that, instead of being shattered in breaking open, we can emerge from the shell newborn, alive, fresh.

Can we see that being broken is what practice requires of us? Not that practice is being broken, but that self-centered holding creates breaking. Each time we hold self-centeredness against the world, we bang self-centered functioning against the moment as it is. We refuse to be the moment we are, and insist on being the moment of thoughts and beliefs. This being so, practice entails being broken, and it entails experiencing the being broken, which is exactly the experience of suffering and dissatisfaction in the many forms it takes in our life.

Basic practice is awakening to, clarifying, and actualizing the truth of our life. In koan practice, this begins with an initial practice such as Mu. Speaking theoretically, the koan Mu is sometimes described as a Dharmakaya koan, embodying the unity of life, True Nature. Dharmakaya is the first of the Three Bodies (Trikaya) of Buddha. However, conceptual theory of itself does not make a live practice and is not of much value. What we know does not aid us in being and living the unity of life, much less the reality prior to heaven and earth. What we know, expect, and believe often is a hindrance in resolving our dissatisfaction, suffering, and stress. "Should" and "should not" keep us from the natural embrace of life as it is.

Therefore, this first Treasure of practice, Buddha, is not-knowing; it is the intimacy of being. Formal sitting is the support and container for embodying this not-knowing, for encountering the thoughts and emotions we hold and attach to, for allowing them to pass. Intelligent practice encourages noticing and practicing with this. Working with noticed expectations and beliefs in practice is not about changing them. It is not any other variation of this. What we meet is exactly our life, not anything else. Seeing and living this is exactly our practice effort.

As we practice, we discover how we want others to be different than they are. Do we notice this belief? We think problems and stress come from the circumstances and the encounters of the day. Do we notice these thoughts as thoughts, and make our practice effort? Embodying this moment beyond the narrow limits of the thoughts about this moment is the task of being this moment. A well-known koan begins, "You know the sound of two hands clapping." We start with what we know. But if what we know is the limit, the guide of how we proceed, then we cannot resolve, embody, and function as the koan that asks, "What is the sound of one hand?"

One morning, I stepped out of my front door and saw our greyhound Milo sniffing at something in the grass. Approaching, I saw four baby bunnies, about six inches long, fur fully formed, lying still on their sides. Bending down closer, I saw blood punctures on their sides. All of a sudden, a larger bunny hopped off, and the dog started chasing it. Gathering up the baby bunnies, I began a small funeral service, chanting and lighting incense.

For many years, it has been my practice when seeing dead animals on the road to put my palms together in *gassho* (or one-handed gassho when I was driving), and chant briefly for the passing of this being from this realm of existence. Chanting *Namu dai bosa* ("Being One with the Great Bodhisattva"), encountered right here on the road in this birth-death passing, acknowledging, embracing, this birth-death life that this is.

Buddha is the first of the Three Treasures, yet Buddha is the diversity of Dharma. Buddha life, Buddha death: we want it our way. Saying things like "unity" is nice, but we know very well all the aspects of the unity diversity that we dislike, reject, and are repelled by. When we look closely, we see these things are the anger, upsets, and problems that we believe hinder our life. These are all the encounters throughout our day.

We all want lives of happiness and joy. Indeed, this is who we are. Yet we suffer and are unhappy. Indeed, the stress and dissatisfaction, the suffering and agitation that we experience in life in particular forms, is what drives us to practice. We try all sorts of things to deal with our suffering, believing that the circumstances of our life are the cause of this. External causes seem to be easier to attend to, so these external causes are often our focus of attention. Indeed, grasping and pushing away, in extreme forms such as greed and anger, are general attitudes for dealing with the circumstances of life that seem to cause unhappiness or prevent happiness. Even when we focus on seemingly internal causes of unhappiness, grasping and pushing away are our major modes of acting.

Unfortunately, grasping and pushing away do not produce the results we seek. As a result of an inaccurate understanding of life, an inaccurate understanding of the cause of unhappiness and suffering, our grasping and pushing away only perpetuate what we are trying to end. In traditional terms, it is greed, anger, and ignorance, the three poisons, that create and perpetuate suffering.

Diversity is our life, the encounters we meet throughout the day and night. Diversity is exactly the many forms of life. Yet we do not see this. Instead, we see circumstances that we encounter that we do not want, are not what we believe they should be, or are what they should not be.

My cousin Elliot was two years older than me. I looked up to him, literally and figuratively, when I was very small, following him around and trying to copy him. He did not want to have much to do with me because I was just a little kid to him. Though he lived a block away, I usually saw him only on the Sabbath when he and his father came to the shul for prayer. I do not remember how his father and my father (older and younger brothers) got along, and because my dad died when I was six, I never had much memory of the two of them together.

In the shul, which was the ground floor of the building that I lived in until I was eight, I would follow Elliot around. Right after the start of a long series of prayers, the little kids would leave. We often played in a front vestibule outside the main prayer hall. On Yom Kippur eve, the shul was more crowded than usual. The men were wearing long white robes (*kitel*) over which they had their long white-and-black prayer shawls, many trimmed with bright gold or silver collars. The cloth covers on the Torah Ark, on the lectern, and on the *bimah* (Torah reading platform) were also covered with the special high holiday white cloths, which were shining with gold and silver embroidery.

After the start of prayers, dressed in our finery, the younger boys went out to the vestibule hall to play. My cousin and a friend were playing; I wanted to play with them, but they disregarded a three-year-old as too little for them. Their play turned to sliding down the banister of a long staircase, catching and stopping themselves on the end post, which was even with the rest of the banister. I thought, "I'll show them!" So after they slid down several times, I followed them up the long staircase. After they slid down, I slid down, too. I was terrified on the way down, but I could not stop myself.

I do not recall hitting my head on the marble floor, the disruption to the Kol Nidre service that this caused, my mother's distress as she came down from our third-floor apartment, the ambulance arriving, the travel on the holiday necessitated by the injury, or the days being unconscious and in critical condition. To this day, looking out from the edge of heights, my insides tighten up and queasy feelings arise. When I first shaved my head, I discovered scars from the concussion and treatment.

This head injury did not stop my acting before looking. A year later, I was with my parents in Prospect Park in Brooklyn. It was a warm Sunday afternoon; I do not recall my brothers being there. I was climbing the park benches and metal fences. There was one fence that was composed of fence posts with two heavy black horizontal bars in between them. The top bar was too high to hoist myself over, so I climbed between the two bars. Unfortunately, the top bar was loose and it fell on me, hitting me just above my right eye. Blood pouring down, screaming, my father holding me up while the sirens of ambulance and police sounded. Disruption. Several stitches took care of it.

Luckily, I did not have major damage to my eye or vision at the time. Now, almost sixty years later, I had to have seven eye surgeries in less than a year on the same eye in an attempt to save the retina, and in the process I lost sight in this eye.

I bring up these events because they arise in thoughts and feelings in the process of living this life now. There is no need in our practice or our life to go looking for "past," or to try to figure these things out. No thing remains, no thing abides. This is cause-effect now. This is arising-passing now. And when "things" arise, if we get caught up in them through various forms of reactive habits of body-mind, we may act out of that entanglement and entangle our self and others, thereby sustaining stress and suffering in thoughts and actions. This arising moment, these thoughts, these feelings, all the functioning of our body-mind universe, are an opportunity to encounter the truth of our life; they are an opportunity to reveal the Buddha's teaching, which is the truth of this life that we live and the reality that we encounter this moment.

In seeing this truth now, in seeing this existence, we have the opportunity to be this life that we are. We are transparent; from the beginning, this life is transparent. Circumstances, conditions, and events arise and pass. In the midst of this, we are fortunate and able to be born this moment. We are able to be alive, we are able to be fresh.

PART FIVE

Jukai, Three Treasures, Three Pure Precepts

36

Jukai

Receiving the precepts is receiving our life. Nothing more, nothing less. It is receiving what we are, who we are, and what we have. And it is most valuable to receive what is so. In Jukai we are revealing this that we are, and we are manifesting our life, beyond any limits that we might hold or beyond any belief of who we are. And in going beyond, despite our limited understanding, we are being beyond, functioning beyond, and seeing beyond. This beyond is intimacy right here now. Because right here now, we are not limited to our understanding and concepts of right here now, and therefore we can be right here now.

The word *Jukai* literally means to receive the precepts. *Ju* means "to receive," and *kai* means "precepts." "Jukai" ("Ju" pronounced as Joo, as the "oo" in too) is the Japanese pronunciation of the characters; in Chinese this is pronounced "shòu jièis." Jukai is a form that enables us to receive the precepts, and the forms of Jukai support us in doing so. Jukai allows and supports us to manifest this joy that we are. Being who we are is receiving the precepts, continuing to practice with and through the precepts, and manifesting the precepts as our life.

Different lineages and different groups use slightly different forms for Jukai, but many of the basics are similar. I will explore the form that I use, which is an adaptation of what I learned from my teacher Hakuyu Maezumi Roshi, as well as my teacher Joko Beck. I continue to adapt this form for use in my Sangha. The Jukai form is the basis of wedding ceremonies and funerals, as well as some other formal ceremonies.

I was very fortunate to be Taizan Maezumi Roshi's attendant (Zendo Jisha) for several years. During that time he officiated at many Jukai, priestly ordination, as well as many weddings and other ceremonies. I was at his side during most of these ceremonies. I made it my practice to chant subvocally and inaudibly along with him as he gave the precepts. I started doing this spontaneously, not thinking about it nor intending to do it. But although I did not plan to do it, little by little, I was doing it regularly. For me that was part of Jukai, part of my practice as attendant to Maezumi Roshi. And after doing it for a while, it continued without my doing it.

I never told anyone else about my chanting during Jukai, including Roshi. But despite my never having brought it up, once when Roshi and I went back to his house (where I also lived for some time as his House Jisha), Roshi alluded to this chanting as good practice. We spoke about it a bit, and he never mentioned it again. I continued this practice even when I was no longer his Jisha. This has enabled me to appreciate Jukai, and especially his efforts and teaching while officiating and giving the precepts.

Each Jukai is unique, a coming together of those who are partaking of this right here now. It is a public ceremony in which we formally take the Buddhist teaching as our own, receive the Bodhisattva precepts, and publicly declare our intention to live the precepts. We bring our life, our karmic habits, and our patterns into the midst of this moment of practice.

Jukai is primarily the preceptor and the recipient, but we

should not limit our vision or understanding. The Buddhas and Ancestors are all present in Jukai. And the Sangha / audience is an integral part of Jukai—though we might miss this part if we are not attentive to this aspect of practice. The Sangha is big, the audience is boundless. This boundless universe participates as the Preceptor and the recipient.

Recipient makes three full bows to Buddha,
Makes three full bows to parents,
Makes three full bows to Kaishi (Precept Teacher).

After a formal bow to the Preceptor (the precept teacher, or Kaishi in Sino-Japanese) in the zendo where the Jukai will occur, the recipient(s) makes three full bows to the Buddha. Often this occurs at a special altar. The Jukai can be for one individual or a group of individuals; nevertheless, it is always one to one.

These bows to the Buddha are expressing our deep gratitude and appreciation for the Buddha, which enables us to practice and share the Buddha's awakening. Without the Buddha, we would not have the opportunity to encounter the teaching and to encounter the life that we are. Without the innumerable efforts of the Buddha in his practice to awaken, to realize the Way, to actualize and teach the Way through all the years of his life, we would not have the opportunity to encounter the Way and to receive Jukai.

Our task is to clarify the Dharma, to see for our self the *Diamond Sutra* clarification: "In the teaching of Dharma, there is no Dharma that can be spoken of. Therefore it is called 'teaching of Dharma.'" This is bowing to Buddha. Bowing is just bowing. We will explore this further when we examine the Three Treasures and look at the Buddha Treasure.

We also make three full bows to our parents, who have enabled us to come to this point and who have given us this human form in order to encounter the Dharma and to embrace the Dharma. Where possible, we do this with our parents present. If they are not alive, not able, or not willing to be there, we do the bows to them nevertheless, sometimes with photographs or some other representation of them.

Some of us have considerations regarding our parents, complaints and criticism about how they raised us or did not raise us. And there may be justification in these considerations; there are even cases where our parent or parents have abused us, or worse. Nevertheless, in the midst of the issues about this most basic relationship, our practice is based on a deep appreciation of the opportunity of our life that comes out of our parents giving life to us. What would have happened if they had not done so? We do not know.

Even if our parents do not want us to practice or receive the precepts, still we bow to them for the incalculable gifts that they gave us: our mother who carried us for nine months, and both our parents who nurtured us, as best they could, through infancy and childhood. How they did this is reflective of their karmic condition, their habits, and their attachments. Nevertheless, in the midst of this, they enabled us to be here now. And our parents embody all of our ancestors, in the many forms that they manifest.

What are the karmic connections that brought our parents to us? What are the karmic connections that brought us to our parents? The mystery of these questions is something we might only get a glimpse of, if even that.

Nevertheless, to enter the precepts is to enter into the mystery of our life to appreciate the support and nurturing we have received and continue to receive so we can practice—and the first of these supports is our parents. Our parents are the source of our opportunity to practice, and perhaps we are the opportunity that will allow them to encounter the Dharma. Do we appreciate their efforts, their actions to nurture and feed us, the way they cared for us when we were sick? Our parents may teach us the first point in practice: forgetting the self, going beyond self, compassionate giving.

Of course, we can evaluate and judge our parents' actions; we can criticize and point out how they were limited, how they created ideas of family versus not-family, and how they taught us ideas of better or worse. Nevertheless, from our life in utero and from our infancy onward, our parents have manifested the Dharma teaching of forgetting self, and they have given us the opportunity of being awakened by myriad dharmas throughout their life, with their death. And we can extend our appreciation to all our ancestors, to our grandparents and so on, to all the known and unknown beings who have brought us to this moment. Even the worrying and fears of our parents throughout our life, skillful or not, are their efforts expended for us.

In his poem "Old Granny's Tea-Grinding Songs," Hakuin Zenji says, "Your debt to your parents is deeper than the sea. If you forget it, you are lower than a dog or a cat. One filial act, even one's descendents prosper. Parents are a field of fortune in an unsure world."

In fact, aspects of Dharma relationships and teaching are couched in terms of a parent's care or a grandmotherly nurturing. Three times Huangbo responds to Linji's questions about the Dharma by hitting him. When Linji speaks of not knowing his faults in relation to Huangbo's blows, Dayu describes Huangbo as grandmotherly for the way he has exhausted himself while teaching Linji. Hearing this, Linji awakens. Do you see this? After Linji returns to the monastery, Huangbo comments on his coming and going, and Linji responds, "It is all due to your grandmotherly kindness."

In a different vein, Dogen writes, "When you handle water, rice, or anything else, you must have the affectionate and caring concern of a parent raising a child." Dogen was seriously ill just before his death, and there are a number of recorded occasions where Dogen encourages his disciple Tettsu Gikai to develop "parental mind." Dogen withholds Dharma transmission from Gikai because he lacked this quality, and Gikai ultimately received transmission from Dogen's successor Koun Ejo only when this quality was matured. Myriad beings parent us, we parent myriad beings. Myriad dharmas serve and nurture us, we have the opportunity to serve and nurture myriad dharmas—this is our practice life.

Dogen also points out in "Gakudo Yojin-shu": "Buddhas' deep compassion for sentient beings are neither for their own sake nor for others. It is just the nature of Buddha-Dharma. Observe how even insects and animals nurture their offspring, enduring hardships in the process. They gain nothing from this, even when their offspring are grown. The deep compassion of small creatures for their young naturally resembles the compassion of all Buddhas for sentient beings."

In talking with Joko, we both agreed—based on our own practice and based on our work with students—that the many facets of the attachment of being a parent was one of the deepest and strongest attachments that one had to work with in practice. Of course, this is a natural attachment, no problem. And yet, parental care in its many forms of attachment to parents, attachment of parents and attachment to children can become an attachment habit that blinds us in seeing, in being present, in responding to circumstances. This can cause all sorts of problems and reactions, and generate habits of anger, greed, and so forth.

What is appropriate parenting? What is the appropriate way to be raised and parented, in all the many forms of parenting? What serves to allow a full person to emerge and a true Dharma to manifest? Whether we are parents or not, whether we were raised by our parents or not, and this is our ongoing practice. Practice is allowing others to manifest themselves; it is allowing the manifestation of their karmic circumstances and opportunities and the dependent origination that is their life. We allow this in the midst of our relations with them, in the midst of our attachment to them as parent, as child, or as other relationships. This is our opportunity to respond intimately and skillfully, and to see our own attachments and reactive habits as these things arise.

As we will see, Jukai includes the the Three Treasures Refuge. Jukai also includes a lineage and karmic / Dharmic connection. These are "mysterious"; they are not adequately dealt with by cognitive habits, by "ordinary knowing" and "ordinary explaining." (I do not want to use the word "mystical," especially because of the Western connotations of that word.) As Dogen says in a different context, "When one side is illuminated [realized], the other side is dark." This is simple, straightforward, not special. This is ordinary everyday functioning; this is intimacy.

The theme of parental and ancestral relationships is one aspect of the lineage, of the *kechimyaku,* which is part of the Jukai ceremony, and I will explore this further later in this chapter. But we can see that the bows and appreciation at the beginning of the ceremony set the framework for what we do later.

Our relationship to all sorts of ancestors is not about the past. Otherwise, if ancestors are past, that much we see our self as separate and fixed in the present, that much we see our self as being the recipient of something coming from a past, whether genetic material from DNA, social and psychological habits, or Dharma teaching. We see the past moving to the present and to the future, or we see our self moving through the past, to the present, and into the future. This moment present has a past and future. Nevertheless, there is not a past ancestor of any sort that we are appreciating. It is the past ancestor right now that we are bowing with, it is the Ancestor that we are manifesting in bowing in appreciation. It is the boundless present that makes this ancestral appreciation possible.

In many ways, my relationship with Maezumi Roshi included

aspects of a parental relationship. And in some ways I could say that, despite being an adult, an aspect of my Dharma relationships was that I had a Dharma father in Maezumi Roshi and a Dharma mother in Joko. Nevertheless, my teacher was never my father, my mother, my therapist, or my friend. While the student-teacher relationship can be any of these things for the time being, it is always face-to-face, Buddha meeting Buddha.

As our practice matures, we deepen this independence, this interdependence, just as an adult child does. Maezumi Roshi once said to me, "Genmyo, I can't keep you at my side always." So let us manifest this intimacy of independence, of interdependence, of relative and absolute. Not anywhere else, right here. This intimacy is Buddha Dharma.

In a Pali sutra called *Life's Highest Blessings,* there is the following statement: "The support of father and mother, the cherishing of wife and children, and peaceful occupations—this is the Highest Blessing."

Bowing, we have an opportunity to appreciate and express our thanks for what we cannot be thankful enough for—even if we judge it as inadequate or problematic. Bowing is manifesting giving away self, giving away to enable us to arise and serve this moment.

Most fundamentally, bowing is body-mind giving away self, putting everything down. Bowing is a wonderful practice. There are so many ways to bow and so many forms of bowing; these opportunities appear throughout our life. Sometimes we notice these opportunities, sometimes we have to be reminded by practice forms and prompts, and sometimes it is only in stress and upset that we see what to do. In Jukai we bow many times on many different occasions. We can see Jukai as a punctuation in this ongoing process of practice life. It is a milestone, and yet the Jukai continues and reverberates, past and future. The matters that come up are not finalized, but continue to be matters for ongoing clarification. This is one of the reasons we should consider every Jukai that we attend as our own, whether we have already received Jukai or not. Therefore, all those who participate in Jukai are taking and receiving Jukai, in whatever state they are in.

The bows to our parents are followed by three full bows to the Preceptor. She or he is our connection to our lineage, to the various ancestors who are coming forth here in our receiving the Three Treasures, the Three Pure Precepts, and the Ten Grave Precepts. It is only through the ancestors' efforts to accomplish the Way that we have this opportunity. Whatever the nature of our connections with them, we must appreciate this.

Scholars have argued about and challenged the historical veracity of various aspects of Zen transmission lineages. However, those scholarly discussions have nothing to do with our appreciation for all the named and unnamed and all the known and unknown ancestors, which include those in our formal lineage as well as all others who have practiced the Way, accomplished the Way, and enabled the Way to come to us. Appreciating this is appreciating our life right now—and this is our practice. Unless we do so, we cannot really receive the Three Treasures and the Precepts. Just as we carry the genetic materials of countless known and unknown ancestors, humans and nonhumans, so too we carry the practice efforts and realization of countless Dharma Ancestors. Our Preceptor here and now in Jukai, in this very human person, is the embodiment of these Dharma Ancestors for us, and so we bow.

There are many times during the Jukai when we offer incense. What is this? The most simple aspect of incense for me is that we are taking the pinch or stick of incense, and in bringing it to our forehead we are making it ours; we are making it our self in whatever way we see our self. Then in offering the incense, whether we are dropping it onto hot charcoal or putting it into a bowl to burn, we are giving self away to the Way, just as we do in bowing. Even if we say that this giving self away is symbolic, the fact that it is symbolic does not exclude the real and immediate. Offering incense is immediate, and we have the opportunity to be this immediacy. Do not miss this. Just offer incense.

There is much to explore about the role of incense in many cultures, particularly the Asian cultures where Buddha Dharma developed. I leave this to scholars and others. Incense is a form of giving that we use, but need not be attached to. In fact, the very evanescent, impermanent nature of incense is nonattachment. So give self away, offer self, offer incense. I will refrain from further listing all the times we offer incense during Jukai.

Let us now invoke with a short period of silence the presence of the Three Treasures, all Awakened Ones of past, present, future—all beings who guide and support us on the path of wisdom and compassion.

What is invoking? The dictionary definition includes "to petition for support," "to appeal to," "to call forth," and "to bring about." So this silence allows the presence of the Three Treasures, of the Awakened Ones. It allows what is so; it allows the Dharma that is always being preached to be sensed and to be heard. You are so, therefore you can be so, and therefore you can invoke so. This is the wonderful opportunity of receiving the precepts, of receiving who we are.

I follow my teachers and use the form of invocation that includes the Three Treasures, the historical Shakyamuni Buddha, the bodhisattvas Kanzeon, Samantabhadra, and Manjushri, and as well as Dogen Zenji (Koso Joyo Daishi) and Keizan Zenji (Taiso Josai Daishi).

INVOCATION OF THE THREE TREASURES:

Namu ji po butsu
Namu ji po ho
Namu ji po so

Namu honshi shakyamuni butsu
Namu dai zu daihi kyu ku kanzeon bosa
Namu daijin fugen bosa
Namu daishin manjusri bosa
Namu koso joyo daishi
Namu taiso josai daishi
Namu riki dai soshi bosatsu

Being One with Buddha in the ten directions,
Being One with Dharma in the ten directions,
Being One with Sangha in the ten directions,
Being One with Original Teacher Shakyamuni Buddha,
Being One with Kanzeon Bodhisattva of Great Love and
 Great Compassion,
Being One with Great Compassionate Samantabhadra
 Bodhisattva,
Being One with Great Wisdom Manjushri Bodhisattva,
Being One with Eminent Ancestor Joyo (Dogen) Great
 Teacher,
Being One with Great Ancestor Josai (Keizan) Great
 Teacher,
Being One with Successive Great Ancestral Teacher
 Bodhisattvas

Having invoked the Three Treasures and the Buddhas and
Bodhisattvas, we now prepare to receive the Three Treasures as
our life. In order to do so, we must go beyond the habits of body
and mind; we must release the habits of body and mind right here
now. This is atonement.

Atonement is the path and practice of opening the mind-
heart. The power of atonement is beyond calculation, puri-
fying all intentional actions of body, mouth, and thought.

Atonement is timeless; it is reaching "across" ideas of past, present, and future. Being time is just right now; we are just right now. And "now" includes so-called past and so-called future—now. The simple gloss on the word "atonement" as being "at-one-ment" is not just words. We can truly be at one right now. In being present, we are able to enter this moment that is not limited by and yet includes our conventional ideas of past and future, just as this moment being is not limited by and yet includes conventional visions of self and not self. So endless dimensions in all senses are right now in this atonement. This is our opportunity to atone.

Atonement is for harmful actions; these actions are evil karma in the sense that they result in suffering and harm, which manifest in this cause-and-effect moment. Harmful actions grow out of intentions that are blinded by self-centeredness, and they grow out of habits that are misperceiving who and what we are, and what our life is.

Anger is not seeing clearly cause and effect; it is not seeing clearly dependent origination. Instead, we take events as having to do with so-called others and their failings, whether the others are individuals, groups, social entities, or even natural phenomena. Or we take events as an indicator of our so-called inadequacy or failings, again missing the cause-and-effect dependency that originates this moment.

If we see this cause-and-effect dependency as what it is, without self-centeredness (or with "less" self-centeredness), then the basis for anger lessens and dissipates. The anger habit might still arise, because beginningless greed and anger are ours through the human body-mind condition, but we need not be trapped by it, and we need not be run by it. We can see more clearly how and where to skillfully respond to the cause and effect manifesting this moment, to the karmic stream flow right now. Skillful response is the manifesting of myriad Bodhisattvas, the manifesting of the

Dharma right now, the countless beings that are being liberated right here.

Greed and anger are the manifesting of holding to self. And with holding to self comes ideas of other. Only if there is some fixed permanent self can there be clinging to anger and greed, in all their many forms. Look closely at what getting angry is, look closely at what there is greed for. Who is angry? Who is greedy? The karmic cause-and-effect conditions that manifest as our life right here, that manifest as this moment dependent arising, is our wonderful opportunity, as well as the source of greed, anger, and misperceiving ignorance.

Sometimes it is important to emphasize confession as part of atonement, although during the Jukai we do not specify what we are confessing. In our daily life, what hinder appropriate and skillful confession are our self-centered fears of the consequences of confession, such as what others might think of me or do to me if I confess. As long as we hold those fears, we are hindered and blocked in the at-one-ment.

Of course, atonement is not a onetime event. In some zendos, there is atonement at the start of every morning service; this atonement makes the morning service possible. Over and over, we can atone; over and over, we should atone. Of course, there is no burden we carry unless we hold to it. And yet, atone, atone again and again. So although those doing Jukai atone, everyone else participating also atones.

Atonement is not merely a personal matter. In the "Shushogi" ("The Meaning of Practice and Verification"), Dogen says of the merit of atonement, "This merit skillfully increases unhindered pure faith and striving. When once pure faith is realized, both oneself and others are equally transformed. The benefit is shared with sentient beings and insentient beings."

In the marriage ceremony that I use, this confession and atonement are extended into ongoing practice through the following vows:

To accept my mistakes without making excuses for them.

and

I accept full responsibility for action and reaction, for motive and effect.

There are a number of ways to translate the "Atonement Gatha." The following is the form that I use:

Being one with Awakened Ones in the ten directions,
Being one with awakened actions in the ten directions,
Let us recite the verse of atonement.
(Preceptor [Kaishi] recites each line, and Sangha follows):
All harmful actions ever committed by me since of old,
On account of beginningless greed, anger, and ignorance,
Born of my body, mouth, and thought,
Now I confess and atone for them all.

Beginningless greed, anger, and ignorance, born of body, mouth, and thought, are part of the DNA body-mind package of being human. Hardwired and softwired, so to speak, these physiological, psychological, genetic, social, and personal habits are the cause and effect manifesting right now as this person, this body-mind. There is ongoing scientific research that is clarifying the extent of the biological and genetic predispositions for becoming angry and the variations among people. Nevertheless, greed, anger, and ignorance are is our inheritance, along with the ability and opportunity to go beyond this, to practice and manifest the Dharma truth of our life.

Body-mind habits are not a fixed, permanent thing; they arise and they pass. This is the mysterious world of our life, the mysterious opportunity of human birth. Therefore our practice and our atonement are ongoing moment by moment in the midst of this impermanence, in the midst of this moment arising-passing. We can call this the unfolding of karmic circumstances.

Our choice is not whether a body-mind habit or a body-mouth-thought habit arises. Our choice is whether we attach to this habit and build on it with reactions like greed and anger, or whether we are able to let this habit go in order to skillfully work with it. This practice effort allows habits and circumstances to be transparent in the midst of arising-passing. Our ongoing practice also creates karmic habits that counter our reactive greed, anger, and ignorance. Thus it is possible for us not to cling to these three poisons and not to be caught by them, or to be able to practice with them whenever we see the practice opportunity.

> I am now going to ask you to accept and maintain the Three Treasures and the precepts. These are the formulations of inherent good. This good is not the opposite of bad; this good can be called self-nature, Buddha-nature, no-nature, the absolute.

It is most important to see that the Three Treasures are not limited to our ideas of them, nor to any words that we try to put on them. Nevertheless, we use the words, the intentions, and the actions to enable us to go beyond. This is not only for the recipient of the Jukai; all of us have this opportunity right now. And we accept the Three Treasures with all beings and for all beings. So everyone present at the Jukai is encouraged to repeat this chant (and many of the chants) along with the recipient(s).

> All beings are this wisdom and compassion, the perfection of good! Only our delusions and attachments prevent us from witnessing to the good. Precepts are a guide, leading us from self-centered delusion and attachment to a more

complete realization and manifestation of wisdom and compassion as our lives. They point the way to the fulfillment of our true nature.

The Preceptor chants, and the recipient(s) and participants repeat. According to circumstances, sometimes I lead this in Sino-Japanese, sometimes in one of the English forms, sometimes in Pali, and sometimes in all three languages.

Sometimes we take refuge only once, sometimes we take refuge three times. We cannot take refuge too often. Dogen writes in "Shushogi": "Once refuge is established, it is ever strengthened, life after life, place after place, and always accumulates merits, and results in the unsurpassed right complete awakening." Taking Refuge in the Three Treasures is being intimate.

The Three Treasures (Sankikai) (repeated three times)

Japanese version:
Namu ki e butsu
Namu ki e ho
Namu ki e so
Ki e butsu mujo son
Ki e ho rijin son
Ki e so wago son
Ki e bu kyo
Ki e ho kyo
Ki e so kyo

Pali version:
Buddham saranam gacchami
Dhammam saranam gacchami
Sangham saranam gacchami

Dutiyampi Buddham saranam gacchami
Dutiyampi Dhammam saranam gacchami
Dutiyampi Sangham saranam gacchami
Tatiyampi Buddham saranam gacchami
Tatiyampi Dhammam saranam gacchami
Tatiyampi Sangham saranam gacchami

The English version of the Japanese is as follows:
I take refuge in the Buddha.
I take refuge in the Dharma.
I take refuge in the Sangha.
I take refuge in the Buddha, the incomparable honored
    one.
I take refuge in the Dharma, honorable for its purity.
I take refuge in the Sangha, honorable for its harmony.
I have finished taking refuge in Buddha.
I have finished taking refuge in the Dharma.
I have finished taking refuge in the Sangha.

The English version of the Pali, which I use, is as follows:
I take refuge in the Buddha.
I take refuge in the Dharma.
I take refuge in the Sangha.
A second time, I take refuge in the Buddha.
A second time, I take refuge in the Dharma.
A second time, I take refuge in the Sangha.
A third time, I take refuge in the Buddha.
A third time, I take refuge in the Dharma.
A third time, I take refuge in the Sangha.

An alternative English formulation of the Three Treasures
    refuge is:

I take refuge in the Buddha/unity.
I take refuge in the Dharma/diversity.
I take refuge in the Sangha/harmony.

Preceptor: Will you maintain this?
Recipient: I will. (Makes three full bows.)

Asperging is when the officiant, after "blessing" the "wisdom water," the purification water, with a mantra, hand mudra, and incense, sprinkles the water on their own head three times, then sprinkles it on the recipient's head three times, and then returns it to their own head three times. This is done with a small branch of pine needles, though sometimes other evergreens are used, and even flowers have been used. A flower bud is especially appropriate at a wedding. This is receiving the wisdom water of all Buddhas and Ancestors in the transmission of the precepts.

THE THREE PURE PRECEPTS

Preceptor: I vow to be nonharming, to cease all harmful actions.
Will you maintain this well?
Recipient: I will. (Bow.)
P: I vow to do good.
Will you maintain this well?
R: I will. (Bow.)
P: I vow to do good for others, to serve all existence.
Will you maintain this well?
R: I will. (Bow.)

THE TEN GRAVE PRECEPTS

P: Now, the Ten Grave Precepts.
First precept: I vow to practice nonkilling.
Will you maintain this well?

R: I will. (Bow.)

P: Second precept: I vow to practice nonstealing.
Will you maintain this well?

R: I will. (Bow.)

P: Third precept: I vow to practice not being greedy, not misusing sexuality.
Will you maintain this well?

R: I will. (Bow.)

P: Fourth precept: I vow to practice telling the truth.
Will you maintain this well?

R: I will. (Bow.)

P: Fifth precept: I vow to be aware of my ways of clouding the truth by my ignorance.
Will you maintain this well?

R: I will. (Bow.)

P: Sixth precept: I vow to abstain from speaking of the errors and faults of others.
Will you maintain this well?

R: I will. (Bow.)

P: Seventh precept: I vow not to elevate myself or put down others.
Will you maintain this well?

R: I will. (Bow.)

P: Eighth precept: I vow to be generous.
Will you maintain this well?

R: I will. (Bow.)

P: Ninth precept: I vow not to indulge in self-centered anger.
Will you maintain this well?

R: I will. (Bow.)

P: Tenth precept: I vow not to speak ill of the Three Treasures, the truth, the teaching, and those who practice the teaching.

Will you maintain this well?
R: I will. (Bow.)

After the recipient has accepted the precepts, the officiant then asks:

> Preceptor: These sixteen precepts—the Three Treasures, the Three Pure Precepts, and the Ten Grave Precepts—are handed down by Shakyamuni Buddha generation after generation to me. Now I give them to you. Will you maintain them well?
> Recipient: I will.
> P: Will you maintain them well?
> R: I will.
> P: Will you really maintain them well?
> R: I will. (Three bows.)

We maintain what is so. No need to add, no need to change, but in seeing what is so, in committing to what is so, in receiving and taking what is so, we are able to maintain what is so—and in doing so we are so, and we support others in being so.

> Rakusu is placed on recipient.

The rakusu is made of strips of black cloth sewn together into a rice-field-like pattern of a rectangular bordered area with vertical and horizontal strips within the border. It is worn around the neck like a bib. In Zen traditions deriving from Japan and Korea, the rakusu is given to both lay and ordained practitioners who have received the precepts.

The rakusu originated in China in the Sung dynasty, and is a miniature version of a kesa or kasaya, which is the robe worn by an ordained person. There are a number of different rakusu forms within different lineages, and there are also different traditions of sewing the rakusu. Sewing the rakusu is an ongoing practice and preparation for receiving the precepts, along with actual precept study and practice. It is the robe of the Buddha, which is our robe, our life with which we are clothed. The "Verse of the Robe" that we chant, which is an English translation and reframing from the Japanese, is:

Vast is the robe of liberation,
A formless field of benefaction,
Wearing the universal teaching,
Harmonizing all being.

Kechimyaku is given to recipient.

The kechimyaku is the particular lineage chart of the Preceptor. It is a list of names from Shakyamuni Buddha to the present, to which the recipient is added as the last name. There is a red "blood line" from the name Shakyamuni Buddha, at the top of the chart, which wends its way through all the names up to the recipient's new name, and from whom the "blood lineage line" is "reconnected" to the name Shakyamuni Buddha. Some lineage charts are in the form of a circle, with Buddha in the center, and some are a combination of vertical and horizontal, with Buddha at the top.

There are a number of different forms of kechimyaku. In the ceremonies I officiate, I have provided the recipients with a form beforehand, and I usually have the recipient write the names of the lineage ancestors in the months before the Jukai, (except the names of my immediate teachers, my name, and their name). In writing the names of our ancestors, becoming familiar and intimate with them, reflecting on who they are, and appreciating their practice and understanding, we become intimate with our ancestors, and with our connection and interrelationship to them.

There is also further study of the lineage. It is important to see that it is the Buddha and Ancestors who give "birth" to us, whose Dharma connection births us and enables us to receive this treasure of Buddha Dharma and practice—and at the same time, it is important to see that we are birthing and sourcing the Buddha and Ancestors.

Dharma name given and explained.

A recipient can be given one or two Dharma names. I give two Dharma names, both in Sino-Japanese, along with the English translation. When two Dharma names are given, usually the second name is the one that is used regularly. The Dharma names can be used in Sino- Japanese or in their English equivalent; therefore attention is paid to how the names sound, as well as to their meaning.

Most important is that the Dharma names reflect the Dharma, the truth of reality, and at the same time articulate the specific person's nature, practice strengths, and potentialities. The Dharma names are a Dharma gift, a support and encouragement of practice, as well as an ongoing koan for the recipient.

The Jukai ends with the "Gatha on Receiving the Precepts":

> When beings receive the precepts,
> They enter the realm of the Buddhas,
> Which is none other than the great enlightenment.
> Truly, they are the children of the Buddha.

As I said, receiving the precepts is receiving our life. So we enter, or reenter, the life we have always been. Living this life is dependent on our willingness to accept this life; once we accept this life, then we can be this life of interbeing. The life of the great enlightenment is the ongoing change we call Buddha-nature.

Through skillful efforts as needed, we are re-minding our self in our practice that our life is the life of the Buddha. Thus we are enabled to live the wisdom and compassion of the Buddha.

Not only can we do live a life of wisdom and compassion, but we must do this. And in accepting the precepts and vowing to maintain them, we undertake to live Buddha's wisdom and compassion, and support our self in doing this. Supporting our self, being supported, acknowledging that we are children of the Buddha—this is how we support the whole family of the Buddha. This family is our family, namely all the beings that we encounter from morning to night. Now that we see this, we manifest this.

37

The Buddha Treasure

I AND ALL BEINGS

On seeing the morning star, Shakyamuni Buddha attained enlightenment and said, "I and all beings of the great earth have together attained the Way." This is most important for us all to see. So, what is this?

Taking refuge in the Buddha, the Dharma, and the Sangha is taking refuge in Buddha's Awakening. Without this, there is nothing to say about refuge, nothing to say about Three Treasures. From what do we need refuge? We seem to live in a world of conditions and circumstances arising, in which we face storms of conditions and our seemingly natural reactions to them, which result in discomfort, dissatisfaction, and suffering. Look closely for your self: What do you see? We try all sorts of things to alleviate conditions and their consequences; we try to change others, to change our self, to change conditions. Does this work?

The Three Treasures are treasures because they are refuges that enable us to live the life that we are amid what seem to be storms of arising conditions and circumstances; they enable us to live amid feeling battered by the self-centered habits of greed and anger that can wreak such havoc in our life. These storms seem to be a natural part of who we are, but at the same time they are unsatisfactory and troublesome.

So we ask: What are the Three Treasure? How are they refuges? How do we take refuge in them? How do we face and embrace what is painful and hard to accept? Clarifying this is what practice asks of us, and at the same time this is what practice enables us to do.

In the *Transmission of Light,* Keizan Zenji says, "This so-called I is not Shakyamuni Buddha; even Shakyamuni Buddha is born of this I. Certainly you, I, all beings are born of this I." The whole of the great earth and all beings come forth from it as well. Attaining the Way is seeing and realizing this. It is seeing that from the beginning, we are all nothing but this unborn Buddha mind. What is this? Making this unborn Buddha mind clear for our self and for others is the core of our life practice. This is taking refuge in the Buddha, the first of the Three Treasures, the first of the Three Jewels.

Keizan Zenji also says, "When a great net is hauled up from the sea, all the openings in the net are hauled up with it. Likewise when Gautama attains the Way, beings of the earth also attain the Way. . . . Not only beings of the earth but Buddhas, enlightened ones of past, present, and future."

This is the central point of practice: to be intimate in all the circumstances that we encounter—and this is because everything we encounter is our intimacy. This is seeing the morning star; this is seeing our own face. Attaining the attained; that is why it is possible to say, "I and all beings of the great earth have together attained the Way." That is why we can say, "All beings are the wisdom and the compassion of the Tathagata." This is acknowledging what is so: not something that we create, not something that is personal and mine, and not anyone else's. This is really acknowledging what is mine because it is everyone's, and because it is not dependent on my conditions and circumstances.

And yet, I need to make it my own, and you need to make it your own. Buddha is not someone or something out there; any such Buddha out there, any taking refuge in something else, makes us miss this. Zazen is clarifying this in our ongoing practice life. Taking refuge is making this my own.

Keizan Zenji continues, "Even so, don't hold a false notion of Gautama becoming Shakyamuni and realizing enlightenment."Or to say it in another way: "For Shakyamuni there is no thought of attaining the Way." Keizan Zenji's commentary is a way to question us about this attaining the Way; it's a way to question us about this Buddha. Or saying it differently: What is it that we think is not the Attained Way? What is it that we think is not Buddha? What is it we think is I? What is it we think is not-I? When you take refuge in Buddha, all beings take refuge in Buddha. If this is not so, then you are not taking refuge. And yet, do not depend upon all beings taking refuge; you yourself must take refuge.

Do you see "I and all beings of the whole earth have together attained the Way"? Do you see at the same moment all are together attaining? This is our life: this is who and what our life is, this is what awakening is. Always this is our practice, awakening to the universe that our life is right now, the face that we encounter every moment of our life. Sitting is the intimacy of this "I" that is the Attained Way, this "I" that is exactly our life. When we speak, walk, lie down, and work, this is it. We are awakening to this that we always are from the beginning. However, if we believe and think otherwise, if we function as if it is otherwise, then it is otherwise for us.

Keizan says, "It is the solitary body revealed in the midst of myriad forms." This is our functioning; "the solitary body" is our life "in the midst of the myriad forms." We are always encountering this solitary body, which is the myriad forms of everyone and everything that we encounter. If the solitary body is seen as some self and the myriad forms are seen as something elsewhere, which is the way many of us function much of the time, then we miss this. We live a dualistic life with its resulting storms, which seem to cause such difficulties for us, and from which we are often trying to escape.

These phrases are the encouragement of practice; they encourage us to see and be the harmony of the myriad forms. This Buddha Jewel is always revealing our life. We can see all the ways that we resist, all the ways that we believe otherwise, all the ways that we act otherwise. Taking refuge is alive in the specifics of our life, in this moment life practice. Then the refuge in Buddha Jewel is so for us.

When we are practicing together, when we are walking together, each of us is walking individually, and yet we are all this whole walking together. The same when we chant: we are all this whole chanting together. Unfortunately, sometimes we don't quite hear this or do this. So when we are chanting the *Heart Sutra* in the morning, for instance, it is important to do it with our ears so that it is the ears chanting—which are at the same time hearing and responding with everyone else. It's not just me chanting with my mouth. Of course, all of us hear to our own capacity; some of us have a harder time hearing, and a harder time chanting. But within our own capacity, we can go beyond this seeming capacity.

This is the same with other circumstances, such as when we meet people. What is it to meet and see our self? Whoever we are meeting is seeing our self, and yet we are meeting the other, so how do I respond by feeling with them? By being compassionate. This means feeling who and what their life is, and what they are doing and saying. This way, our response grows out of that harmony of the two of us speaking, of the two of us functioning, of the three, four, or five of us functioning. Our response grows out of the harmony of being in the world with people, animals, trees, snow, and cars. All these things are this great earth that together attains the Way. It is the "solitary body revealed in the midst of the myriad forms."

If we are caught up in myriad forms, then we are on one side, and we miss the solitary body that is exactly our life. We miss the harmony. It's the same when we are chanting: if we are only attentive to our voice and what we want, that much we miss the whole chanting. The same with our sitting: even though our sitting is this body-mind right here, yet it is this body-mind in the midst of the zendo with everyone else. Not thinking about them, not doing anything specific, but being this functioning moment of being present.

In the Zen tradition, we celebrate Buddha's enlightenment on December 8. In some Buddhist traditions, it is celebrated in the spring at Wesak. Every morning you can celebrate this enlightenment, because every morning is attaining, encountering, embracing, and being intimacy—the life that we are.

I grew up in New York City and didn't learn to drive until I was eighteen. For the first eight years after I had a license, I didn't drive more than two hundred miles altogether. The way I learned to drive was driving to California to move to the Zen Center of Los Angeles (ZCLA) in 1976. I was determined that either I had to get there or I would not survive.

When I was Maezumi Roshi's attendant at ZCLA, one of my jobs was to drive Roshi to various meetings and so forth, despite my limited experience in driving. At one point while I was driving, he said to me, "Genmyo, you are driving the car; really, just let the car drive the car."

It is this way in all sorts of activities and functioning. It is not so easy to see this sometimes, to see what to do, to give our self away. This is being intimate with the circumstances and activities, to see, respond, act, and function out of this present moment. This is zazen: just sitting, just breathing. Otherwise, in our everyday functioning, if we are not seeing and not being our connectedness, our actions may gouge out gaping wounds in the fabric of our life. We do not see the myriad forms that are our body, that are our life.

A car doesn't drive itself, and yet it does drive itself, our self. The car and our self are not separate when we are driving the car. This is the intimacy of self and car. This is the point. From morning to night, we are encountering all sorts of people and circumstances, we are encountering many forms of life functioning. It is a dance, a dance of our self and this other that we encounter—and this other that we encounter is our self. And yet, we may get caught up in ideas and beliefs, and we may be puzzled: "I'm dancing with them, they're dancing with me, but am I leading or are they leading?" We get caught up in all sorts of dreams. We dance with the car, and both we and the car dance with the road. But it is hard to dance because we often want to lead.

How do you see the morning star? If you think seeing the morning star creates something in here because the morning star out there just happens to be a good trigger, that much we don't realize "I and all beings of the great earth have together attained the Way." We have to chew on this to see what this is.

"Even though spring, summer, fall, and winter come with their changes, and mountains, rivers, and land change with time, you should know that since it is all old Gautama raising his eyebrows and blinking his eyes, it is the solitary body revealed in the myriad forms" (Keizan). This is what we are talking about; this is who and what our life is. All we encounter is our own face—and yet we don't see that.

This Buddha Treasure is a very nice koan. This is our life; this is our ongoing practice. In traditional koan practice, we clarify the various aspects of the Unified Three Treasures, the Manifested

Three Treasures, the Abiding Three Treasures. We can chew on all the many different aspects of this. We do not clarify this in order to get someplace, to get some special words or phrases. We clarify this to allow this to be ours, to allow us to manifest this and to manifest all the aspects of our life.

38

Dharma Treasure

ENTANGLING NOT-KNOWING

The teaching of the Buddha, the Buddha Dharma, is exactly this life that we are. The Dharma Treasure is descriptive of what is; it describes the reality of this life. The Dharma Treasure is also prescriptive; it tells us the way to be the life that we are. Because we are so, we can be so. Buddha's Teaching, Buddha's Dharma, is "not-knowing." Because we are not-knowing, we can be not-knowing. So taking refuge in the Dharma is taking refuge in this as this is; it is enabling this to be manifest for us, as us. The Dharma Treasure is being genuine.

We are all very fortunate that we are able to hear and see this Dharma in this moment life. We may not realize what this Dharma life is, and yet unless we realize this Dharma, our deep habits and self-centeredness turn us from this very life moment we are. Many times we take for granted the human capacities and opportunities that we have, assuming that we and all beings are entitled to this. The wonderful truth is that we can study the Dharma, we can practice the Dharma, and we can manifest the Dharma.

"Knowing" that you know things now can be a practice support to enable you to open knowing. The more you see this "knowing," the more it is an opportunity this moment to be this, to go "beyond" the knowing. Knowing is just another human habit, just another habit of thought arising and passing—except if we clutch it and build on it, and thereby miss our life. This is important: being not-knowing is our choice and our opportunity. It is hard sometimes, but by being sitting and entering into this moment not-knowing, rather than sitting and holding to knowing what is and what is going to be, that much we can *be* what is. Not-knowing is embracing suffering, not-knowing is embracing arising-passing, not-knowing is embracing this moment cause and effect—not-knowing is embracing just this.

Just this here-now is the Dharma Treasure revealed; just this here-now is the Dharma Treasure manifested.

This is simple, but simple means taking care of what needs to be taken care of. We could say "incomparably profound and minutely subtle," but that is only on one side. The other side, which is most basic, is that it is simple and straightforward, which is why it is always accessible. "It" means our life. "It" means if there is noise, it is noisy. "It" means if we need to record, we turn on the recorder. "It" means sitting, and whatever arises is the opportunity to experience our life without clinging to, or being determined by, the characteristics and form of life. Therefore, it is not the characteristics that determine us, because all characteristics are of the nature of arising and passing; all characteristics are our original nature. Sometimes we talk about form and emptiness as a way of expressing this.

Despite being in the midst of the particularities of form, sensations, conceptions, discriminations, and awareness, form isn't form except as form that is empty. Therefore, form is exactly form, characteristics are exactly characteristics. In the midst of characteristics is the opportunity for being free of characteristics. To explain it further, we can say the "backside" of form is empty, so if we truly enter this form, if we truly inhabit this form moment, we also enter this boundless empty. But as form is exactly emptiness, emptiness exactly form, so simply be this form completely.

Therefore, our ideas about these forms—"I like it, I don't like it; this is what I want, this is what I don't want; this is what I planned on, this isn't what I planned on"—need not determine how we are, and need not determine our suffering or lack of suffering. To use Dogen's phrase, "when the self advances and realizes the myriad dharmas, this is delusion." Despite the "backside" of not-knowing, of essential nature, of boundless emptiness, we do not penetrate through to this because we hold to self, we "hold our self back" to only one side of the coin. When we penetrate through so that we can freely be the front side with the backside, and be the backside with the front side, then the myriad dharmas, this very moment dharmas, "advance and realize the self" in the midst of this realized life.

There is a story about Hakuin that illustrates this. Once in a public talk, Hakuin said, "Buddha is one's own being. When Buddha appears, everything in the world radiates great light. If you want to perceive this, just turn your own mind and seek single-mindedly."

A woman heard Hakuin say this, and she thought, "That is not too hard." Returning home, she sat with this day and night, keeping it in mind in the midst of all activities, awake or asleep.

One day she was washing a pot, and suddenly she woke up. Tossing aside the pot, she went to see Hakuin. She said, "I've come across the Buddha in my own body, and everything radiates light. Marvelous, marvelous!" She was so happy she danced. Hakuin said, "What about a cesspool? Does that radiate light?"

The old woman slapped him, saying, "This old fellow isn't through yet." Hakuin laughed.

We usually think and act based on the thought: "If I'm going to suffer, it is because of A, B, C, D. But if I get rid of A, B, C, D, then I won't suffer." We are seeing and living as if the characteristics and conditions, the thoughts and feelings, are the basis for happiness or suffering. The truth is that we are not determined by or dependent on the characteristics and conditions. We are able to enter into the characteristics, and at the same time be free of them.

Saying this is one thing. Our capacity to do this over and over is ongoing practice; it is sitting together, it is walking, it is functioning throughout our life. This is to be simple and straightforward in the characteristics and conditions of the moment. That is why I say that practice is simple and straightforward, nothing special. This fundamental simpleness and straightforwardness of practice is the truth of how we are.

A calligraphy I received in China reads: "Buddha light shines everywhere." That doesn't mean that there is some Buddha whose light is shining and reaching everywhere. Light shines everywhere. Don't think that light is something different from darkness.

So everywhere light is shining, everywhere is shining Buddha. What does that mean? What about the cesspools? Practice is not to believe the words but to simply and straightforwardly enter into the cesspools that we think are cesspools; these are the characteristics, the thoughts, and the conditions that we think are not shining light. The nonabiding nature that we are enables us to enter and leave these characteristics, thoughts, and conditions; it enables us to come and go as they appear. The truth of reality is that we can be everything, we can be anything. As these things appear in our being present, as they appear in this moment of life, our ability to enter them is only limited by our thoughts and beliefs about these characteristics.

So every opportunity is an opportunity to enter, to awaken, to open to this moment as it is. Or to skillfully work with the characteristics, to work with the thought that we have about this moment as it is: "I don't like this. This shouldn't feel this way. He shouldn't do that." I picked a few easy ones, but those might not be the ones you have. You have to see what "your" characteristics and forms are right this moment. Or you don't have to see anything; just straightforwardly do, without being blinded by the characteristics. Straightforwardly breathe, right where you are. Straightforwardly experience this light, the way this seems to you. Smell this cesspool: what a wonderful cesspool—no light anywhere else, just this rotting shit.

The willingness to straightforwardly experience this moment life in the midst of how it seems to you is exactly what opens this life moment up to being what it truly is. This is the Dharma Treasure. It isn't your characteristics; it isn't what you call it. The Sixth Ancestor says, "Without characteristics is being free of characteristics while being in the midst of characteristics." This is the basis of who we are, the basis of this practice, the basis of "original nature."

Being without thought is the core. How is it the core? The core is not thinking in regard to thoughts. Thoughts arising and passing is never an issue, because it is just one consideration of how we are. Hooking on to the thought as who and what we are is what hinders us. And this hinders all of us: every one of us in our own way hooks on to some of our thoughts and beliefs. I am using the word "thoughts," but you could say "feelings," you could say "emotions," you could say "evaluations." We hook our self onto it: "I'm thinking that, I'm shouldn't feel that, I should have that."

So thoughts are not the issue; the issue is hooking on to them and thinking about them. Either we see how we can do something about this, or we don't see and it does something about us. That is why we say that being without thought is not being stained by thought. It is being free from the thought hook.

Being is not-knowing. Just sitting in not-knowing. We think not-knowing is some special state. Not-knowing is the simple openness of doing, of being right where you are. It only is difficult when we cling to our knowing habit, or when we don't see our knowing habit. Not-knowing is not something you have to add on. It is very simple and straightforward. It really is.

39

Sangha Treasure

THE BALLOON OF OUR LIFE

Our life is a balloon. As we all know, a hole in a balloon affects the rest of the balloon. More than affects it; every point in the balloon is connected to every other point.

Often it is hard for us to have a sense of this connection in our life. We tend to live our life as if there is "me" and "others"—other humans, other beings, other things of all sorts—and we tend to live as if we are all separate. In one sense, of course, this is true. And in another sense of course, this is not true.

Sometimes it is hard for us to see that this is not true. Not only in terms of other beings but sometimes even in terms of our so-called own life. Whether physically, mentally, or emotionally, there are many aspects that we don't include in the balloon of our life, much less the balloon of the whole universe. We may see that we are one part of the balloon, but we miss that we are exactly the whole of the balloon. Not the h-o-l-e, but the w-h-o-l-e. And if we don't see the whole, we can become the hole that deflates the balloon of our life.

Seeing the morning star, the Buddha said, "I and all beings of the great earth have together attained the Way." This "I" is not some historical person, but this "I" is exactly the "I" that we all come forth from, that Shakyamuni Buddha comes forth from. This is the "all beings of the great earth." Not just humans, but all beings of the great earth. This is the whole universe that is our life.

So any place in the balloon that you pull on will pull the rest of the balloon. And any place in the balloon that someone else pulls on will also pull on so-called your part of the balloon. This analogy goes in all directions, but the point of the analogy is not to have more ideas; the point of the analogy is to enable us to clarify our life, to see and be what is so, to see where we get stuck. The analogy helps us see where one aspect, one set of ideas, or one perspective can somehow limit and blind us in our functioning.

Literally, the Sangha Treasure refers to those who practice the teaching of Buddha. Most narrowly, it is those who have left home and taken monastic vows. In a broader sense, we in the West often use the term "Sangha" to refer to everyone who practices. Dogen Zenji says zazen "is the front gate of the Buddha Dharma." What is practice? There is formal practice, there is the commitment to practice, and there are the various forms of Buddhist practice. Truly, all people we encounter are practicing, whether they know it or not, whether their practice is skillful and effective, or whether their practice is blundering in the midst of life and causing harm and suffering. Being human is the opportunity to practice, and to discover the gift of the opportunity of this life.

In an even broader sense, Sangha is all beings of the great earth, not excluding the stones, trees, mountains, clouds, and stars. The Dharma is vividly revealed and preached by myriad beings, sentient beings and insentient beings. Who is sentient? Who is insentient? What is the light that we all are? Look closely; do you see this? This is the refuge of endless dimension universal life that is our Sangha, that is our refuge. Taking refuge in the

Sangha is taking refuge in the life that we are, not taking refuge in some narrow vision or self-centeredness. It is going beyond. The Sangha Treasure is the harmony of this, the merits of harmony, the virtue of harmony.

As a practice exercise, I suggest that you pick two particular aspects of your life to attend to. Of course, practice is being present, and is not limited to two aspects; nevertheless, this is an exercise to explore. Pick a bodily physical aspect like a hand, a foot, your face, or any place that you are not usually attentive to during your everyday functioning. Throughout the day or at various times during the day, be aware or include awareness of your left hand, for example, in the various things that you are doing. This does not mean you should do anything special with the left hand; just do what you are doing, but make sure from time to time to remind your self to feel, to be that left hand, and to include that hand with whatever else you are doing—talking, cooking, working, eating, walking, or exercising. Make an effort at various times during the day to just include how that hand feels, inside and outside.

The other aspect is a little different. Include someone or something else that is so-called outside your self. For instance, what does it feel like being here with this tree? Or this wall? If I was spending much of the day in this room, my practice would be at various times to just to notice the wall, to include the wall as the wall, in whichever way awareness includes the wall. You can choose a particular physical object or something at a particular place, or the other person who you are with. It could be sound, which might mean the traffic noise or the store noise or the sound in the room where you are.

I want you to find what works in your life. But pick something so-called inside, something bodily, and something so-called outside. Notice these aspects of the balloon that is your life, these things that are so-called inside and so-called outside. How it is to include and be these things at various times during the day?

Being listening, at various times just be listening in wherever you are as you are, whether it's at a party with people, walking down the street, driving on the highway, or waiting at an airport. Some of you have done this formally: you have a watch that signals every hour on the hour, reminding you to be present practice. All of us can make an effort at various times during the day to just notice, to be present in this way. This is a way to begin exploring this not-two. You don't need to have any ideas; just begin exploring the not-twoness.

You might pick tasting at various times during the day, making a point to taste whatever is in your mouth, whether there is nothing in your mouth or whether you have something in your mouth. If you spend a lot of time in the car, it might be just noticing what is in front of or in the car. You know your self and your life very well. Therefore, use this form as a support for your practice. See what works, and see what would be useful for your practice.

When we sit, especially for long periods, sometimes there is physical pain. Often we react with thoughts such as "I can't take this pain any more, I gotta move" or "No, I'm not going to move, no matter how painful it is." Either one of these reactions are places where we can get trapped. Being intimate with the pain, the pain is you, and any movement or adjustment grows out of the appropriateness of moving, because that is what is called for.

Explaining can become a new position, a new idea: "No, I've got to be intimate with my pain." But I say it anyway. Words sometimes allow us to see how we are being used by the words rather than simply using them, or how we are being used by the attitudes and habits that the words are expressing. Are we being used by words, ideas, and circumstances? Do they trap us? Do they limit us from being who we truly are because we believe them? Or can we use them freely as appropriate?

Whether we know it or not, whether they know it or not, all day we are encountering Bodhisattvas. We encounter them at home, at work, in the store, on the road, and also in the zendo. And yet, if we miss it, we need to be reminded of this wonderful Sangha Treasure, this harmonious functioning that exists even in the midst of not seeing harmony, or even when we are seeing not-harmony.

Once I was in a van with Soen Nakagawa Roshi going from Dai Bosatsu Zendo in the Catskill Mountains to New York City. We crossed the George Washington Bridge to enter Manhattan and paid our fee at the tollbooth. Soen Roshi suddenly pointed out: "Wonderful Dharma transaction! Namu Dai George Washington Bosa! Crossing the George Washington Bodhisattva Bridge, giving two George Washington Bodhisattvas [two dollars bills for the $1.50 toll] and receiving two George Washington Bodhisattvas!" [two quarters for change].

It does not matter if the toll collector, the Bodhisattva who supports us in this Dharma transaction, knows this is a Dharma transaction or not. In fact, knowing and not-knowing have nothing to do with this. It does not matter if the toll collector acts how we think a Bodhisattva should act. It is up to us, and up to our practice exertion, to make it so for us and to make it so for the toll collector—and we do this in the midst of not-knowing. Making it so, it can be so for the toll collector. This is doing good for others.

Do we see the Bodhisattvas we encounter? Do we appreciate the Bodhisattvas we encounter? Do we appreciate the so-called sentient, the so-called insentient? Our transactions are Bodhisattvas giving and receiving, Bodhisattvas being given and being received. Are we present? Do we live the harmony of the Buddha and Dharma? Our transactions are Dharma transactions, the opportunity to practice the Sangha harmony, the opportunity to harmonize the Sangha practice, the opportunity to liberate transactions. When you are in the store, on the phone, at the Department of Motor Vehicles, it is Bodhisattvas serving Bodhisattvas. Do not miss this Sangha.

Being "I and all beings of the great earth together" is the functioning of this "I and all beings of the great earth," this functioning of the "together." This is the perfection and wisdom of Buddhas and Bodhisattvas. Speaking about it is one thing, but we each have to live this. It is not about explanations or reading. Our practice is living this, actualizing this, manifesting this. This is the live Sangha Treasure.

40

First Pure Precept

NONHARMING

Each of us is fully embodying this truth that we are, the truth that is our life. Zazen is complete and whole. It doesn't need extras, like Dharma talks, explanations, or all sorts of other things. Life is complete and whole as is. Nevertheless, all sorts of supports enable us to be just this that we are. So these few words are supports and encouragement.

The Three Pure Precepts are nonharming, doing good, and doing good for others. Often the first Pure Precept is translated as "Refrain from evil" or "Not doing evil." You could translate the precept this way, but the English word "evil" has all sorts of connotations and denotations that can mislead us, and then the Pure Precept becomes an entanglement of more thoughts and beliefs to which we attach. So I say "nonharming," and maintaining "nonharming," which is maintaining who we truly are.

Just doing zazen, all precepts are taken care of. There's no need to talk about anything. All the paramitas are taken care of right here. And yet, being just this moment, we discover all sorts of emotion-thought that we are caught up in, all sorts of notions of self and others arising. So I will discuss the first Pure Precept by talking on nonharming.

Usually we understand the precept of nonharming as referring to "self" harming others. This is one side. It's just as important to see the side of the precept that's related to the belief of harm coming to "self," our beliefs about what can harm us. Despite the fact that we are nonharming, we believe "my self" can be harmed. Of course, even the very holding to self is harming. We don't see how holding to these beliefs harms in and of itself, but when we hold to beliefs about how and what will be harmed, this precept of nonharming is not maintained.

This is not a matter of theory or concepts. Fear is inherent in holding these beliefs, these seemingly natural bodily beliefs. It is only the beliefs and reactions that cut off the Awakened Way. This precept enables us to notice what we believe and how we are reacting—and then to make the appropriate effort of practice, of experiencing, of being exactly this life we are, this Buddha-functioning.

Some aspects of harming are easy to see, such as "I will be harmed if I get ill." Sometimes it is easy to say, "Too much pain, too much cold," without looking closely to see if it is really too much. We may think these thoughts seem self-evident. And yet even in what seems self-evident, there is an aspect of nonharming that we can clarify and practice. Yes, we get old, we get sick, we get weak, and we have pain. All sorts of physically or emotionally painful circumstances arise. In fact, being human and being conditioned guarantees these things. Illness is difficult and pain hurts, sometimes terribly so. It is hard to inhabit, and it is hard to tolerate.

And yet if we look, we can see what we have added on; we can see our notions about how the circumstances and conditions harm us over and above the actual pain. What is the harm of illness? What is the harm of pain? Look closely. This is not a matter of saying, "No, I shouldn't believe that I am harmed." Just the opposite: it is a matter of seeing and really embodying the belief moment; it is a matter of noticing and opening up bodily to experiencing. Over and above the ache of hunger, is it "I am harmed if I am hungry"? Is it "I am harmed when my muscles ache, I am harmed when I am sick"? Emotional circumstances also get mixed with ideas of harm: "I am harmed by them speaking about me that way, I am harmed by them disagreeing with me"; "I am harmed when he doesn't like me, I am harmed when she thinks she is smarter."

Noticing and experiencing, and at the same time maintaining nonharming, does not mean that we stop acting and responding to circumstances. However, it shines a light on the harm and fear that we create, that we add on and react to in the midst of the circumstances; it shines a light on the so-called harm to our "self" by others. Believing harm, that much we are cut off from life. Some of this is self-evident and easily seen, and some of this is more subtle.

One of my teachers, Soen Nakagawa Roshi, was abbot of Ryutaku-ji, a monastery in Japan. Nevertheless, he still did sesshin with Harada Roshi at Hosshin-ji in order to clarify his practice. He was criticized by some people for this: "Why are you going to sesshin with another roshi? You are an abbot, you have monks." Nevertheless, Soen Roshi would go, and he would also do private retreats as a hermit. He was always polishing and clarifying his practice.

During or after one of these sesshins, Soen Roshi "had" a "great" enlightenment. Several months after this experience, he told his monks the following story, which I will paraphrase. Soen Roshi often went to Tokyo and elsewhere to lead zazen meetings. On the train, there was an elderly woman who would always come over to him and talk about all sorts of things. She would chatter on endlessly, telling him about her family and all the latest gossip.

Soen Roshi didn't particularly look forward to this. He would sit there and listen and be very nice and polite, but, to put words in his mouth, "Ah well, I'll put up with her." You all know about this sort of thing. I am sure there are people you meet who go on and on about whatever. Though one may say, "Emptiness of all forms, oneness of multitude of dharmas," in these kinds of situations, this remains conceptual. Even if you try to "act" this out, it is not actualized as your life. And though you are polite and even friendly, there is a trace of annoyance.

After this enlightenment experience, Soen Roshi said he noticed that whenever he encountered the old woman, he was delighted to see her. When she started talking, there was not even a trace of annoyance. In fact, just the opposite: he felt enormous love for her just as she was. Circumstances and conditions did not change; she did not change, and he did not do anything different. And yet, just of itself, something was completely transformed.

Being just this moment compassion: this is nonharming. There is nothing in the universe that is not our self. There is nothing that can harm us, there is nothing that can be harmed. The compassion and love that is who we are naturally manifests.

The verse on this precept of nonharming in Keizan's *Kyujukaimon* (Giving and Receiving the Teaching of the Precepts) is clear: "It is the dwelling place of all the Buddhas, Dharma, and precepts, the very source of all the Buddhas, Dharma, and precepts." What is this? Life is our opportunity to clarify and actualize this.

I bring this matter up not to add any new rules, but to point out that maintaining nonharming is being who we are. When my teacher Maezumi Roshi gave Jukai (the precepts), he asked, "Will you maintain this well? Will you maintain this well? Will you really maintain this well?" Maintaining is not adding something new. It is being who we are, it is being what life is.

Unfortunately, self-centeredness keeps us from maintaining this well. Our ongoing practice effort, our ongoing life effort, is to maintain well this all-inclusive Pure Precept that is the source and dwelling of our life. Clarifying this enables us to begin to see when traces of beliefs about "what can harm us" arise. Of course, we also notice thoughts and beliefs about all the things in the universe, all the people, beings, and events that we don't like, that we want to do something about, that we want to "harm." Actions involving physical "harm" seem easy to see. But even with mental reactions, it is vital to notice harming of so-called others; it is vital to notice our anger and upset with persons and events; it is vital to notice the condition of this body-mind.

These various aspects of harming are different sides of the same thing. We want to harm when we feel we are harmed; we want to harm when fear arises. If we feel harmed, there is a trace of both wanting to harm and believing we have been harmed. This is not a matter of blame or judgment. This precept is a perspective to enable us to notice beliefs, since only in holding to beliefs and thoughts do we cut off from this life that we are right now.

Harming may arise in our sitting or in all sorts of circumstances. Sitting and practicing we notice the thoughts and beliefs that arise, and which we pursue, cling, or attach to. We each have our own way of functioning, and therefore we need to practice with this in a way that is appropriate for this body-mind functioning that we are.

All the precepts are like this. The whole practice is like this. Zazen is being this body-mind-world that we are; our own practice is this experiencing. And it is more than adequate to fill our life; it is more than adequate to sustain and nourish us. Yet it is easy to miss, because most of what we learn in our culture encourages us to believe harming and being harmed, to believe that evil is being done to us and to believe that we need to punish evil. Yes, events result in hurt. But almost imperceptibly, along with pain, comes this side of emotion-thought: "I am being harmed." This is our practice opportunity.

We maintain nonharming by noticing when we get caught up. Noticing when we get caught up is the opportunity of experiencing, the opportunity to be this moment. My teacher Joko Beck had an expression: "Stop and pop." "Stop" is noticing being caught up in or holding to emotion-thought; noticing is the "stop" of the moment. Then you "pop" into this moment, or open as this body-mind moment. Having a nice phrase like this is of value when it leads to our practice effort of this moment. Zazen is that opportunity for all of us sitting here; zazen is an opportunity to nurture life, to inhabit this compassionate life that we are, being just this moment.

I bring this up to encourage us in our practice effort, whether during formal sitting, walking, or working, whatever we are doing throughout our everyday life. Clarifying what we do, this is the opportunity of being together; this is the opportunity to embody this life that we are, this moment. In the dwelling place of Buddhas, you meet only Buddhas. Just turn the wheel of Dharma and nurture precepts from morning to night.

41

Doing Good

BEING JUST THIS MOMENT

Being just this moment is our life. It is simple and straightforward, not requiring anything extra, not requiring anything except being as you are right now. This is our practice opportunity and effort; this is doing good. Truthfully, there is only this moment, and being this moment is being time.

Unfortunately, many of us live within a fictional story, and that is exactly where difficulty and problems arise. What seems natural to most of us is a fiction, a story of my life from before to now to some future, a story of the world I live in. This story results in missing our life, and then no matter what we do, we miss this good.

We often hold an image of self that extends from past to present to future. Look closely: Is that so? Practice is going beyond an image; going beyond is zazen. Being present is being this body-mind world, this impermanence reality right here. Impermanence is this moment as is; cause and effect is the functioning of this life—these are two interconnected aspects of this life that we are.

Impermanence reveals this nonself, this not fixed, not permanent, not separate self. This is not holding to the story line, which is a horizontal image of this "I" life that was yesterday and is today. Holding to a horizontal line, or a variation of it, has consequences, consequences that we sometimes bemoan and suffer through. This "I" life creates and separates us from not-I other people, from beings and the great earth, from this arising-passing moment, from conditions and circumstances. This image of a horizontal stream life insures that we miss this very life we are.

The Three Treasures and the precepts are the formulations of inherent good. This good is not the opposite of bad; this good can be called self-nature, Buddha-nature, the absolute, no-nature. All beings are this wisdom and compassion, this perfection of good! Only delusions and attachments prevent us from seeing this, and prevent us from testifying and manifesting the good. Precepts are a guide leading us from self-centered delusion and attachment to a more complete realization and manifestation of wisdom and compassion as our life. They point the way to the fulfillment of our true nature.

Dogen Zenji writes: "Every good is not existent, not nonexistent, not form, not emptiness, nor anything else; it is only devoutly practicing. . . . Devoutly practicing even one good among the every good causes the entirety of dharmas, the whole body and reality itself to devoutly practice together."

Being right here—nothing extra. It is only in the arising of a habit of ignorance and delusion of self that the turning wheel of self-centeredness following through a time line of an ongoing past, present, and future is believed. Practice is seeing this as it arises, as it is here—at the moment you see it. The willingness to see it, the willingness to enter it body-mind when you see it, is our practice opportunity and courage. Holding on and attaching to a believed image is closing off this moment. As a result, all sorts of body-mind habits and beliefs are fed and nurtured. If so, we miss this that we are. Yet, right here we have the opportunity to enter this moment, and in doing so we can unbind what is never bound, and we can liberate what is never not-liberated.

Being right here is not bound in a separate horizontal stream of I-past, continuing to I-present, continuing to I-future. Experiencing this moment, this life right here is seen. Being right here is forgetting the self horizontal story life. Because it is this moment unbound, we can taste and discover this for our self. Truthfully, this moment extends in all directions, this endless dimension universal life. It extends boundlessly because it need not be bound in a horizontal life story. And it is right here, this moment.

But there's no need to agree with this. Simply look and see what is so; simply be what is so. This is zazen. This is zazen functioning in our daily life activity. Doing good is practicing and being practiced.

"Buddha's wisdom is cause and effect with no I at the core," writes Yasutani Roshi. And this cause and effect right here, this not-I, has past and future right here. Cause and effect is action and consequences. Cause and effect is consequences here now. To paraphrase Dogen's "Genjokoan," firewood does not turn into ash, and ash does not turn into firewood, yet firewood has its own past and future, and ash has its own past and future. This cause-and-effect aspect of impermanence reality counters nihilistic and depressive suffering tendencies, which might arise when we attach to ideas of impermanence, or more accurately, when we attach to an experience a holding to distorted and narrow ideas about impermanence, and when we act out of this one-sided view.

So what is this moment? Please do not be satisfied with a simplistic idea or understanding here. In "Shoaku Makusa," Dogen encourages us to look deeply into this: "Although causes engender results, it is not a case of before and after because of the truth of the sameness of before and after."

Being right here is equanimity being present in the midst of what is painful, in the midst of what seems not satisfactory. Being right here is the strength of equanimity and of practice mind. Being present is the willingness to be in the midst of habits where we are reacting to the arising circumstances—reacting to conditions with fear, reacting to circumstances and becoming angry, greedy, and confused. It is bodily inhabiting these arising habits and reactions, and yet not acting them out further, and responding right here. Or in the midst of acting out the reactions, noticing and releasing the habits of self in the practice effort of being present as this is, right here now. Being present is responding.

Equanimity is the not-holding to the story line of self past continuing to self present continuing to self future; equanimity is forgetting self. And just as the self past-present-future fiction is not a basis for holding, so also the self-of-others past-present-future fiction is not a basis for justifying anger, greed, or hatred. Other is the arising-passing of cause and effect, with no "I" at the core. The whole universe, our life right now, is other-no-self arising.

Equanimity arises out of not-holding to the story line of self or other-self past-present-future; equanimity arises out of being this moment arising cause and effect. By seeing the arising-passing right here that we call other, rather than seeing the fictional otherself, compassion naturally flows from this wisdom. This compassionate functioning of wisdom is being right here. Being right here, numberless beings are saved.

We all know very well the obvious impermanence of body and the obvious impermanence of various states of mind. Despite this, the very attachment to body-mind is a source of maintaining the past-present-future sense of self that seems natural to most of us much of the time. So our wonderful life opportunity in the midst of arising attachment habits is, as Joshu says, being a ball tossed on rushing water—nonstop flowing. Being right here is body-mind dropped away, not being bound in a horizontal body-mind life story, and not being bound in attachment habits.

Being this moment is most simple, unless we hold to body-mind habits that feel natural. When we are not bound by reactive habits of the horizontal story, we are not bound by ideas of others, by ideas of fixed, permanent, separate selves out there. Because we are not bound by these things, the basis of the poisons of greed, anger, and ignorance is undercut. Not holding to these right now is inexhaustible desires ended. Entering this moment is this boundless freedom, the dropped-away body-mind manifesting this endless dimension universal life. Then wisdom and compassion are naturally functioning; there is nothing special and nothing added.

This endless dimension life is our intimacy here. This is our ongoing practice effort of right now in the midst of dependent arising of cause and effect, nonstop flowing.

Please enjoy your life right now as this is. Do good.

42

Doing Good for Others

NONABIDING SERVICE

Our life task is being awake. Being awake, we serve all that appears. Serving is how we manifest who and what we are. Together here in the zendo, on your cushion, in the dokusan room, walking, eating, our job is to be awake.

Actually, this is not a good way to say it, because we might think there is this thing called "being" and this thing called "awake." I could say "awakening," but then we might think there is a state called "awakening" versus some other kind of state.

The Sixth Ancestor was awakened by a phrase from the *Diamond Sutra:* "Bring forth the mind that abides nowhere." Our task is nonabiding; being nonabiding not as something extra, but as what and who we are. The *Platform Sutra* says: "Nonabiding (*wuzhu*) is our original nature." This is transcending ordinary, transcending special; this is liberating others, liberating self.

Nonabiding is being awake. Awakening, awakening, awakening this moment. The only thing that hinders this awakening is abiding or clutching to some aspect of this, whether we call it "my thoughts, my feelings, this circumstance," whether we call it "inside" as opposed to "outside," a "physical" state or a "mental" state, memories about the so-called "past" or the so-called "future." So it is vital to see when and how we abide. What and where is abiding? Or to use another word, where is attaching? Where is getting caught? We are addicted to self; we are a self-aholic. We add self to this arising-passing, which is similar to an alcoholic adding alcohol to all sorts of life circumstances—and in both cases, this leads to suffering and harm.

Our simple task is serving. Life is serving. Most basically, zazen is serving; serving is sitting in the midst of this cause-and-effect universe that is right here now. Easy; nothing extra you need to do. This is shikantaza, or "just sitting." Just sitting is opening to right here; it is nonabiding; or when abiding, you are releasing attaching, releasing abiding, to right here.

Sometimes our practice is to enter through the body-mind abiding into being just where we are. Sometimes we have to cut away holding; in other words, we have to use more forceful effort to be right here. It could be skillful to do that, maybe because of the strength of the agitation, maybe because of the strength of the body-mind habits. We do this not in order to create nonabiding, but to enable us to be this nonabiding that we are.

Practice is to clarify this. You are clarifying this not so you have more ideas, but so you can see what is so, and you can see what to do—or see what not to do. Of course, you don't need to do anything. See, nonabiding is this. It is not even accurate to say that nonabiding is instantaneous, because that itself makes it something extra, something that you need to go to. You don't need to go anywhere. You are right here. This is instantaneous.

The Sixth Ancestor says, "Sitting [zazen] means from the beginning not attached to mind, not attached to purity." This is being without obstacle and without hindrance. "Not giving rise to any thought externally in regard to whatever object and internally seeing nature." This means to see our nature without perturbation.

What does it mean "not giving rise to thought with regard to objects"? What is your experience when sitting? What is your experience when walking? What is your experience when serving a meal to another? What is your experience when answering another? It doesn't mean that thoughts shouldn't arise. Thoughts arise, feelings arise. In fact, you can't help but see them, because that is the nature of who you are. When you are awake, you see what is here. And if "here" at this moment is thoughts arising, they arise.

But what is it when you grasp onto thoughts? What is it when you attach to thoughts and believe them? That is our part; that is where the "I" connects to thoughts." Saying "my thoughts," I've already connected. "I feel"; "I sense"; "I am going"; "I want." That is the linchpin of where we get into trouble, or where we can release trouble. Where and when we notice the self-aholic "I" habit, we can release the abiding to allow this natural nonabiding that we are, and then we can taste and function as this natural nonabiding that we are.

The problem isn't with thoughts or phenomena, with so-called outside sounds arising or so-called others appearing, nor with using the word "I." That is not the problem. The problem is when we attach to the thoughts, to the dualistic division; in a sense, we create our self around that arising. The task is always right there, right where we attach—right here where we don't see what this is. We don't see what is so right here, because we see it through a distorted lens, as one way or another, as having these characteristics or not having these characteristics, as having this past or having this future, as being self or not-self.

As the Sixth Ancestor says, "How is it while in the midst of characteristics to be free of characteristics (*wuxiang*)?" (The Chinese word used can also be translated as, "How is it while in the midst of form to be free of form?") This is our practice; this is what we are, without form. This is form is empty, empty is form, as the *Heart Sutra* states.

This does not mean sitting here and being deaf and dumb. It is to sit here in the midst of arising, in the midst of passing, and not grasping, not holding on to, not abiding. This is to be free of the characteristics while we are in the midst of them. Or to notice the holding to form, the holding to characteristics, and right there make practice effort.

It is very simple: this body, this life, even this mental functioning, are all characteristics that arise. All sorts of characteristics seem to arise, and all sorts of thoughts seem to arise and pass. And yet our practice isn't about stopping thoughts, and our practice isn't about going someplace where there aren't characteristics. This is to be free from characteristics while in the midst of characteristics. This is not thinking about thoughts, not holding to thoughts about "I feel good, I feel bad, I feel achy; He is loud, he is agitated, he is quiet." This is not clinging to the thoughts that appear and disappear, and not holding to ideas of "I need to help him," "She is not deserving," "I will do good for her," and so forth. This is not even holding on to some idea of "being free." Do not even abide in "free"; be completely unfree—be as this is. Naturally, not holding to thoughts is not reacting as a result of thoughts. Be this original nonabiding nature that we are. This is liberating our self and others.

Explaining further, practice and sitting is being nonabiding; it is awaking, awaking, awaking. "Awaking" is a strange word usage in English, but that is OK, because I want to be careful that we don't think "I have to be awake." I want to be careful that we don't create this subject-verb-object called "I" and "awake," much less some specific state. Awaking is right now mind nonabiding. Nonabiding is serving all beings. Nonabiding is not holding to dualistic ideas of me serving others, or ideas of self and not-self.

When I was Maezumi Roshi's attendant, one of my duties was to take care of his guests. Roshi impressed upon me the importance of serving his guests in the ways that would suit them best.

We might say this is obvious, but we often miss this if we hold to our ideas and beliefs of how to serve or what others need. Often guests arrived with little or no notice. Sometimes Roshi did not know them; they had received a recommendation from a friend or an acquaintance, and sometimes those making the recommendation only had a casual acquaintance with Roshi. Whether they were long expected or sudden arrivals, Roshi would put aside his work and planned activities to whatever extent possible and welcome his guests. In the midst of a busy schedule, the arriving guest was the matter at hand.

I remember some guests who acted in ways that made continuing demands upon Roshi's hospitality, and even damaged the house. In the time that I served him, I never saw Roshi withdraw his hospitality. After the guest left, we might speak of what occurred and clarify how we could do things differently in the future.

This openhanded, openhearted hospitality is exactly the teaching of guest and host, exactly the teaching of doing good for others. Of course, there may be a killing sword and a life-giving sword in hospitality. As a lifetime ongoing practice, serving is doing good for others. It may be easy to see this, but as Roshi sometimes said, "Realizing this is one thing, actualizing this is lifetime practice."

Don't know how to do it? That's fine. Just see what you know how to do, and see where you say, "I don't know how to do it." Work with that; enter there. Because nonabiding is who you are. You don't have to know how to do it. In fact, the things we know sometimes get in the way, because our knowing becomes another thing that we are trying to do, another thought that we are clinging on to.

So as a skillful means, when you find yourself clinging to your thoughts, what do you do? That is your practice. Taking care of right now, serving all beings right now, nonabiding serving right now. In zazen, open the hand of clinging, and while being this body-breath-moment, allow thoughts to arise and pass, and look at "Who is clinging?" Or if you have a particular koan practice, be that in the midst of this habit clinging that you find yourself in. I don't mean habitually yesterday or habitually because you figured out that you have this habit, but habitually right now. Habits only are right now. Habits are cause-and-effect right now. I'm not interested in habits from the past and habits in the future. Even saying, "Habits are only right now," be careful; otherwise we turn it into something.

Some of you are familiar with a nice phrase in the *Diamond Sutra:* "Past mind is ungraspable, present mind is ungraspable, future mind is ungraspable." See, this is truly nonabiding. Right now this is listening, right now this is reading. Nonabiding is listening; listening is serving this moment. But do not get caught in some idea: "I am listening to her." If you do, then doing good for others is gone. And yet, when we find our self abiding, right here there is something to do. Look! Doing is nonabiding. This is not anything else.

We are capable of practicing; we are capable of making that effort. Not an effort to get somewhere else, or an effort to get better. We are not trying to better our self or better others. This is being the original nature that we are. Original nature enables us to make this effort; original nature enables us to do good for others. Original nature right here now.

Student: What is nonthinking, and how is that different from thinking or not-thinking?

Genmyo: Thinking and not-thinking are dualities. There is A, and then the absence of A is B, or some form of that. I would explain this by saying that nonthinking is the bigger container of nondual. Of course, if I say much more I am in trouble, because then it is dual.

But even saying "bigger container" is nonsense, because then we get an idea of "bigger," and then we try to be something we think is bigger as opposed to something we think is smaller. I only say "bigger" to counter the sense of limited "I" that we hold, and that we might think resides in our body, in our personal space and senses. Not bigger, not smaller; then right here we see that we are not limited to any ideas or any sense of the size of right here.

If we hold to thinking or not-thinking, that can hinder this functioning and hinder serving. It is inherently problematic to figure out nonthinking with thinking. In the midst of thoughts arising and passing, nonthinking. Then we serve this life; then we do good for others.

Student: So nonthinking contains thinking.

Genmyo: Be careful. Don't create a picture of it; jump into it. Then you will discover that you are in the midst of it; you will discover that you jumped from where you are to where you are.

Your job is to allow nonthinking to manifest as your function-ing and serving; your job is to be this nonthinking that you are. In fact, this very serving allows nonthinking; it allows nonthink-ing. When you taste it, then you may see it, then you may know it. So manifest what you are; serve the conditions of this moment, serve the arising circumstances right now.

But this is not something that you are going to create. Notice when you are believing thinking, notice when you are grasping thoughts, notice when you are grasping on to the characteristics that you believe about inside and outside. Then see the very grasp-ing for what it is. You will see this very seeing, you will taste this very seeing—nonthinking thoughts.

Student: Is there a time for thinking?

Genmyo: Sure. Thinking is another aspect of functioning. But what is nonthinking in regards to thought? What is functioning with thoughts in the midst of nonthinking? All sorts of states and characteristics are part of this functioning, this functioning aris-ing and passing.

For example, if you want to make tea, you have to know what leaves go into the pot, and you have to know that the water needs to be a certain temperature. At some point you were taught this, and now you make choices about which tea, which cup, and so forth. And yet, we are without characteristics, we are without form. What is nonabiding?

When there is something to think about, think about it. Practice throughout life is going beyond the usual habits that most of us live out of, which include thinking much of the time, thinking about "our" thoughts, thinking about others, thinking about our so-called future and so-called past. No problem when you need to plan where you are going, but it is not necessary much of the time, such as in the midst of doing the dishes, driving, or during zazen.

Taste who you are so that you can function this way in the midst of thinking, in the midst of not-thinking, in the midst of characteristics. This is nonabiding. Not being obstructed by all the dharmas, by all the conditions that arise and pass, be the activities and functioning right here. Do not add self to thoughts and conditions and actions—unfortunately, this is what we often do with thinking. This obstructs serving, and it obstructs doing good for others.

The forms of practice enable and support us to be without thought in the midst of thoughts arising and passing. In fact, we are without abiding in the midst of arising and passing all the time, because this is who we are. But most of the time, we miss this. In fact, we are sure this is not so; we are sure that we and others are our thoughts, our characteristics, our judgments. So this is a little break from that sureness, that certainty of our thoughts, feelings, and characteristics.

And in going beyond, in being the bigger container that we are, we can see that we are not bound by thoughts, feelings, and characteristics. We are not enslaved by them. Therefore, we can

JUKAI, THREE TREASURES, THREE PRECEPTS

taste and we can be; we can manifest this liberation that we are right here, we can do good for others right here. Not abiding in self, not abiding in other.

Student: It seems that thinking and not-thinking implies some "I." But nonthinking doesn't seem to imply that.

Genmyo: Don't get caught up in theory; the point isn't theory. My words aren't to give us more ideas. I encourage you in your practice so that you can taste your life, just as I can taste this tea. Our practice is to be who we are.

See when you latch "I" on to the thought, see when you latch "I" on to the feeling—keep seeing that. Then look: What is skillful practice in the midst of that? And then do it. Because you are without that attached "I," despite the fact that this "I" appears to be so. Who you are is not limited to the "I" that you attach to thoughts, actions, and characteristics.

There's no problem with "I." "I" is a fine word to use. If I want tea, I need to say, "Please, may I have some tea?" Then "I" is something we can pick up and put down, whereas most of the time it picks us up and it puts us down.

So our practice is nonthinking in regards to thoughts. It is not giving rise to thoughts. Otherwise we just create an illusionary state that "I have to be this way, I have to not be that way." All along we are sneaking in this "I" have to be and this "I" have to not be.

Practice is very simple: it's being awake, awaking, being present. Or if you wish, call it awareness or attention. Whatever word resonates for you, practice is the doing right here. And practice is seeing what to do when you are caught up. Being breathed, wonderful. Just sitting, wonderful. Just doing, right now.

In the midst of just sitting, what happens to the thoughts that you are spinning around in? If you can just let them go, then just let them go like that. If you can't, then do something with them.

Student: I notice that I have a belief that by the end of a sesshin, things are going to go more smoothly. There are a lot of details in my life right now, and details are not really my forte. That is a story of mine, I would say. But sometimes the details get to be so much that I have to pull back just to get a perspective on them. And yet, it does seem sometimes after sesshin that things go a little more smoothly.

Genmyo: It does! They do! This is a by-product of sesshin. It is good that you like this; that's fine. But it is important to see that this is a by-product of being present, a by-product of being who you are.

Saying that things go more smoothly doesn't mean that there aren't going to be all sorts of things that you have to deal with after sesshin. You might still have the same so-called things to deal with. And yet, the dealing with is more smooth. This is serving; this is doing good for others. And that's because there is less grasping and attaching and abiding. But "less" and "more" are still dualistic conditions.

Yes, things do go more smoothly after sesshin, but this is always a by-product of the fundamental nonabiding that is who you are. Nonabiding is who we are, despite our habits that insist on holding to characteristics and habits. By-products are fine, but don't get attached and judgmental if they do not arise or if they are not the way you want them.

Student: Let's say I'm at work. There are a lot of details to take care of, and I've got all these lists of things to do. In those circumstances, how can I be that nonabiding?

Genmyo: Give yourself away to one doing as you are doing. Take care of the detail you are taking care of. It is not about, "How can I be that?" It's like my asking, "How am I supposed to breathe? How am I supposed to speak?" even as I am speaking and breathing. If I wasn't breathing and speaking, you wouldn't be hearing me. See clearly that it is the very breathing and speaking that asks, "How am I supposed to breathe? How am I supposed to speak?"

Look at your doing right here; look at your doing throughout the day. This very doing is the wisdom that is who you are. This is the wisdom that functions you, this is the wisdom that thoughts grow out of. This is serving all beings, this is doing good. It is not something extra; it is right where you are, and it is who you are. It is who asks right now, who responds right now, and who hears right now.

Continue your practice, and together we will continue to taste and be who we truly are. Together we will continue serving and being served.

Notes

1. Shunryu Suzuki, *Zen Mind, Beginner's Mind* (Boston: Shambhala, 2010); Maharshi Ramana, *Talks with Sri Ramana Maharshi* (Tiruvannamalai, S. India: T. N. Venkataraman, 1955); and Ram Dass, *Remember, Be Here Now* (San Cristobal, N.M.: Lama Foundation, 1971).

PART ONE: *Practice*

1. Ps. 46:10.
2. Spoken by the Buddha upon his enlightenment (*Avatamsaka Sutra*).
3. Lev. 19:18.

PART TWO: *Impermanence*

1. "Gatha on Opening the Sutra": "The Dharma, incomparably profound and minutely subtle, is rarely encountered, even in hundreds of thousands of millions of ages. Now we

see this, hear this, receive and maintain this. May we completely realize the Tathagata's true meaning."

2. Master Huangbo, *Essential Transmission of Mind-Dharma*, trans. Alexander Mayer (unpublished).

PART THREE: *Nonself*

1. Guanyin is the Chinese name for Avalokiteshvara.
2. Beata Grant, *Daughters of Emptiness* (Somerville, Mass.: Wisdom, 2003), 17.
3. Eihei Dogen, *Eihei Koroku,* trans. Taizan Maezumi Roshi, *ZCLA Journal* (Fall 1972): 1.
4. Taizan Maezumi, *Appreciate Your Life: The Essence of Zen Practice* (Boston: Shambhala, 2002).

Glossary

ABBREVIATIONS:
Chi. for Chinese
Jp. for Japanese
Skt. for Sanskrit
Pali for Pali
n.d. for no dates

Ashvaghosha (80?–150?) Indian philosopher, poet, and twelfth Indian Ancestor in Zen lineage, purported author of "Awakening of Faith in the Mahayana," but some modern scholars question this attribution.

Avalokiteshvara (Skt.; Chi.: Guanyin; Jp.: Kanzeon) Literally, "Lord who looks down." Bodhisattva of Great Compassion. *Kanzeon* means "one who hears the sounds of the world."

Awakening of Faith in the Mahayana (Skt.: Mahayana-shraddhotpada-shastra; Jp.: Daijokishinron) Chinese version written in 553. Attributed to Ashvaghosha, but since the earliest extant versions are in Chinese, it may have been written by the "translator" Paramartha.

Baizhang Huaihai (Chi.; Jp.: Hyakujo Ekai) (720–814) Chinese Ch'an master. Teacher of Huangbo, he was a Dharma heir of Mazu.

Blue Cliff Record (Chi.: Biyen-lu; Jp.: Hekigan-roku) This is a collection of a hundred cases compiled in the eleventh century, and edited by Xuedou Chongxian with commentary and verse. Later, Yuanwu added introductions, capping phrases, and commentary. Though Yuanwu's successor Dahui Zonggao burned all the copies he could find because Chan students were becoming attached to and dependent on the book, later new editions were published, and it is considered an especially important text in the Linji/Rinzai school.

Bodhi mind (Skt.) Literally, "awakened mind."

Bodhidharma (Skt.; Chi.: Puti Damo, Jp.: Bodai Daruma) (450–530) Considered by tradition to have brought Zen from India to China. The twenty-eighth Zen master after the Buddha, and the First Zen Ancestor of China.

Bodhisattva The state before full awakening; one who postpones their own full awakening to the benefit of all beings.

Book of Equanimity (Chi: Congrongan Lu; Jp.: Shoyoroku) Collection of a hundred cases and verses compiled and edited by Caodong Master Hongzhi Zhengjue, with added introduction, commentary, and capping phrases by Wansong Xingxiu. This text is especially treasured and used by the Soto school.

Buddha Names Sutra (Chi.: Fo-ming-jing; Jp.: Butsumyo-kyo) The sutra was translated into Chinese about 520. It lists the names of more than one thousand Buddhas and Bodhisattvas. Recited as part of confession in some traditions.

Caoshan Benji (Chi.; Jp.: Sozan Honjaku) (840–901) Chinese Ch'an master. A successor of Donghshan Liangjie. The first character of his name, Cao, is sometimes considered the source of the first character of the name of the Caodong (Soto) School.

Changsha Jingcen (Chi.; Jp.: Chosha Keishin) (800–68) A disciple of Nanquan Puyuan.

Charlotte Joko Beck (1917–2011) American Zen Teacher, cofounder of Ordinary Mind Zen School. Author of *Everyday Zen* and *Nothing Special.* One of the first major female Zen teachers in America, she emphasized practice in all aspects of life, using daily life activity as practice, and the importance of being "as awake as possible in each moment."

Daitsu Chisho Buddha Literally, "Distinguished Wisdom of Great Transcendent Faculty." A Buddha referenced in Buddhist mythology as having lived in prehistoric era.

Dayu (Chi.: Gao'an Dayu; Jp.: Koan Daigu) (n.d.) A successor of Baizhang Huaihai. His prominent female disciple is Moshan Liaoran, one of only a few early Zen female teachers.

dependent origination (Pali: Paticca Samuppada; Skt.: Pratityasamutpada) Basic Buddhist teaching of cause and effect and the twelve links of interdependent arising, starting with ignorance. Sometimes called the wheel of becoming.

Dharmakaya (Skt.; Jp.: Hosshin) Literally, "Reality Body" or "Truth Body." "Absolute Truth." The first of the three bodies of the Buddha (Trikaya), manifestation of all things as one.

Dharma transmission Designation by Zen master of person to carry on the Dharma lineage and in turn name Dharma successors. Sometimes referred to as "mind-to-mind" transmission.

Diamond Sutra (Skt.: Vajracchedika Prajna Paramita Sutra) Belongs to the large corpus of Prajna Paramita Sutras, emphasized by the Sixth Ancestor and by the Ch'an tradition after him.

Dogen (Dogen Kigen, Eihei Dogen, Koso Joyo Daishi) (1200–53) Japanese Zen Master, who received Rinzai transmission in Japan about 1226. After that went to China 1227–33 and received Caodong transmission from Tiantong Rujing (Jp.: Tendo Nyojo). Founder of Soto Zen School in Japan. Author of *Shobogenzo* and other important Soto texts. Founded Eiheiji monastery.

Dogen's Extensive Record (Jp.: Eihei koroku) A collection of short formal talks to monk trainees, koans with commentaries and verses for various formal and informal occasions, ten volumes.

Dogo. *See* **Tenno Dogo**

dokusan (Jp.) A one-to-one, face-to-face meeting of Zen master and student in which practice is the focus and the student's understanding and clarity are probed and tested.

Dongshan Liangjie (Chi.; Jp.: Tozan Ryokai) (807–869) Chinese Ch'an master considered founder of Caodong (Soto) Ch'an lineage in China.

Eido Shimano (b. 1932) Dharma heir of Soen Nakagawa and founder of Daibosatsu zendo and New York zendo in the United States.

Fazang (643–712) Chinese Huayan Master. Considered Third Ancestor of the Huayan School. Prolific author of sutra commentaries. Legend has it that he assisted the great translator monk Xuanzang.

five skandhas (Skt.) Literally, "five aggregates" or "five heaps." Form, sensation, conception, discrimination, and awareness. The components of human existence.

four great elements Earth, air, fire, and water. The elements that combine to produce existence.

gassho (Jp.) Buddhist mudra of putting palms together upright as expression of appreciation, gratitude, and respect.

The Gateless Gate (Jp.: Mumonkan) Collection of forty-eight Ch'an (Zen) koans compiled in the early thirteenth century by Mumon Ekai with commentary and verse. Begins with koan "mu."

Gautama. *See* **Shakyamuni Buddha**

Bernie Glassman (b. 1939) First Dharma Heir of Maezumi Roshi. Founder of Zen Peacemaker Order and a major figure in Engaged Buddhism and of White Plum Sangha.

Guanyin. *See* **Avalokiteshvara**

Hakuin Ekaku (1685–1768) Zen master who revived Rinzai Zen in Japan; almost all Rinzai Zen masters today trace their lineage through him. Author of many koan commentaries and "autobiographical" works. Emphasized importance of kensho awakening and after-kensho training.

Hakuyu Taizan Maezumi (1931–95) Japanese Zen teacher, established Zen Center of Los Angles and White Plum Sangha. Inherited three Zen lineages, that of Baian Hakujun, Hakuun Yasutani, and Koryu Osaka. A Soto teacher, he integrated koan practice into his teaching.

Harada Roshi (1871–1961) Daiun Sogaku Harada. Soto Zen Master who trained under both Soto and Rinzai masters; Abbot of Hosshin-ji and other temples. Integrated koan practice with Soto style practice. Dharma teacher of Yasutani Roshi.

Hongzhi Zhengjue (Chi.; Jp.: Wanshi Shogaku) (1091–1157) Chinese Ch'an master. Caodong Master who revived the lineage. Collected koan cases and wrote verses that were the basis for *Book of Equanimity*.

Hsuansha Shih-pei (Chi.; Jp.: Gensha Shibi) (835–908) Chinese Ch'an master.

Huangbo Xiyun (Chi.; Jp.: Obaku Kiun) (770–850) Chinese Ch'an master. Dharma heir of Baizhang, Dharma father of Linji. Author of "Essential Transmission of the Mind-Dharma."

Hui Chung *See* **Nanyang Huizhong**

Jianzhi Sengcan (Chi.; Jp.: Kanchi Sosan) (d. 606) Chinese Ch'an master. Known as the Third Ancestor. Purported author of *On Believing in Mind* (Chi.: Xin xin ming).

Joshu Jushin (Jp.; Chi: Zhaozhou Congshen) (778–897) Chinese Ch'an master. Successor of Nanquan (Jp.: Nansen). One of the most cited masters in koan literature; cases are excerpts from his "Recorded Sayings." It was said that his "lips emitted light" because of his pithy style.

Joshu Sasaki Roshi (b. 1907) Founder of Mt. Baldy Zen Center and many other temples in the United States. Major Rinzai Zen Master in the United States since the 1960s.

Jukai Ceremony of receiving the precept, formally becoming a Buddhist in the Zen tradition. "Kai" (Skt.: Sila) means precepts in Japanese.

Kanzeon. *See* **Avalokiteshvara**

Keizan Jokin (Taiso Josai Daishi) (1268–1325) Japanese Soto Zen Master. After Dogen, considered second most important founder of Japanese Soto Zen school. Author of the *Transmission of Light*. Founder of Sojiji monastery.

kensho (Jp.) Also referred to as Satori Experience of Awakening, literally "seeing into one's nature."

koan (Jp.) A text case, often an exchange between a Zen Master and student or on a Master's Enlightenment experience, assigned as a practice focus for resolution.

Kodo Sawaki Roshi (1880–1965) Japanese Soto Zen master. Teacher of Uchiyama Roshi.

Kol Nidre Opening prayer of Yom Kippur Jewish Day of Atonement, "on the first evening."

Koun Ejo (1198–1280) Japanese Soto Zen master, Dharma heir of Dogen, second abbot of Eiheiji. Editor of some of Dogen's writings.

Life's Highest Blessings (Maha-mangala sutta)

Linji Yixuan (Chi.; Jp.: Rinzai Gigen) (d. 866) Considered founder of the Linji (Jp.: Rinzai) School of Ch'an. Known for his short, forceful, direct style of teaching.

Maezumi Roshi. *See* **Hakuyu Taizan Maezumi**

Maitreya The future Buddha who will arise for an era after the present.

Manjushri (Skt.) Literally, "Gentle Glory." Bodhisattva of Transcendent Wisdom.

Mazu Daoyi (Chi.; Jp.: Baso Doitsu) (709–88) Chinese Ch'an master. Considered one of two major Zen masters of his time, said to have had more than 120 Dharma heirs.

Mumon Ekai (Jp.; Chi.: Wumen Huikai) (1183–1260) Chinese Ch'an master; author of *The Gateless Gate.*

Nanquan Puyuan (Chi.; Jp.: Nansen Fugan) (748–835) Chinese Ch'an master, Dharma heir of Mazu and teacher of Joshu (Chi.: Zhaozhou).

Nanyang Huizhong (Chi.; Jp.: Nanyo Echu) (675–775) Chinese Ch'an master. Also known as Hui Chung. Dharma heir of Sixth Ancestor, also known as "National Teacher."

Nanyue Huairang (Chi.; Jp.: Nangaku Ejo) (677–744) Chinese Ch'an master. Dharma heir of Sixth Ancestor and Dharma Teacher of Mazu.

Nicholas of Cusa (1401–64) Also referred to as Nicolaus Cusanus and Nicholas of Kues, cardinal of the Catholic Church from Germany (Holy Roman Empire).

On Believing in Mind (Chi.: Xin xin ming) Also known as the *Faith Mind Sutra*. Attributed to the Third Ancestor of Ch'an, Jianzhi Sengcan (Jp.: Kanchi Sosan).

Paramartha (499–569) An Indian monk who translated Sanskrit texts into Chinese.

Platform Sutra (Chi.: Fabao tan jing) The only Ch'an text with the title *Sutra*. Contains purported autobiographical section on the life of the Sixth Ancestor and his practice/doctrinal teaching.

Precepts (Bodhisattva Precepts) Set of practice and life guidelines used in Mahayana Buddhism.

The Record of Master Linji (Chi.: Linji lu; Jp.: Rinzai roku) Account of life and teachings of Ch'an Master Linji Yixuan (see "Linji Yixuan").

Rinzai school (Jp.) (Chi.: Linji School) Major school of Zen in China and in Japan. Considers Linji as founder.

roshi (Jp.) Literally, "venerable teacher." Zen master.

samadhi A concentrated, one-pointed state of mind, a nondualistic awareness.

Samantabhadra (Skt.) Literally, "Universal Worthy." Bodhisattva of Action.

Samyutta Nikaya (Pali) Literally, "Connected Discourses" or "Kindred Sayings." Early Buddhist scripture found in the Pali Canon.

Sandokai (Jp.) (*Identity of Relative and Absolute*) (Chi.: Tsan-Tung-Chi) A major text of the Soto school. Written by Shitou Xiqian (Jp.: Sekito Kisen).

sesshin (Jp.) Literally, "touching the heart mind." A period of intensive Zen practice (usually three to seven days, but sometimes longer) at a Zen monastery or center.

Shakyamuni Buddha (Skt.) (Gautama) The historical Buddha. Although scholars disagree on the dates of his birth and death, he is commonly believed to have lived during the fifth century B.C.E. Buddha literally means Awakened or Enlightened One.

shikantaza (Jp.) Literally, "nothing but precisely sitting." The prototypical and "official" Soto practice, inspiration for which is found in the writings of Dogen.

Shinji Shobogenzo (Jp.) Three hundred koan cases compiled by Dogen. Many are the subject for Dogen's commentaries and poems in the *Shobogenzo* and *Eihei Koroku*.

Shobogenzo (Jp.) Literally, "Treasury of the True Dharma Eye." Collection of essays by Dogen; there are editions with twelve, twenty-eight, sixty, seventy-five, and ninety-five fascicles or chapters.

Shoju Rojin (Dokyo Etan, Keitan Dokyo) (1642–1721) Japanese Zen master. Considered Hakuin's Dharma Teacher. Being his heir connected Hakuin to the O-To-Kan Rinzai lineage.

Shunryu Suzuki (1904–71) Japanese Soto Zen teacher who established San Francisco Zen Center and Tassajara Zen Mountain Center. Author of *Zen Mind, Beginner's Mind* and other books.

Simchat Torah Annual Jewish holiday in the fall celebrating the completion of the weekly reading of the Torah.

Sixth Ancestor (Chi.: Dajian Huineng; Jp.: Daikan Eno) (638–713) Sixth Patriarch of Ch'an (Zen) Buddhism. Subsequent Ch'an and Zen schools trace their lineage through him and his disciples. The Platform Sutra is attributed to him; questions of authorship exist.

Soen Nakagawa (1907–84) Japanese Rinzai Zen master, abbot of Ryutaku-ji; taught and led sesshin in the United States. Seminal figure in the development of American Zen, teacher to a number of American Zen masters.

Soto school (Jp.; Chi.: Caodong) In China one of five major Zen schools. In Japan one of two major Zen schools. Dogen is the founder of Soto school in Japan.

Tathagata (Pali; Skt.) Literally, "One who has thus gone" (tatha-gata) or "one who has thus come" (tatha-agata). The historical Buddha, Shakyamuni, often referred to himself with this term after Enlightenment.

teisho (Jp.) Dharma discourse. Suzuki Roshi called this "tongue-less speech" or speaking of what cannot be talked about. A non-dual formal presentation by Zen Master on Zen text or koan.

Tenkei Denson (1648–1735) Japanese Soto Zen master and major commentator on Zen texts.

Tenno Dogo (Jp.; Chi.: Tianhuang Daowu) (748–807) Chinese Ch'an master.

Tettsu Gikai (1219–1309) Third Ancestor in Japanese Soto lineage, student of Dogen and Dharma heir of Koun Ejo.

Tiantong Rujing (Chi.; Jp.: Tendo Nyojo) (1163–1228) Dogen's Chinese Ch'an master.

Toshi. *See* **Tosu Daido**

Tosu Daido (Chi.: Touzi Datong) (819–914) Chinese Ch'an master.

Transmission of Light (Jp.: Denkoroku) Text by Keizan of cases and commentary on the Enlightenment and Dharma Transmission of the Soto lineage from Shakyamuni Buddha up to Koun Ejo.

Valjean McLenighan (1947–2008) Prairie Zen Center member who lived in Chicago and had an affiliate sitting group at her home.

Xuedou Chongxian (Chi.; Jp.: Setcho Juken) (980–1052) Chinese Ch'an master. Selected and wrote verses for one hundred koan cases that became *Blue Cliff Record*.

Yasutani Hakuun (1885–1973) Japanese Zen Master, Dharma Heir of Harada Sogaku. Seminal figure in development of Zen in the West. Combined koan practice and Soto teaching. Founded Sanbo Kyodan and teacher of Maezumi Roshi, Aitken Roshi, and Kapleau Roshi, among others.

Yom Kippur Jewish Day of Atonement.

Yongjia Xuanjue (Chi.; Jp.: Yoka Genkaku) (665–713) Chinese Ch'an master and Tiantai master. Dharma heir of Sixth Ancestor.

Yuanwu Keqin (Chi.; Jp.: Engo Kokugon) (1063–1135) Chinese Ch'an master. Compiled *Blue Cliff Record* based on Xuedou's work, added introduction, extensive commentary, and capping phrases.

Yunmen Wenyan (Chi.; Jp.: Ummon Bun'en) (864–949) Chinese Ch'an Master, considered founder of Yunmen School. Famous for his pithy responses that form the basis of many koans.

Yunyan Tansheng (Chi.; Jp.: Ungan Donjo) (780–841) Chinese Ch'an master. Teacher of Dongshan.

zazen (Jp.) Sitting meditation.

zendo (Jp.) Zen meditation hall.

Zengen Chuko (Jp.; Chi.: Shishuang Qingzhu) (807–88) Chinese Ch'an master.

Zenji (Jp.) Title meaning "Zen Master." Formal term showing great reverance, reserved for lineage founders and heads of lineage; sometimes used for revered Ancestors.

Reb Zusha (Rabbi Meshulam Zusha) (1718–1800) Jewish Chassidic master.